VERB MEANING AND THE

The relationship between the meaning of words and the structure of sentences is an important area of research in linguistics. Studying the connections between lexical-conceptual meaning and event-structural relations, this book arrives at a modular classification of verb types within English and across languages. Ramchand argues that lexical-encyclopedic content and structural aspects of meaning need to be systematically distinguished, and that thematic and aspectual relations belong to the latter domain of meaning. The book proposes a syntactic decompositional view of core verbal meaning, and sets out to account for the variability and systematicity of argument-structure realization across verb types. It also proposes a novel view of lexical insertion.

GILLIAN CATRIONA RAMCHAND is Professor of Linguistics at the University of Tromsø. Her previous publications include *Aspect and Predication* (1997) and *Handbook of Linguistic Interfaces* (2006, with Charles Reiss).

CAMBRIDGE STUDIES IN LINGUISTICS

Verb Meaning and the Lexicon

A First-Phase Syntax

In this series

Earlier issues not listed are also available

VERB MEANING AND THE LEXICON

A FIRST-PHASE SYNTAX

GILLIAN CATRIONA RAMCHAND

University of Tromsø, CASTL

CAMBRIDGE
UNIVERSITY PRESS

CAMBRIDGE UNIVERSITY PRESS
Cambridge, New York, Melbourne, Madrid, Cape Town, Singapore,
São Paulo, Delhi, Dubai, Tokyo, Mexico City

Cambridge University Press
The Edinburgh Building, Cambridge CB2 8RU, UK

Published in the United States of America by Cambridge University Press, New York

www.cambridge.org
Information on this title: www.cambridge.org/9780521182348

First published 2008
Reprinted 2009
First paperback edition 2010

A catalogue record for this publication is available from the British Library

Library of Congress Cataloguing in Publication data

Ramchand, Gillian, 1965–
    Verb meaning and the lexicon : a first-phase syntax / Gillian Catriona Ramchand.
        p.   cm.
    Includes bibliographical references and index.
    ISBN 978-0-521-84240-2
    1. Generative grammar.   2. Lexicology.   3. Grammar, Comparative and
    general—Verb.   1. Title.
    P158.R36 2008
    415'.0182—dc22   2007050190

ISBN 978-0-521-84240-2 Hardback
ISBN 978-0-521-18234-8 Paperback

Contents

Acknowledgements

This book could not have been written without the generous engagement of many of my friends and colleagues in the field. It would be impossible to name them all, or to do justice to all their comments and criticisms. For lengthy discussions, arguments and advice I would like to single out David Adger, Miriam Butt, Raffaella Folli and Peter Svenonius. I also thank CASTL (Center for the Advanced Study of Theoretical Linguistics) and the University of Tromsø for being one of the best and most stimulating places in which to write a book. Much of the material for this book arose out of interaction with colleagues and students during the course of seminars and lectures. My debt to all of those interactions and the other research going on at Tromsø can be seen clearly in the pages of this book. For the final stages of writing and revising, I am once again grateful to Peter Svenonius, who commented on more drafts than time or sanity should allow.

Abbreviations

The following abbreviations are used in the glosses:

ACC	accusative case
CAUSE	causative
CLASS	classifier
DAT	dative case
DEC	declarative
DIR	directional marker
ERG	ergative case
F	feminine agreement
FUT	future tense
IMP	imperfective
INF	infinitival form
INSTR	instrumental case
LOC	locative marker
M	masculine agreement
NOM	nominative case
OBL	oblique case
PASS	passive
PAST	past tense
PERF	perfective
PERFPART	perfect participial form
PL	plural agreement
PRES	present tense
PROG	progressive
SG	singular agreement
TOP	topic
1	first-person agreement
3	third-person agreement

1 Introduction

Classical generative grammar partitions linguistic competence into three basic components: lexical knowledge, phrase structure rules and transformational rules (Chomsky 1965, 1981). One of the fundamental debates over the years, and one which is still alive today, concerns the division of labour between information and processes that reside in the lexicon and those rules and processes that are part of syntax.

In this book, I explore a view of the architecture of grammar whereby the lexicon is eliminated as a module with its own special primitives and modes of combination. By this, I do not intend to deny that there are items within the language that need to be listed/memorized, or that they are associated with grammatical information. Rather, I will seek to claim that to the extent that lexical behaviour is systematic and generalizable, this is due to syntactic modes of combination and not to distinct lexicon-internal processes (Hale and Keyser 1993, etc.). The general ideology is not novel; I am attempting to implement an old idea in the light of current, accumulated knowledge concerning the nature of 'lexical' generalizations and patterns. In pursuing, as I will, a radically unstructured view of the lexicon, I engage with recent ideas of constructionalism (Goldberg 1995, Marantz 1997b, Borer 2005) and make my own proposal based on what I take to be the core empirical issues of 'thematic' roles, event structure (aktionsart) and selection.

One of the things I will take for granted in this work is that human beings' linguistic competence includes, minimally and crucially, a (linguistically specific) combinatorial system.[1] It is this combinatorial system that I will be referring to with the term 'syntax', and I will assume that the system itself is universal, in

---

[1] Here I also wish to abstract away from the debate concerning whether this combinatorial system is representationally innate in the sense of all the basic knowledge existing in a hardwired repository of brain structure, or whether it emerges inexorably as a result of the learning strategies abstractly encoded in a language acquisition device. In fact, it is not even relevant to my argumentation whether the combinatorial system that emerges is specific to language, or whether it is part of a more general human symbolic capacity.

the sense of underlying all instantiations of human language. Under the view I will be pursuing here (and one that is implicit in much work within minimalist syntax, and even earlier), this is the *only* linguistically relevant combinatorial system that there is, i.e. we are dealing with only one set of primitives and one set of operations.

Two distinct types of lexical information have always been recognized: unstructured encyclopedic information with its infinitely variable web of association and nuance; and the grammatically relevant, more systematic, class of information that interfaces with the syntactic system (Chomsky 1965, Jackendoff 1983). The classical assumption has been that two such types of meaning coexist in a module that is termed 'the lexicon', with the latter level being the linguistically relevant 'subset' of the former (cf. Levin and Rappaport Hovav 1995, Levin and Rappaport 1998).

Taking the existence of a lexical module of some sort for granted, many early generativist debates were concerned with the location within the grammar of particular sorts of linguistic generalizations, i.e. whether they should more properly be considered 'lexical' or 'syntactic' (see Chomsky 1970 for foundational early discussion, as well as later debates staged in Baker 1988 and Belletti and Rizzi 1988 vs. Alsina 1992 and Bresnan and Moshi 1990). Importantly, claiming that there are generalizations that can only be stated at the level of lexical information is different from merely accepting that lexical items possess syntactic information, hence the debate. In general, some theories such as LFG sought to establish the validity of separate modules with their own primitives and modes of combination, linked by correspondence rule (Bresnan 1982); whereas GB theory and its descendants took the view that the lexicon should be seen as the repository of essentially idiosyncratic/memorized information with no independent combinatorial primitives (Di Sciullo and Williams 1987, Chomsky 1981). It is a version of the latter position that I will be arguing for in this book, although the details prove stickier than one might imagine if one is intent on not begging the important questions.

The main challenge to the unstructured lexicon view has always been the existence of thematic, or argument-structure generalizations,[2] captured in GB theory via the D-structure level of representation, or by Hale and Keyser via L-syntax (an encapsulated syntax for the building of lexical items). In more recent minimalist work (Chomsky 1995, 2000), presumably no such additional

---

[2] I am concerning myself purely with syntax here. Lexical phonology, if it exists as a set of operations distinct from postlexical phonology, might constitute another such challenge. I will assume optimistically, for the purposes of this book, that those challenges can also be overcome.

level of representation can exist, but the operation of 'initial' Merge is potentially available as a locus for these generalizations. Since this operation is triggered by selectional features (Chomsky 1995), capturing generalizations at this level will depend on the nature of the features involved, and the nature of selection and insertion of lexical items.

The key here is therefore the features on lexical items and how they might be deployed to create selectional generalizations. One approach to the problem is to deny that such selectional generalizations exist. This is the view most recently taken by Marantz (1997b) and (1998, 2005), whereby lexical items possess no syntactically relevant information that could constitute a constraint on their insertion possibilities (not even category information). The actual limits on variability reported in more standard accounts would then have to be due to limits based on real-world knowledge and convention (extralinguistic). While I will be sympathetic to the attempt to void the lexicon of argument-structure information and processes, I will still seek to encode some notion of selectional information that constrains the way lexical items can be associated with syntactic structure (so in this sense I will consider myself responsible for at least some of the data cited by the lexicalist camp, e.g. Levin and Rappaport 1998, Reinhart 2002).

In order to frame the particular proposals of this book more concretely, it is useful to compare schematic versions of the architecture of the grammar with respect to the lexicon that have emerged either explicitly or implicitly over the years. My descriptions of the main options are not necessarily specific to a particular researcher, although I will attempt to associate the different abstract positions with various prominent proposals in the literature. Every individual proposal has its own subtleties and makes specific decisions about implementation, which I will abstract away from here. The purpose in what follows, rather, is to characterize the extreme options in an idealized way, in order to clarify what is at stake, and to contextualize the view I will develop in this book.

The core questions that any theory of the lexicon must address are the following:

(i) Is the lexicon a 'module' of the grammatical system, with its own designated primitives and operations?

(ii) If the answer to (i) is yes, what is the division of labour between 'lexical' operations and the recursive/generative syntactic computation (which must exist, by hypothesis)? [3]

---

[3] See, for example, Wasow (1977) for an argument for the lexicon-internal treatment of passive, and Dubinsky and Simango (1996) for a discussion of adjectival passives in English and Chichewa, also Marantz (2001) for a recent reassessment.

(iii) What is the relationship between lexical information and nonlanguage dedicated parts of the mind/brain?

According to a common-sense standard view of lexical entries, lexical items used in language contain both language-specific and non-language-specific memorized information. I represent a possible listing in the toy lexical entry in (1).

(1)

> RUN
>
> $/ r \wedge n /$
>
> Verb, $< 1 >$
>
> +dynamic; −telic
>
> argument 1: Theme; argument 1: animate
>
> *continuous directed motion undergone by* $< 1 >$
>
> *motion involves rapid movement of legs,*
>
> *no continuous contact with ground*
>
> $\vdots$
>
> *Associations: exercise, boredom, heart attacks*

In principle, anything can be memorized; nevertheless, certain lexical entries do not exist in natural language. For example, lexical entries where the agentive instigator of an action is realized as the direct object, while the passive undergoer comes out as the subject, do not seem to be attested. This kind of pattern is clearly not arbitrary. The generalizations about thematic linking to grammatical function, and the fact that intransitive verbs with 'more agent-like' arguments behave linguistically differently from intransitive verbs with more 'patient-like' arguments (the unaccusative hypothesis, Perlmutter 1978), are generalizations we would like our theory of grammar to capture. There are two clear strategies for implementing the generalizations we need:

(I) The **lexical–thematic** approach, which allows for the semantic classi-fication of role types within the lexicon, readable by a 'linking' theory that places these different roles in different places within the structure. In this approach, the relevant information is *projected from the lexicon*. Under this view, the lexicon is a 'submodule' of the language faculty since it has its own distinct primitives and modes of combination.

(II) The **generative–constructivist** approach which allows free building of syntactic terminals, but allows general encyclopedic knowledge to mediate whether a particular lexical item may be inserted in those terminals or not (Borer 2005, Marantz 2001). Under this view, the lexicon is *not* a submodule, since it contains no grammatically relevant information or processes.

1.1 Capturing argument-structure generalizations

1.1.1 The lexical–thematic approach

If we embark on the first strategy, and take the lexicon to be a genuine module dealing with argument structure, then the linguistically relevant part of the lexical entry looks perhaps as follows (with more or less internal structuring) (2).

(2)   RUN;   V

         <1>

         Theme

However, the most important challenge when pursuing this view lies in stating the correspondence or linking rules between the lexical module and its internal structuring and the syntactic module and its internal structuring. One traditional way of doing this includes postulating the existence of a 'thematic hierarchy' which mediates the assignment of thematic participants to grammatical function or structural position. Some examples of thematic hierarchies are shown in (3) and (4) below, with examples of rules of argument realization in (5) taken from Larson (1988).

(3)   Larson (1988)

       AGENT < THEME < GOAL < OBLIQUES(manner, location, time)

(4)   Grimshaw (1990)

       Agent < Experiencer < Goal/Source Location < Theme

(5)   *Principle of Argument Realization 1* (Larson 1988)

       If α is a predicate and β is an argument of α, then β must be realized within a projection headed by α.

       Principle of Argument Realization 2 (Larson 1988)

       If a verb α determines θ-roles $\theta_1, \theta_2 \dots \theta_n$, then the lowest role on the Thematic Hierarchy is assigned to the lowest argument in constituent structure, the next lowest role to the next lowest argument, and so on.

It is important to note that there has not been consensus on the number and types of thematic relations the theory should employ, nor on the exact nature of the thematic hierarchy involved. Dismay at the lack of reliable and objective linguistic diagnostics led at least one researcher, Dowty (1989), to despair of the enterprise altogether. Dowty himself offered a more flexible alternative to thematic generalizations in his 1990 article, advocating a more fluid kind of linking based on the relative weighting of a number of different proto-properties. These are listed in (6) below.

(6)   *Dowty's proto-roles (1990)*
        Contributing properties for the *Agent Proto-role*
        (a) volition
        (b) sentience (and/or perception)
        (c) causes event
        (d) movement
        (e) referent exists independent of action of verb

        Contributing properties for the *Patient Proto-role*
        (a) change of state (including coming into being, going out of being)
        (b) incremental theme (i.e. determinant of aspect)
        (c) causally affected by event
        (d) stationary (relative to movement of Proto-agent)
        (e) Referent may not exist independent of action of verb, or may not
            exist at all.

        Dowty's argument selection principle (1990)
        The argument of a predicate having the greatest number of Proto-agent prop-
        erties entailed by the meaning of the predicate will, all else being equal, be
        lexicalized as the subject of the predicate; the argument having the greatest
        number of Proto-patient properties will, all else being equal, be lexicalized as
        the direct object of the predicate.

In fact, this is even more of a retreat than it appears to be, since the principle of argument selection given above cannot be seen as a fact about the synchronic computational system (since, plausibly, decisions about what gets to be the 'subject' are not computed on-line or subject to variability in cases of 'ties'), nor as a fact about memory (if one assumes that memory does not calculate, but merely retrieves information). Dowty's principle basically gives up the idea that the generalizations we see should be represented in the core grammar – the properties he gives must have the status of general cognitive tendencies which ultimately underlie how various concepts tend to get lexicalized (memorized) in natural language. Dowty's proto-roles are nevertheless interesting and instructive, because they are the ones that he judged to be most criterial of linguistic behaviour. As we will see, I will argue that these general properties (as opposed to thematic role labels) are in fact the right level of abstractness for stating systematicities concerning the mapping between syntax and semantics.

One further view on thematic linking is worth mentioning here, that of Baker (1988) and subsequent work. In Baker's view, thematic roles are linked to structure/grammatical function not via a relative ranking system as in theories employing the thematic hierarchy, but in a more *absolute* sense. In other words, each type of thematic role has its own special structural position that it is associated with.

(7)   *The Uniformity of Theta Assignment Hypothesis (UTAH)*
       Identical thematic relationships between items are represented by
       identical structural relationships between those items at the level of
       D-structure.   (from Baker 1988: 46)

In recent work, Baker (1997) claims that the notion of thematic role that is relevant for this principle is somewhat more abstract than the traditional list, but rather contains such thematic categories as: Agent (specifier of the higher VP of a Larsonian structure), theme (specifier of the lower VP of a Larsonian structure), Goal/Path (complement of the lower VP). Still, the principle (and, in fact, many systematic principles of linking) receives its major challenges from data pairs such as (8), (9) and (10) below, where apparently identical thematic configurations are differently aligned in the syntax.

(8)   *Experiencer object vs. experiencer subject*
       (a) Wolves frighten John.
       (b) John fears wolves.

(9)   *The dative/double object alternation*
       (a) John gave the book to Mary.
       (b) John gave Mary the book.

(10)   *The spray-load alternation*
       (a) Bill loaded the cart with hay.
       (b) Bill loaded hay on the cart.

A lexical theory containing linking principles such as those described above essentially has three main options in dealing with such flexibility. The first option is to make the linking principles themselves flexible and nondeterministic. This is in a sense the option taken by Dowty (1990) and certain versions of LFG (cf. Bresnan 2001). The second option is to claim that the (a) and (b) sentences above involve the same underlying configurations, but at least one of them involves a nontrivial syntactic derivation. This, for example, is the option taken by Larson (1988) in his treatment of the double object alternation, and the solution advocated by Baker (1997) for one set of alternations as well. The extent to which this general strategy is plausible will depend on the syntactic principles at stake being independently justifiable, and not ad hoc additions to the syntactic tool box merely to save the UTAH and its kin. The third strategy, of course, is to claim that the thematic roles in the (b) sentences are actually different from those in the (a) sentences (cf. Oehrle 1976, Pesetsky 1995 for the double object construction). This is in fact the claim Baker (1997) makes for the 'spray-load' alternation, although not for the 'double object' alternation. The success of this strategy revolves around resolving the tension between the need to use fairly abstract thematic labels to capture the natural classes which exist but which are nevertheless subtle enough to distinguish between thematic relationships in the closely related pairs above.

Thus, assuming a lexicon which contains at least some annotations from a syntactic vocabulary encompasses a wide range of theories from different ideologies, I think it is possible to distinguish two clear extremes.

(i) *The static lexicon*
The lexicon contains argument-structure information which correlates in a systematic and possibly deterministic way with syntactic structure. The lexicon has its own vocabulary, but there are no lexicon-internal manipulations prior to insertion. Syntactic transformations can alter the manifestation of a particular set of lexical information in a sentence.

(ii) *The dynamic lexicon*
The lexicon contains argument-structure information which correlates in a systematic and possibly deterministic way with syntactic structure. The lexicon has its own vocabulary, as well as lexicon-internal manipulations prior to insertion. Syntactic transformations to account for alternations are kept to a minimum.

Both types of approach necessitate a linking theory because each module uses a different vocabulary, but independent differences also arise relating to whether that linking is assumed to be deterministic and absolute, deterministic and relative, or even one which involves optionality (nondeterministic). I take Baker (1988) to be a representative of the (deterministic) static lexicon view, with Levin and Rappaport Hovav (1995) being proponents of the dynamic lexicon view.

Flexibility in verbal meaning exists on the level of aspectual specification as well, prompting the postulation of lexicon-internal processes such as 'template augmentation' (cf. Levin and Rappaport Hovav 1995) and event-type shifting (van Hout 2000a, 2000b).

Thus, while there are many differences of approach within this broad class of theories, the very notion of 'linking theory' presupposes that two distinct vocabularies from two distinct modules are being connected. Which 'rules' and 'transformations' exist in one or the other, or indeed both modules (the lexicon and the syntax), constitutes an important debate in the context of this kind of architecture, and has a direct impact on the nature of the labels and natural classes proposed for the thematic roles as listed in the lexicon. In this book, I will pursue the view that there is only one module where rules and transformations can be stated (I will call this the narrow syn–sem computation). However, the patterns uncovered through these classic debates will form much of the descriptive base for the proposal, and the general intuition behind the UTAH, which correlates structure with meaning fairly directly, will be present in the implementation. The bottom line is that lexical theories must either invoke 'lexicon-internal' processes, or tolerate massive stipulated homonymies. To the extent that the processes that need to be assumed can actually be elegantly captured in the syntax, it should be preferable on grounds of parsimony to assume only one such system if we can get away with it.

1.1.2 Generative–constructivist approaches

Under an extreme constructivist view, lexical roots contain *no* syntactically relevant information at all; they are just bundles of cognitive and encyclopedic information. Consider the revised 'lexical entry' below in (11).

(11)

RUN
continuous directed motion undergone by animate entity
motion involves rapid movement of legs,
no continuous contact with ground
⋮
Associations: exercise, boredom, heart attacks etc.

The complete lack of syntactic or argument-structure information on the file card makes it in principle compatible with many different syntactic frames.

Thus, Borer (2005) offers the following range of examples for the English verb *siren* (which significantly is also compatible with nominal syntactic structure).

(12)   (a) The fire stations sirened throughout the raid.
        (b) The factory sirened midday and everyone stopped for lunch.
        (c) The police sirened the Porsche to a stop.
        (d) The police car sirened up to the accident.
        (e) The police car sirened the daylights out of me. (from Borer 2005)

The well-known problem with this view is of course the fact that argument-structure flexibility is *not* as general as it would suggest. For example, some intransitive verbs resist causativization (13a), and others resist telic augmentation (13b):

(13)   (a) *John slept the baby.
        (b) *John watched Mary bored/to boredom.

How does one account for this kind of selective behaviour in a theory where the lexical item contains nothing written in the syntactic vocabulary? For Borer (2005) the (only internally consistent) answer is given: convention, habits of speech and real-world knowledge make certain combinations of root plus syntactic/functional information unusable or infelicitous.

Under the Borerian and Marantzian views, the distinction between lexical and functional categories hardens, lining up with real-world vs. linguistic meaning respectively. The root is the only lexical category under these views, although ironically, of course, it does not even carry category information. All category information and linguistically manipulable meaning come from the functional structure that sits on top of the root. Once again, there are many versions of this position out there in the literature, with slightly different choices of functional projections and labels for any particular effect. In Borer's structure, there is an aspectual quantity phrase that sits on top of the VP and is responsible for both telicity and object quantity effects. In Travis's work, there is an event phrase (EP) higher than VP and an aspectual phrase (AspP) sandwiched in between Larsonian VP shells, the latter of which is correlated with telicity (Travis 2000). In Ritter and Rosen (1998), there is an initiational aspectual projection on top of TP, and a delimitational aspectual projection in between TP and VP. The general approach also varies with respect to how much information is allowed to the lexical root and how much is relegated to the functional structure. In Kratzer (1996), the lexical root contains information about the internal argument, but the external argument is introduced by a hierarchically superior functional head *v*. The idea of little *v* in its turn has had many proponents, different types of external argument being introduced by different 'flavours' of the little *v* head (cf. Harley 1995, Folli and Harley 2004). Within this spread of opinion, in a sense the same debate is being staged – the division of labour between the syntax and the lexicon. Once again, we can distinguish two extremes.

(i) *The naked roots view*
   The root contains no syntactically relevant information, not even category features.

(ii) *The well-dressed roots view*
   The root may contain some syntactic information, ranging from category information to syntactic selectional information and degrees of argument-structure information, depending on the particular theory. This information is mapped in a systematic way onto the syntactic representation which directly encodes it.

The latter position is virtually indistinguishable in practice from the static lexicon view in the section above, and could be made perfectly compatible with it provided the technical issue of selection and selectional features is decided. In practice, the majority of researchers in the 'decompositional' or 'constructivist' camp actually fall between the two extremes described above. In essence, the theoretical questions revolve around deciding how much functional structure (which heads precisely, and in which order(s)) related to so-called 'argument-structure' generalizations can be justified in the syntactic representation. It should be clear that this question corresponds empirically to the question of how many and what type of thematic roles we have and how they line up with syntactic position in the deterministic static lexicon view.

In discussing the general class of 'constructivist' approaches, it is necessary to say a word about 'Construction Grammar', which I think must be clearly distinguished from those above, even though it shares with them the view that 'structures carry meaning'. The theory of construction grammar, as found for example in Goldberg (1995), allows that structures carry meaning but seems to make the opposite architectural claim to that of the constructivists discussed above: it analogizes constructions to lexical items that have to be listed and memorized. In this sense, it downplays the generative character of the natural language system and allows large templatic chunks to be simply memorized. The view taken in this book will be that the reason constructions have meaning is because they are systematically constructed as part of a generative system (syntactic form) that has predictable meaning correlates. Thus, the view proposed here will be 'generative–constructivist' in spirit, but not 'constructionist'.

1.2   Excursus on the role of encyclopedic knowledge

One of the important ideas in this system, which I share with many others, is the need to make a strict and principled distinction between linguistic meaning and encyclopedic content. In this context, it is useful to examine another prominent view of the lexicon, as espoused by Pustejovsky (1991). Pustejovsky's 'generative' lexicon is interesting because it explicitly contains two different sorts of information, which he acknowledges to be different. Specifically, Pustejovsky acknowledges that (i) there is no way that meaning can be divorced from the structure that carries it and (ii) that the meanings of words are also the reflections of deeper conceptual structures, i.e. the 'image' of nonlinguistic conceptual organizational principles.

> *Information in the lexicon according to Pustejovsky*
> A Argument structure: the behaviour of a word as a function, with its arity specified. This is the predicate argument structure for a word, which indicates how it maps to syntactic expressions.
> B Event structure: identification of the particular event type (in the sense of Vendler) for a word or phrase, e.g. as state, process or transition.
> C Qualia structure: the essential attributes of an object as defined by the lexical item.
>   • The relation between it and its constituent parts *constitutive role*
>   • That which distinguishes it within a larger domain *formal role*
>   • Its purpose and function *telic role*
>   • Whatever brings it about *agentive role*
> D Inheritance structure: how the word is globally related to other concepts in the lexicon.

Rather than assuming a fixed set of primitives in lexical-semantic representations, Pustejovsky assumes a set of generative devices to construct semantic expressions for *one* aspect of the lexical representation. These 'generative devices' are basically located in the event-structure module of Pustejovsky's system and the recursive rules that combine them.

While I am completely in sympathy with the distinction made by Pustejovsky, I differ with respect to the architectural decision that he makes. Basically, since event-structure composition is productive and does not actually need to be memorized, it is not clear whether it really belongs in a designated module separate from syntactic generative devices proper, i.e. it looks as if these principles need to apply to 'constructions'. If the combinatoric devices proposed are essentially redundant with syntax, then they do not belong here. During the course of this book I will attempt to show that it is a mistake to take argument structure/event structure facts as a property of the lexicon, or even single lexical items, since the same structural organization can be detected in languages that use single words or analytic constructions to express verbal meaning.

The second problem with Pustejovsky's position is in a sense the converse of the first. This concerns the amount of cognitive information that is claimed to be specified in an item's lexical entry. I think it can be shown that this is a slippery slope, and that the effects of qualia structure are not in fact distinguishable in any reliable way from real-world knowledge whose effects are unpredictable. Consider the following example.

(14)   (a) John began a book.
            (began writing it, or began reading it)

The qualia structure of the item *book* contains information about its telic role and its agentive role in the above sense, and this is what is supposed to license the two different types of inference in (14) above. But, of course, other readings are possible. If John and Mary are systematically going through all of Bill's magazines erasing all the 'e's, one can say (14a) to indicate the start of that process applied to a book. Given this kind of interpretational possibility, it is not obvious where one stops annotating a lexical item with how it can potentially interact with the real world.

In some cases, the effects feeding off qualia structure seem to be even more than just specificities of interpretation, but actually have syntactic consequences. In the pairs of examples in (15) and (16) below, the only thing changed is the choice of DP object.

(15)   (a) John baked a cake.
         (b) John baked a potato.

(16)   (a) John painted a picture.
         (b) John painted a wall.

Pustejovsky uses the contrast in inferences between 'bake a cake' and 'bake a potato' to argue for different qualia structure for 'cake' and 'potato' in their lexical entries. On the other hand, real-world knowledge makes equally great differences to the inferences licensed. In the case of a potter making clay miniatures of edible items, the judgement concerning (15b) is rather different.

At the same time, the creation sense allowed for the 'bake a cake' and 'paint a picture' examples is probably in fact a different structure within the verb phrase, with further distinct linguistic consequences. So, while the creation sense use of 'paint' can give rise to a benefactive construction, as in (17), or a resultative construction, as in (18), the incremental theme interpretation of an object does not, as the (b) examples show.

(17)   (a) John painted me a picture.
        (b) ??John painted me a wall.

(18)   (a) John painted a wall red.
        (b) ??John painted a picture red.

The point here is that there is no a priori way of deciding what goes into the lexical entry with respect to qualia structure. There is no evidence that differences in inference properties at this level are linguistic at all. Rather, it seems more as if language allows different structures, but the real world determines felicity and detailed inferential patterns.

In this book, I will indeed be taking seriously the distinction between lexical-encyclopedic content and structural correlates of meaning. The decisions about what kind of meaning fall on which side of this divide is of course a subtle and empirical question, and should not be prejudged. The theoretical point, though, is that if all so-called lexical content can be reduced to either one or the other, the structural-generative aspect of meaning can be profitably analysed as part of the syntactic component. The lexical-encyclopedic side is a matter for general cognition. The lexical entry itself is the memorized link between chunks of conceptual structure and conditions of insertion; it does not need to reside in a module with its own combinatorial primitives.

The distinction I am making has always been acknowledged in the lexicalist proposals of Levin and Rappaport Hovav (1995), for example. The abstract templatic aspects of Levin and Rappaport's representations are the ones that I will give syntactic representation. The insertion of lexical items into these structures will be analogous to the association of 'constants' to the variables of those abstract templates in the lexicalist views. Thus, the lexical item will contribute conceptual content to structural aspects of meaning, and will be tagged with category labels as a way of constraining that insertion. Thus, unlike the radical generative–constructivist position, I will not be assuming that lexical items are free of syntactic information, and neither will I be assuming that they are inserted always at the 'bottom' or 'root' of the tree. The pure naked roots view seems too strong, and only appears to work when it ignores the substantial empirical and technical issues surrounding selection. Moreover, it defines away the central property of the lexical item as an associative web of properties from different modules, *including*, crucially, the narrow syn–sem computation.

The entry for *run* in (19) is an idealization of the distributed nature of the information involved. It can be represented in one box, but only as a convenient idealization, because of strong links of mental association.

(19)

> RUN
> Label seen by PF: / r ∧ n /
> Label seen by narrow syn–sem computation: *v*, V
> *continuous directed motion undergone by animate*
> *motion involves rapid movement of legs,*
> *no continuous contact with ground*
> ⋮
> *Associations: exercise, boredom, heart attacks*

Thus, lexical items in this system will associate to syntactic representations via their syntactic labels. Constructional-semantic and lexical-encyclopedic contributions are unified to form a proposition at the interface with the cognitive/interpretive systems of the mind/brain.

Under the kind of view explored in this book, the lexicon cannot exist as a module because it is not encapsulated, but associates representations from radically different cognitive modules (conceptual, articulatory, formal).

To the extent that variability of use within syntactic structures is systematic, the primitives and processes involved are the same ones that are used by syntax. I will take as a starting point that it is more parsimonious to assume that they are part of the same system with syntax. On the other hand, there may well be cognitive generalizations about conceptual structure, but we know that conceptual structure must exist outside language. Lexical-encyclopedic knowledge is of a piece with real-world knowledge and does not give systematic compositional effects (the crucial distinguishing property of language).

Syntactic category information appears to be unavoidable for mediating the association of 'functional' lexical items and syntactic structure. If we can reduce all the 'selectional' constraints of so-called 'lexical' categories to this type of association too, then there is no argument against it from parsimony. As with all proposals concerning the architecture of the system, one makes a choice as to where the complexity of that system resides. Under this view, there is only one combinatorial system, and the primitive modes of combination will be minimalist (i.e. confined to (Re)Merge and Agree, triggered by the need to check uninterpretable features), but the complexity will reside in the extended functional sequence assumed in the syntax and the larger set of category features that implies.

The other main point that I want to argue for in this book concerns the nature of the syntax–semantics interface. The basic combinatoric system of the lowest part of the clause emerges as something which encodes semantic information as well as the traditionally syntactic. An inevitable consequence of the separation of lexical-encyclopedic information from the structural is that the structures themselves will be seen to determine abstract predicational and event-compositional semantics. However, unlike the 'constructional' grammar of Goldberg (1995), this semantics will not be associated with arbitrarily large syntactic objects, but constructed systematically on the basis of primitive recursive syntactic relationships. I will argue that once the most atomic predicational relations among basic formatives are taken into account, it is possible to see complex event-structural and argumental relations as being decomposable into simpler ones, which moreover correspond to the simplest primitives of *syntactic* combination (here taken to be MERGE and a distinction between specifiers and complements). Thus, the decomposition of verbal meaning will lead to a proposal concerning the functional sequence of the lowest part of the clause, and universal combinatoric semantics that goes along with it. Isolating this systematic semantic combinatoric component of the grammar is only possible once a principled line is drawn between it and the lexical-encyclopedic and real-world knowledge that goes along with every actual verb in context.

The problem of what constitutes the lexical information determined by a verb carries us first into the domains of argument-structure specificity and flexibility, and event-structure/aktionsart specificity and flexibility. What will emerge from the initial empirical discussion and summary from the literature in chapter 2 is that a particular set of featural or combinatoric primitives seem to be implicated in the linguistic generalizations we find. The challenge of expressing the lexical information in both these domains is to express both the flexibility and the limitations that exist, and the interplay between different elements of the structure in a systematic way. In chapter 3, I make a specific proposal concerning the nature of what I will call the first, or event-building, phase of the syntax (the 'first phase') and the relation between it and the lexicon. The central feature of 'first-phase syntax'[4] is that it decomposes the information classically seen to

---

[4] I use the term 'first phase' here to imply logical priority. The event-building portion of a proposition is assumed here to be prior to case marking/checking, agreement, tense and modification in general. I make no assumptions about what the 'second phase' is or what it should look like. Moreover, if the piece of syntax I am investigating here does not actually turn out to be a 'phase' in the sense of Chomsky (2001) and others, it will not greatly affect the proposals here, since I use no arguments from phase theory to circumscribe the scope of my concerns.

reside within lexical items into a set of distinct categories with specific syntactic and semantic modes of combination. Lexical items in English will be seen to be featurally complex, with their argument-structure properties and flexibility deriving ultimately from the association rules that link the particular feature bundle to the syntactic combinatoric system. In chapter 4, I will use the system to spell out the decomposition of basic verbs in English in their different uses, including a reconceptualization of the classic conflation-type verbs of Hale and Keyser, and an analysis of the double object construction. In chapter 5, result augmentation is considered. Here I examine in some detail the range of resultative and path augmentations in English, including prepositional phrases with motion verbs, and adjectival resultatives. The verb–particle construction is also discussed here as one of the most abstract morphemes in English contributing to the first phase. I compare the particle construction in Germanic with completive complex predicates in South Asian languages and lexical prefixes in Slavic, arguing that the same underlying first-phase syntax is involved, but with different morphological composition. In chapter 6, I tackle the process of first-phase syntax augmentation in the form of causativization, using the productive morphology of direct and indirect causation in Hindi/Urdu as a test case. The final chapter is the conclusion and summarizes the proposals made in the book, and includes some speculations about how the system argued for interacts with the rest of the combinatoric system with its more extended functional sequence.

2 *The empirical ground*

2.1 Selection versus variability

Over the years, it has been acknowledged that in addition to syntactic category information, lexical entries need to contain information related to their selectional properties. The specification of syntactic complementation can account for the difference between transitive and intransitive verbs, for example (1), or for the difference between the verbs that take CP complements vs. IP complements on the other (2).

(1) (a) John saw the lizard./*John saw.
     (b) *John dined the tortellini./John dined.

(2) (a) John hoped that the rain would fall./*John hoped the rain to fall.
     (b) *John got that the rain would fall./John got the rain to fall.

Syntactic selectional information however, is not always deemed to be enough since there seem to be generalizations related to the *type* of semantic participant that make a difference to the linguistic behaviour of different verb types. So, for example, transitive experiencer subject verbs behave differently from transitive verbs with agentive subjects (3) (Grimshaw 1979, Pesetsky 1982), and intransitive verbs with patient arguments (unaccusatives) seem to behave differently from intransitive verbs with agent arguments (unergatives) (4) (Perlmutter 1978, Williams 1980, Marantz 1984, inter alia).

(3) (a) John fears tigers.
     (b) John kills tigers.

(4) (a) The vase fell.
     (b) John danced.

To the extent that these differences are grounded in genuine linguistic behaviour, and not simply a difference in real-world understanding, it seems as if they need to be represented in the lexical entry of the predicates involved. Thematic roles are one way of dealing with generalizations of this type (Gruber 1965, Baker 1988, Grimshaw 1990). Once thematic role information or semantic selectional properties are enshrined in the linguistic system in the form of theta-marking, it is tempting to try to reduce facts that could be accounted for by syntactic selection to this kind of semantic selection as well, so that only that type of information need be present in the lexical entry (Grimshaw 1979, Pesetsky 1982, and recently in the context of distributed morphology Harley and Noyer 2000). However, there are two basic problems with making the reduction in this direction.

Firstly, there are serious doubts concerning the definability and empirical adequacy of thematic role classifications. The ultimate success of a theory of θ-role types depends on finding linguistically legitimate natural classes of arguments which can be systematically identified and studied. As Dowty (1989) has argued, the θ-role labels as traditionally formulated do *not* give rise to natural linguistic classes in terms of their syntactic or semantic behaviour (see also Croft 1998). In particular, Dowty (1989) has shown that many of the linguistic generalizations traditionally stated in terms of particular thematic relations, on further analysis have turned out to rely on distinctions *within* a particular thematic class[1] or on different semantic primitives altogether.[2] In addition, using principles like the thematic hierarchy to regulate mapping to the syntax does not always give the correct empirical results (cf. dative alternation verbs, psych predicates with either experiencer objects or experiencer subject, or spray-load alternations).

More recent argument-role classifications have zeroed in on the fact that the factors that seem to make a difference to linguistic behaviour are correlated with event structure or aktionsart properties. Vendler's 1967 article presenting the Aristotelian classification of event types and relating it to classes of predicate in natural language is the source of much stimulating work on the aspectual or event-structure classification of verbs (Dowty 1979, Taylor 1977, Kenny 1963). While it is now understood that the original division

---

[1] While the initial generalization was that 'do so' substitution and the progressive both picked out the class of verbs with 'Agent' subjects, it turned out that two different notions of Agent had to be distinguished: one characterized by the presence of motion or instigating change (for the 'do so' test), and the other characterized by volition (for the progressive) (Dowty 1989).

[2] In the case of Dutch, auxiliary selection is argued in Zaenen (1993) to be sensitive not to 'Theme' subject vs. 'Agent' subject, but to the difference between definite and indefinite change of state (accomplishment vs. achievement).

into *states, activities, achievements* and *accomplishments* cannot correspond directly to what is specified in the lexicon, many theories attempt to use lower-level aspectual *features* that are derived from these larger natural classes. In particular, notions such as *telicity/boundedness, dynamicity* or *durativity* have played an important role in subsequent theories of event-structure decomposition and lexical classification. In general, many researchers have attempted to classify verbs by means of their inherent aspectual properties (Grimshaw 1990, Hoekstra 1984, 1992, Hoekstra and Mulder 1990, Tenny 1987, Levin and Rappaport Hovav 1995) as a way of capturing important linguistic generalizations.

Recently, many linguists have attempted an explicit aspectual classification of thematic roles and relations themselves, often primarily to account for aspectual compositional effects. Most notable in this class are the proposals introducing lower-level features such as +ADD-TO (which represents the verb's incremental or 'additive' properties), +SQA (which encodes whether a specific quantity of matter is denoted by the DP) (Verkuyl 1989, 1993) or QUA (a general quantization property for both objects and events) and Mapping-to-Objects (a particular kind of thematic relation between verb and object) (Krifka 1987) which can combine with the features of the lexical predicate to give telicity under certain conditions. The aspectual thematic role in this sense is defined by the entailments about aspectual structure that it gives rise to (see also Ramchand 1993, 1997). These classifications are more successful than the classical thematic role labels because they are definable on the basis of genuine linguistic diagnostics and are better at accounting for data such as the spray-load alternation and the unaccusative/unergative divide. Researchers in the more traditional thematic role tradition have also increasingly used more abstract and event-structure-based labels to categorize participant relations (cf. Baker 1997).

However, even these more satisfactory classifications of participant relations have to deal with the second problem facing any attempt to reduce lexical classification to semantic selection. This is the fact that argument-structure information is actually not nearly as rigid as lexical classification in general would imply. Any system of lexical classification of role types (whether classically thematic or aspectual) has to face the reality of argument-structure variability, in a fairly systematic and predictable form. For example, in English, a large class of verbs systematically occurs in an intransitive version with a single 'internal' or theme-like argument, as well as a transitive version with both an agent and a theme (the 'ergative' class of verbs, according to the terminology of Hale and Keyser 1987).

(5)   (a) The glass broke.
       (b) John broke the glass.

These argument-structure alternations, whether mediated by morphological affixation or not, in English and other languages (e.g. middle formation, passive, causativization, etc.), seem to offer evidence for systematic lexicon-internal processes as an alternative to stipulated ambiguity with multiple lexical items (cf. Levin and Rappaport Hovav 1995). Unless such 'lexical redundancy rules' are postulated, representations of lexical information run the risk of failing to capture pervasive generalizations concerning related/phonologically identical lexical items.

At the extreme end of the spectrum, the variability of behaviour seems so rampant as to be virtually unconstrained except by real-world knowledge. Consider for example, the transitive creation/consumption verb such as *eat* in English, which can appear in the following grammatical environments with different aspectual effects (cf. Folli and Harley 2004).

(6)   (a) John ate the apple.
       (b) John ate at the apple.
       (c) The sea ate into the coastline.
       (d) John ate me out of house and home.
       (e) John ate.
       (f) John ate his way into history.

Data like these tempt one into the radical constructionalist approach of Borer (1998, 2005) or Marantz (1997b), whereby no lexical information is present at all, but lexical items are inserted into syntactic contexts according to compatibility with encyclopedic and real-world knowledge. Under this view, the generalizations reside in the systematic ways in which syntactic structures are interpreted by the linguistic computational system, not in the information specified by lexical entries.

At the same time, however, verbal flexibility is not completely general, as the data in (7) and (8) show, otherwise the radical constructionalist view would be unavoidable.

(7)   (a) John arrived.
       (b) *Bill arrived John.

(8)   (a) Mary weighs 100 pounds.
       (b) *Mary weighs.

Flexibility exists on the level of aspectual specification as well, giving rise to proposals for lexicon-internal processes such as Levin and Rappaport's (1998) template augmentation or event-type shifting (van Hout 2000, 2001). The two core cases of event type-shifting involve (i) the adding of a causative subevent to an already possible event structure (as in (9)), or (ii) the adding of a telos to a process verb (as in (10)):[3]

(9)   John jumped the horse over the fence.

(10)   John ate the porridge up.

But once again, these processes are not completely general since some verbs seem to resist causativization (11a), and others resist telic augmentation (11b):

(11)   (a) *John slept the baby.
        (b) *John watched Mary bored/to boredom.

Thus flexibility in event structure and argument structure goes hand in hand with more intangible limits and constraints.

The strategy I will pursue is first of all to reject the existence of formal semantic selectional features in the lexicon, but attempt to account for what rigidity there is in terms of purely syntactic or categorial features, made possible by a more articulated view of the functional sequence within the verb phrase. I will show that once the selectional generalizations are properly understood and isolated from the more heterogeneous and unsystematic felicity conditions based on encyclopedic meaning, they will be seen to be amenable to representation in terms of an articulated syntax with a systematic semantic interpretation. This will allow a radical simplification of the architecture of the grammar by reducing the set of combinatorial primitives and will account for important crosslinguistic data concerning the nature and flexibility of lexical items.

The first step is to establish and motivate the primitives that are empirically necessary in a decomposition of verbal meaning – this is what the remainder of this chapter sets out to do. This sketch is intended as a basic outline of the important distinctions that need to be made in the face of the broadest empirical patterns, not as a complete exegesis of verb types. In chapter 4, after the theoretical machinery has been introduced, I will return to the data in an attempt to offer diagnostics and to be more explicit about the syntax and semantics of individual verb types.

---

[3] Here I am assuming that a telos can be added by a PP, adjectival resultatives and particles.

2.1.1 Causation

The approach I will take here is to argue that establishing the primitive role types goes hand in hand with establishing the primitive elements of event decomposition, since participants in the event will only be definable via the role they play in the event or subevent. The first component of verbal meaning that has received much empirical support in the literature is that of causation. Causation has been shown to be a relevant parameter in verbal differences and shows up very often as overt morphology within the verbal inventory of human languages (cf. Baker 1988, Hale and Keyser 1993, Ritter and Rosen 1998, Rappaport-Hovav and Levin 2000). Moreover, as I will argue next, it is implicated in the external vs. internal argument distinction that has been used as a defining property of verb classes within languages.

Ever since the unaccusative hypothesis of Perlmutter (1978), the existence of an 'external argument' or 'agent' has been cited as criterial of a major division in (intransitive) verb types (e.g. Williams 1980, Marantz 1984). However, Rappaport-Hovav and Levin (2000) show convincingly that it is not agency per se that determines class membership as either unaccusative or unergative. The following intransitives cited by them pass the diagnostics for unergativity in Italian, Dutch and Basque even though they do not possess arguments that bring anything about by agentive action.

(12)   *glow, stink, spew*

Even in English, the fact that these verbs possess an external argument can be demonstrated by their ability to take *X's way* objects under certain circumstances (examples 13) and also show an inability to causativize (examples 14).[4]

(13)   (a) He stank his smelly way home.
        (b) The water spewed its way along the corridor.
        (c) John ran his way into history.

(14)   (a) *Michael glowed Karena's face.
        (b) *We spewed the water out of the sink.
        (c) *We stank the dog by throwing him in the cesspit.
        (d) *John ran Mary by scaring her with a live mouse.

While it is true that many types of external argument can be distinguished according to different semantic properties such as volitionality/agency (Butt 1995 for Hindi/Urdu) or active vs. inactive causing (as in Doron 2003), they

---

[4] These examples are taken from Rappaport-Hovav and Levin (2000).

all seem to be subclasses of argument that behave the same way with respect
to our linguistic diagnostics for unaccusativity as shown above, and differently
from internal arguments. Thus, I will accept the general intuition that there is
an important primitive underlying the distinction between 'internal' and 'external' arguments (cf. Marantz 1984), but I will assume (with Rappaport-Hovav
and Levin 2000 and many others) that the relevant abstract category is that of
'initiator'. An initiator is an entity whose properties/behaviour are responsible for the eventuality coming into existence. Thus, *stinking* has an external
argument which is the initiator by virtue of inherent properties of dirtiness or
smelliness; the water is the initiator of a spewing event by virtue of the fact
that it has the requisite properties of kinetic energy; volitional agents have
intentions and desires that lead them to initiate dynamic events; instrumental
subjects are entities whose facilitating properties are presented as initiating the
event because they allow it to happen. There is a sense in which all of these
'thematic roles' are just real-world instantiations of the more abstract concept
of causation.[5]

Among transitive verbs as well, external arguments can be volitional agents
(15a, b), instrumentals (15c), abstract causes/sources (15d–f), showing the
generality and abstractness of the external argument relation.

(15)　(a) John broke the window.
　　　(b) John built that house.
　　　(c) The hammer broke the window.
　　　(d) The videotape from the secret camera demonstrated the truth of
　　　　　the matter.
　　　(e) The storm broke the window.
　　　(f) John's money built that house.

I'm going to assume, therefore, that even though agency might be relevant
for felicity in certain circumstances, it does not directly determine syntactically relevant class membership. The relevant notion here is that of causation
or initiation, or more abstractly, the existence of a causing subevent, which
has a DP role associated with it via the syntax (similar to Kratzer 1996) and
which is specified more particularly by the lexical encyclopedic knowledge of

---

[5] It is important to be clear that these are not claims about the real world, but about
how human beings systematically interpret the situations they perceive in the world.
Causation appears to be a very basic organizational category in these 'interpretations'
and consistent with a number of different real-world possibilities.

the verb itself.[6] I also leave it open exactly how the truth conditions of causation/initiation should be specified. All that is necessary for our purposes is to establish the existence of a primitive notion at this level of abstraction that corresponds to the linguistic reality of how speakers conceive of events and their components. The details of this position will be taken up again in chapter 3.

2.1.2 Telicity

Telos or resultativity is also a component that has been shown to be isolable as a parameter in verbal meanings, and which has associated morphology and case-marking reflexes in various languages (see, for example, Tenny 1987, Kiparsky 1998, van Hout 1996, Ritter and Rosen 1998, Borer 1998). Semantically, it has been widely argued that the combination of 'process' and 'result' creates complex accomplishments (Parsons 1990, Pustejovsky 1991, Higginbotham 2001). These two subeventual components can be found separately or combined within different verbal meanings, and can even be exploited to create more complex types out of simpler ones in many systems, cf. template augmentation (Levin and Rappaport 1998) or event type-shifting (van Hout 2000a, 2000b).

First, I wish to show that while there definitely are privileged relationships between certain arguments and certain aspectual subevents, the relationship is not as straightforward as it might seem from only examining a subset of verbal types. In particular, there is no general one-to-one correspondence between 'internal arguments' and the semantic feature [+telic], even when the internal argument in question is 'quantized' (in the sense of Krifka 1987, 1992). This is contra the position taken in Kratzer (2004), Borer (2005) and van Hout (2000a). Specifically, I will argue that there are two distinct kinds of aspectually sensitive internal arguments, and that 'quantization' is only relevant for a subtype of one of these.

The arguments for the lack of a simple relationship between the feature [+telic] and the internal argument go in both directions. First of all, the existence of telicity does not actually imply the existence of a quantized internal argument (16b), or even an internal argument at all (16a).

(16) (a) John stood up in a second. (*no internal argument*)
      (b) They found gold in three hours. (*mass term internal argument*)

---

[6] In the implementation that follows in chapter 3, I will not use the device of 'flavours' of little *v* (as in Harley 1995) to capture the different types of initiator found in language, but relegate such differences to the encyclopedic content of the root, or whatever lexical element fills that position.

Conversely, equally basic English examples can be used to show that the existence of an internal argument does not imply telicity (not even when it is quantized) (17).

(17)   John pushed the cart for hours.

Kratzer (2004) builds on work by Kiparsky (1998) and Ramchand (1997) to offer a syntactic analysis that respects the semantic/aspectual correlates of differential object case marking in Finnish and Scottish Gaelic respectively, and found in many other languages. Her account makes a distinction between telicity and quantization, and *conditions* of culmination. In her account, objects are directly or indirectly responsible for establishing measures over the event, and need to move to check their accusative feature (there seen as the uninterpretable counterpart of a [+telic] feature) in a higher aspectual projection just outside *v*. In this sense, the account is fairly similar to that found in Borer (2005), where the quantized object must move to check its quantity feature against the quantity feature in the aspectual head dominating the verb phrase.[7] Both accounts must make extra stipulations to account for the cases where quantized objects do not in fact induce telicity (quantizedness on the part of the event), or cases where a nonquantized argument nevertheless occurs with a telic event. In the case of Kratzer, this comes down to invoking covert measure phrases which must co-occur with objects that are not themselves measures; for Borer, independent (non-object-related) ways are found to check the quantization feature on the aspectual head. However, both of these strategies weaken the system considerably, or rather, weaken the support for a syntactic featural connection between quantization or accusative on the direct object and telicity or quantization on the verbal projection. The exceptions to the correlation, in my opinion, are central and normal enough that they cannot really be seen as 'exceptions'. Instead, I propose to make some finer-grained distinctions in terms of how the direct object maps onto the event, although I will preserve the intuition that some kind of event-topological mapping is criterial of direct objecthood.

The idea which I see as central to the distinctions we need to make is that of a 'path' to the event. By this I mean that dynamic verbs have a part–whole structure, as defined by our human perception of the notion of change. In this sense, dynamic events are generalized 'change' analogues of spatial paths. As we saw in the previous section, a certain class of arguments of a dynamic

---

[7] Kratzer rejects Krifka's (1987) notion of quantization as being exactly the right notion here. So, in fact, does Borer – although she retains the term, she offers a different definition of quantization than the one in Krifka (1987).

predicate can be distinguished as 'external' – they are related to the event as a whole, with a kind of abstract causational or initiational semantics. Internal arguments on the other hand are internal to the path structure of the event. However, I would argue there are a number of semantically distinct ways in which they can be so. The first obvious case to consider is the argument that is interpreted as undergoing the change asserted by the dynamic verb (cf. a general 'Undergoer' role, after Van Valin 1990).

There are two distinct points to be made here. The first is that even if we characterize an internal argument as one that crucially undergoes change, empirically it does not seem true that the change must necessarily entail the attainment of a *final* state.

(18)   *widen, harden, melt, dry*

The verbs shown above satisfy tests for unaccusativity in languages that show these clearly, and yet they are not obligatorily telic. A gap can widen but it doesn't necessarily become wide; the chocolate can melt, but it does not have to become completely liquid.

(19)   (a) The gap widened for three minutes (but still remained too narrow for us to pass through).
        (b) The chocolate melted for three minutes in the back seat of the car (before we rescued it).

While the attainment of a result state can give rise to telicity, mere gradual change on the part of an argument is a distinct aspectual property and one which is logically separable from the attainment of a result (although sometimes one can be implied by context if the semantics of the verb is suitable), and hence is compatible with a lack of temporal bound (see Hay, Kennedy and Levin 1999 for an important discussion of the semantics of scales with regard to change-of-state verbs). Verbs which have an argument that undergoes a gradual change (without attainment of a definite result) often display unaccusative behaviour in the languages where the diagnostics are clear, indicating that they actually have internal arguments in the relevant sense. Correspondingly in English, as Rappaport-Hovav and Levin (2000) note, these verbs do not occur in the *X's way* construction; and many of them *do* causativize.

(20)   (a) John widened the gap between himself and his opponents.
        (b) Karena melted the chocolate in the pan.

It seems that what is crucial here is the notion of the argument undergoing some sort of identifiable change/transition, for example whether it is with respect to its location (21a), its state (21b), or its ullage[8] (21c).

(21)   (a) The ball rolled down the hill.
        (b) The mangoes ripened in the sun.
        (c) The bucket filled with rain.

In the case of transitive verbs, we find direct objects that fulfil this condition of 'undergoing change' as well: DPs can make good 'objects' regardless of whether the change is that of location (22a), state (22b) or material properties (22c) (see Ramchand 1997 and Hay, Kennedy and Levin 1999).

(22)   (a) John pushed the cart.
        (b) Mary dried the cocoa beans.
        (c) Michael stretched the rubber band.

The broad notion of UNDERGOER (after Van Valin 1990) seems to be the one responsible for class membership here, and includes objects of verbs of change of state like *dry*, as well as objects of verbs of translational motion like *push* and *drive*. In other words, the existence of an UNDERGOER does not necessarily imply telicity, even when it is quantized (however we choose to define that).

(23)   (a) The document yellowed in the library for centuries.
        (b) John pushed the cart for an hour.
        (c) Mary dried the cocoa beans in the sun for an hour.

These objects are in a very general sense distinct from the causers/initiators of the previous section. What they all have in common is that they are 'undergoers' of transitional states; this fact holds regardless of the internal denotational constitution of the DP in question.

What then of the notion 'quantized-ness' or 'specified quantity' that has played such an important role so far in the literature on aspectual composition? Is there a class of verbs or class of objects that needs to be distinguished from general undergoers on the basis of their linguistic behaviour? Starting with Verkuyl (1972), the literature on aspectual composition has concentrated on a class of creation/consumption verbs where the denotation of the DP object has a direct effect on the aspectual nature of the verb phrase as a whole. So, to

---

[8] A real, but underused, word of English referring to the volume by which a container is not full.

recapitulate the data, in (24a), we see that a DP with homogenous reference such as a mass noun or a bare plural gives rise to a verb phrase without definite temporal boundary, while a DP with bounded or nonhomogenous reference such as a singular or count term can give rise to a temporally bounded interpretation with the very same verb (24b).

(24)   (a) Michael ate apples/ice cream for an hour/??in an hour.
        (b) Michael ate the apple/five apples for an hour/in an hour.

These facts offer a tantalizing analogy between the denotational properties of the object and the denotational properties of the event that it gives rise to. However, mere transference of a feature of boundedness from object to event (as in, for example, Borer 2005) is a stipulation that does not rest on the semantic compositional analysis of the phenomenon, and extends beyond the domain that the semantic compositional analysis is equipped to cover. We need to ask why such features can transfer not just syntactically (which we know to be possible through general 'agreement' processes), but in a semantically interpretable way from one domain to another. In fact, Krifka (1992) offers just such an account: for a certain class of verbs the relation R between the verb and the object satisfies two crucial properties relating denotation of object and event, Mapping-to-Objects, and Mapping-to-Events. Given the satisfaction by R of these two properties, it can be shown that the right aspectual entailments follow. What is less often built into the systems implemented in the syntax is that, as he himself acknowledges, the aspectual entailments follow only for the class of verbs whose R relation has these particular properties – specifically these are just the creation/consumption class of verbs.

Returning to our verbs describing change, it is only if the nature of the change relates directly to the material extent of the object that the direct mapping between object denotation and event denotation can be found. To transfer boundedness from object to event in the general case of an undergoer is both theoretically unfounded and empirically incorrect. In other words, if the transitions are related to the object's material extent, then quantizedness will produce a telic entailment as in (24).

In fact, the creation/consumption type of transitive verb object is more similar to the notion of 'path' as found in examples with verbs of motion (25).

(25)   (a) John walked the trail.
        (b) Mary ran along the beach.

The notion of path or scale is now understood fairly well semantically and cross-cuts a number of distinct cognitive domains (see Schwarzschild 2002 on measures in general, Zwarts 2005 for spatial paths, Wechsler 2001 and Kennedy 1999 for gradable states). As Hay, Kennedy and Levin (1999) point out, the case of creation/consumption verbs is simply a special case of some attribute of the object contributing the measuring scale that is homomorphic with the event. This property is shared by all paths, whether they are derived from the object as in the case of creation/consumption, whether they come from the scale that can be inferred from a gradable adjective or whether it is a more obvious physical path as contributed explicitly by a PP with a motion verb. Moreover, if one considers the motion verb *push* below, it is clear that path in this sense is not a species of UNDERGOER at all, but complementary to it: in (26), the path describes the ground that the UNDERGOER traverses.

(26)   John pushed the coconut along the beach.

Here the object DP, *the coconut*, is the UNDERGOER because it is experiencing the change of location, and the PP *along the beach*, is the path of motion. Logically, since the transitions are related to the object's change of location, then only the specification of a final *location* will create telicity (27).

(27)   John pushed the cart to the end of the garden.

If the transitions are related to the object's change of state, then only the specification of the final relevant *state* will create telicity (28) (see Hay, Kennedy and Levin 1999 for a detailed discussion of telicity effects with this type of verb.)

(28)   Mary dried the cocoa beans bone dry in only twelve hours.

I would like to entertain the view that with the creation/consumption verbs, the DP argument does not itself travel some abstract 'path of change'; it actually *defines* the path of change, and this is why it creates the quantization effects as noted in the literature.

Thus, we really need to distinguish between UNDERGOER and PATH if the differing linguistic behaviour of these objects is to be understood. We also need to separate the predicational and relational properties described here from the purely temporal notion of telicity.[9] None of these verbs is obligatorily telic;

---

[9] The relation between temporal bound and event-structure notions will be taken up in more detail in the final chapter. At that point, I will end up agreeing with Kratzer (2004) and Borer (2005) on the existence of an aspectual head related to actual temporal boundedness which sits outside the lowest (event-building) verbal domain. However, the notion of temporal bound will not be directly homomorphic with event-topological notions as described here, and which form the basis of the core participant relationships.

they can be interpreted as telic as a result of entailments triggered by the nature of the direct object, and/or the specification of the final state in the syntax (27 and 26). I take the telicity effects in the class of creation/consumption verbs with quantized objects to be semantic *entailments* and not encoded in the lexical determination of the verb or its syntactic reflexes.

One other comment is in order concerning the nature of unboundedness. We have seen that with a creation/consumption verb, the homogenous nature of the direct object translates into an unbounded or homogenous interpretation for the event as a whole. However, this phenomenon, which is once again dependent on the semantic properties of the verbal relation, is distinct from the more general phenomenon of iterative readings, available for all verbs with plural objects.

(29)   (a) John ate TV dinners for years before learning to cook.
      (b) Mary dried the dishes for hours before being released from duty.
      (c) Michael pushed the shopping carts to customers' cars all day.
      (d) Peter threw away those empty jam jars for years before he realized how useful they were.

This is, I believe, a completely independent phenomenon, as evidenced by its complete generality: the unboundedness emerges not because of the homo-geneity of the core event, but because the core event is being indefinitely repeated/iterated once each for every individual within the plural set. As long as the actual cardinality of the plural object set is not determined by the context, such iteration will be unbounded. Notice that in the context of a definite number of objects (30a), or a plural object conceived of as a group (30b), the plural object can indeed be compatible with a PP requiring boundedness.

(30)   (a) John dried the dishes in an hour.
      (b) Bill threw away the empty bottles in a flash.

So the effects here are not related specifically to verb type, nor to general quantizedness (just indefinite plurality). Moreover, such effects are observed with subjects as well as direct objects, with each individual in the group of plural objects determining its own event of the relevant type.

(31)   (a) Tourists arrived at this pleasure spot for years.
      (b) The buccaneers attacked this island for years.

This iteration of fully formed events is a case of external aspect, which needs to be excluded when analysing the phenomenon of aktionsart or event building that will be the job of the lowest portion of the clause. These latter notions will be taken up briefly in the final chapter, when the relation to external aspect and tense is discussed.

To summarize, then, we have isolated a class of verbs which represent a process or set of transitions, where one of the arguments (the UNDERGOER) is the subject of 'change'. We also isolated a class of verbs where the verbal change is directly mapped on to the material extent of the object. I called these objects PATHS, and in these cases, entailments concerning the event's boundedness arise from the boundedness or unboundedess in the material extent of the object.

However, there *are* certain verbs that behave significantly differently in being obligatorily telic, even in English. They systematically reject the *for an hour* test, in contrast to the verbs above where it is always possible to get an atelic reading.

(32)   (a) John broke the stick in a second/*for seconds.
        (b) Mary arrived in two minutes/*for two minutes.
        (c) Michael found gold in just ten minutes.

Clearly, the telicity of this class of verbs needs to be represented differently from the telicity that sometimes arises from the semantic combination of the verb, its object (whether UNDERGOER or PATH), and the presence of a final state (implicit or explicit). The claim here is that these verbs resist the atelicity test because their objects are already defined as holders of a *final* state. They don't just undergo some change, they also end up in a final state as specified by the verb itself. I will call this special type of role relation to the eventuality structure of the predicate the RESULTEE.[10] In the sentences in (32) above: *the stick* attains a criterial identifiable change of state so that its material integrity is ruptured; *Mary* attains a locational state as determined by the deictic context; the result of Michael's actions must be that *gold* has been found. Notice that in (32c), the existence of a result, and by extension telicity, is clear even though we have used a mass term *gold* in object position. The result properties are thus properties of the verbal event structure, not of the interaction between direct objecthood and quantization.

Thus, in terms of subeventual decomposition, we need to distinguish between process or change simpliciter, and the actual attainment of a result state or telos

---

[10] Notice that RESULTEES can also occur in unbounded events, if the unboundedness is created by external modification, as a part of external aspect. For example, as we saw above, a plural distributed object or subject can create an unbounded iteration of events. This phenomenon is independent of the core internal properties of the event as determining a final or result state.

(as in much recent work, e.g. Pustejovsky 1991, Parsons 1990, Higginbotham 2001). Correspondingly, the internal arguments that are the UNDERGOERS of change are distinguishable from the attainers of a final state, although it is possible (and indeed common) for a single argument to possess both properties. We have also seen the necessity of distinguishing PATHS from UNDERGOERS (or indeed RESULTEES), because these former have special transfer properties concerning the homogeneity of object and event. During this discussion we have been careful also to distinguish the effects accruing because of these primitive event role relations from iteration of events and the general availability of distributive readings for all arguments.

2.1.3 *Nonaspectual arguments*

One final class of arguments needs to be considered now. So far we have looked at participant roles that play a particular kind of relation specifying the subeventtal decompositions of dynamic events: the INITIATOR is the direct argument related to the causing subevent (when it exists); the UNDERGOER is the direct argument related to the process subevent; and the RESULTEE is the direct argument related to the result state (when it exists). However, not all arguments of predicates can reduce to participants of this type (I will return to PATHS again in what follows). We need to consider the arguments of stative verbs, DP arguments which do not affect the aspectual interpretation of a dynamic event in the previous ways, and also PP arguments, to complete our typology of the ingredients in the building up of the core event.

To take one obvious set of cases, the objects of stative verbs do not bear the aspectual relations of INITIATOR, UNDERGOER, RESULTEE, but have objects that further specify or describe the state of affairs. In (33), 'the fear' that 'Katherine' has is 'of nightmares', in (34), 'the weight' in question is the weight 'of thirty pounds'. With stative verbs, there is no dynamicity/process/change involved in the predication, but simply a description of a state of affairs. The difference between the DP 'Katherine' and the DP 'nightmares' in (33) is a matter of predicational asymmetry: 'Katherine' is the theme of the predication, i.e. the entity that the state description is predicated of; 'nightmares' is part of the description itself.

(33)   Katherine fears nightmares.

(34)   Alex weighs thirty pounds.

This theme–rheme asymmetry is the main distinguishing semantic feature of stative predicates and the difference between subjects of statives and their predicational codas. Rhematic material in stative verbs doesn't just take the form of Verb + DP object (as in (34) and (33) above), but can also take the form of Verb + AP (35), and Verb + PP (36).

(35)   (a) Ariel is naughty
         (b) Ariel looks happy.

(36)   The cat is on the mat.

Given that there are no subevents to be distinguished here, and no change to be caused or to culminate in any result, it is not surprising that the participant roles discussed in the previous subsections are not applicable here. However, given the existence of genuine internal DP arguments in (33) and (32), we need to acknowledge the existence of DP accusatives (at least in English) which do not bear the aspectual role relations discussed so far. These DP objects of stative verbs I will give the label 'Rhematic Objects', or RHEMES to indicate that they are not subjects of any subevent, but part of the description of the predicate. From our examination of stative predications, it is clear that RHEMES can be PPs and APs as well as DPs.

However, once we turn again to the dynamic class of verbs, the predicational asymmetry between THEMES and RHEMES is present here as well. The THEME is traditionally considered to be the object in motion, or undergoer of a change, and this is what I have been calling UNDERGOER so far in this chapter. On the other hand, I have argued that PATHS are the trajectories covered by the UNDERGOER. In the next chapter, I will argue that PATHS are in fact in a different structural position from UNDERGOERS; they occupy an internal position which helps to *describe* the subevent that is then predicated of the UNDERGOER. We can see that PATHS have a different distribution from UNDERGOERS from the following examples. Consider the verb *jog* (and others like it) in English. It is classically considered difficult for such verbs to transitivize by taking direct internal arguments that are undergoers (37).

(37)   (a) Karena jogged.
         (b) *Karena jogged the child.

Still, it is possible for verbs of this type to take certain direct objects perfectly grammatically, as (38) shows.

(38)   Karena jogged two miles.

However, the DP 'two miles' cannot in any sense be seen as an UNDERGOER (or even RESULTEE): the entity 'two miles' does not suffer any change as a result of the event; it remains the same but merely measures the path that the UNDERGOER traverses in this case.[11] In fact, any DP that describes the path of motion in some way makes a good internal argument for a verb of motion, even when UNDERGOER internal arguments are systematically disallowed.

(39) (a) We walked the West Highland Way.
      (b) Chris ran the Boston marathon.
      (c) We danced the merengue.

The PATH objects briefly discussed in the previous section seem actually to be the dynamic version of RHEMES. PATH complements seem to be particularly common crosslinguistically to co-describe a process, so much so that it very often licenses selected complements. Interestingly, while manners or instruments are often important criterial factors in distinguishing one kind of process from another, it does not appear to be the case that manner/instrumental PPs or APs can be selected as the complement of a process head in this way.

(40) (a) *John pounded a hammer. (meaning John used a hammer to pound something)
      (b) *Mary moved a hobble. (meaning Mary hobbled).

These sentences are strikingly bad, so much so that it might not even seem surprising. But it is nevertheless true that manners and instruments seem to be primarily represented internal to verbal conceptual meaning in many English verbs (*John hammered the metal, Mary hobbled to the pub*), and not as complements.[12] PATHS on the other hand can be selected DPs or PPs, and can also be 'conflated' in the sense of Hale and Keyser (1993).

(41) (a) John did a dance.
      (b) John danced.
      (c) John danced a happy dance.

In the next chapter, I will argue that one of the criterial properties for being the selected complement of a process is that the XP in question denote something

---

[11] 'Karena' must be seen as the UNDERGOER in this sentence since she is the individual that suffers change in location; she is also the INITIATOR since the change emerges because of her own causational efforts. The phenomenon of unified participant roles will be discussed in the next chapter.

[12] Peter Svenonius (p.c.) points out that verbs such as *wield, use, employ* etc. might seem to have instrument objects. However, the information that the object of these verbs is a tool is encoded in the conceptual semantics; linguistically these objects are not modifiers of the process event, they seem to diagnose as simple UNDERGOERS.

that has some kind of scalar structure that can be mapped to the verbal change
in a systematic way. To anticipate, I will argue that the difference between
PATH objects and the RHEMES we find in stative predicates is analogous to the
difference between locations and paths: stative verbs do not have any part–
whole structure as defined by perceptible change and hence they are simple
'locations' and their rhematic content also fails to describe any part–whole
structure; dynamic verbs on the other hand are 'paths of change' and their
rhematic objects must also be PATHS in some generalized sense.

Prepositional phrases are the simplest representations of paths (in the spatial
domain canonically, with extended metaphorical and temporal uses), and the
empirical fact appears to be that while PP arguments systematically never fulfil
the roles of INITIATOR, UNDERGOER or RESULTEE, both DPs and PPs are available to be RHEMES. This asymmetry is what is plausibly behind the 'conative'
alternation shown in (42a) and (42b) below.

(42)   (a) Michael ate the mango (in an hour).
         (b) Michael ate at the mango (for an hour).

While the DP argument in (42a) is a definite bounded PATH, which creates
telicity entailments with creation/consumption verbs, the PP in (42b) denotes
only an unbounded path defined by only a vague relevancy relation to the ground
element (in this case, 'the mango'); it is a PP RHEME of process but unbounded
and so giving rise to atelicity.[13] I will use the term RHEME as a cover term for
the 'ground' elements[14] in both stative and dynamic predications, but also the
term PATH for the subclass that exists only in dynamic ones.

It is also possible to argue for the existence of RHEMES of result, where the DP
in question does not 'hold' the final state, but further describes the final state.
In (43) below 'the room' expresses the final location arrived at by the subject.

(43)   Kayleigh entered the room.

To summarize, it has been possible to isolate a number of different classes
of argument that form the broadest groups with respect to linguistic behaviour
and semantic entailments, especially with regard to event structure. The first

---

[13] The class of DP objects that I am calling RHEME here is the same as the class of objects
that I termed 'non-aspectual' objects in Ramchand (1997).

[14] The terms 'figure' and 'ground' are common terms in the spatial domain corresponding
to the argument structure of prepositions (see Talmy 1978), where 'ground' is basically
the rheme of the spatial predication and the 'figure' is the theme. I stick to the more
general terminology here, although the correlation should be clear.

major distinction was that between the external argument and the internal one. I tried to argue that the differences among different types of external argument were not as linguistically relevant as that basic property of externality. They all relate to the event as a whole, i.e. with its internal arguments already calculated in (see Marantz 1984 and Kratzer 1996); they can all be described as initiators in some abstract sense; they show distinguished syntactic behaviour. Within the group of arguments classified as 'internal', I argued for a number of distinct role relations: UNDERGOERS and RESULTEES were the 'themes' of process events and result events respectively; PATHS, or RHEMES more generally were part of the event description and in the case of PATHS actually provided part–whole structure that could give rise to quantization properties on the part of the event.

In the next chapter, I will lay out the theoretical machinery that I argue makes sense of these empirical patterns.

3   A first-phase syntax

In the previous chapter, I argued for a small set of basic argument relations that are implicated in the linguistic construction of eventive predication. In what follows, I will tie these argument relations to a syntactically represented event decomposition. The reason for this move is the claim that the generalizations at this level involve a kind of systematicity and recursion that is found in syntactic representations. The strongest hypothesis must be that the recursive system that underlies natural language computation resides in one particular module that need not be duplicated in other modules of grammar (i.e. in the lexicon, or in the general cognitive system). At the same time, this means that the semantics that is compositionally built up by the syntax at this level can only include those aspects of meaning that are genuinely predictable and systematic – many aspects of meaning that are traditionally included in descriptions of lexical verbs (e.g. thematic roles, certain kinds of semantic selection) must be excluded. The modularity that this involves has already been acknowledged within many theories of the lexicon as the difference between grammatically relevant lexical information and more general conceptual information, although the separation has mostly been argued to be internal to the lexicon itself (Hale and Keyser 1993, Jackendoff 1990, Grimshaw 1990, Kaufmann and Wunderlich 1998, Levin and Rappaport Hovav 1995). The approach here is a little different in that the grammatically relevant information actually comes from the interpretation of the syntactic structures that the verbs participate in. Any concrete proposal along these lines inevitably involves making a decision about which aspects of meaning should be represented in the syntactic system and which should be seen as coming from lexical-encyclopedic content. The proposal made here represents one set of choices, one that should be evaluated according to the usual standards of descriptive and explanatory adequacy. In this sense the enterprise I embark on here should be seen not as a monolithic theory, but as a concrete starting point for investigating issues of this type.

The actual proposal relates closely in spirit to others in the literature which seek to correlate the morphosyntax and the semantics of event structure in a direct way (see Borer 2005, Ritter and Rosen 1998, Travis 2000, among others). The common idea behind these proposals is that the syntactic projection of arguments is based on event structure. However, the specific position argued for here differs from those in certain points of detail, and I try to be more explicit about the semantics of the structures proposed. In particular, based on the informal discussion of core predicational relations and syntactic argument types in chapter 2, the event-structure syntax will contain three important subevental components: a causing subevent, a process-denoting subevent and a subevent corresponding to result state. Each of these subevents is represented as its own projection, ordered in the hierarchical embedding relation as shown below in (1).

(1)

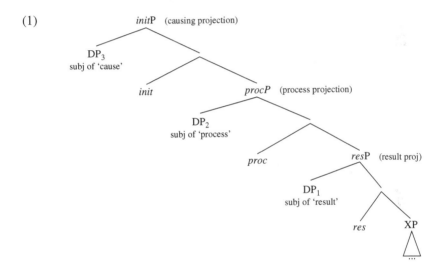

In (1) above, I have chosen the label *init* (for initiation) to represent the outer causational projection that is responsible for introducing the external argument; in many ways it is similar to the external argument introducing *v* as invoked in the recent literature (Hale and Keyser 1993, Harley 1995, Kratzer 1996). The central projection that represents the dynamic process is called *proc*P (for process phrase). The lowest projection has been given the label *res* for result. I have stayed away from more traditional categorial labels such as V, because it is important to realize that this system is actually a splitting up of what we normally think of as V, in the same spirit as Rizzi's (1997) splitting up of the C node to show its fine structure, or Pollock's (1989) splitting up of Infl into T and Agr. All three of my projections are essentially verbal, and no individual piece actually corresponds to what traditional accounts would label V: the notion of verb is always a composite which involves some or all of these elements. Also, the tree in (1) represents the maximal possible decomposition, and a dynamic verbal projection may exist without either the *init* or *res* elements, as we will see.

Under this view, *proc*P is the heart of the dynamic predicate, since it represents change through time, and it is present in every dynamic verb. In other words, a *proc*P is present regardless of whether we are dealing with a process that is extended (i.e. consisting of an indefinite number of transitions) or the limiting case of representing only single minimal transition such as that found with 'achievement' verbs. The *init*P exists when the verb expresses a causational or initiational state that leads to the process. The *res*P only exists when there is a result state explicitly expressed by the lexical predicate; it does not correlate with semantic/aspectual boundedness in a general sense. Specifically, the telicity that arises because of the entailments based on DP structure and the verbal relation do not mean that *res*P exists, i.e. *res*P only exists if the event structure itself is specified as expressing a result state. Conversely, the expression of result can be further modified by auxiliaries, PPs etc. outside the first-phase syntax to create predications that are atelic, but this will not warrant the removal of *res*P in the syntactic representation.

In addition to representing subevental complexity, as motivated by work on verbal aktionsart (Vendler 1967, Parsons 1990, Pustejovsky 1991, Higgin-botham 2001), this structure is also designed to capture the set of core argument roles discussed in the previous chapter, as defined by the predicational relations formed at each level. Each projection represented here forms its own core pred-icational structure with the specifier position being filled by the 'subject' or 'theme' of a particular (sub)event, and the complement position being filled by the phrase that provides the content of that event. The complement position itself of course is also complex and contains another mini-predication, with its own specifier and complement. In this way, the participant relations are built up recursively from successively embedded event descriptions and 'subject' predications.

- *init*P introduces the causation event and licenses the external argument ('subject' of cause = INITIATOR)
- *proc*P specifies the nature of the change or process and licenses the entity undergoing change or process ('subject' of process = UNDERGOER)
- *res*P gives the 'telos' or 'result state' of the event and licenses the entity that comes to hold the result state ('subject' of result = RESULTEE)

This idea has antecedents, for example, in the work of Kaufmann and Wunderlich (1998) who argue for a level of semantic structure (SF) which is crucially binary and asymmetrical and in which possible verbs are formed by constrained embedding.

POSSIBLE VERBS
In a decomposed SF representation of a verb, every more deeply embedded predicate must specify the higher predicate or sortal properties activated by the higher predicate. (Kaufmann and Wunderlich 1998: 5)

Kaufmann and Wunderlich see their SF level as being a subpart of the lexical semantics, and not represented directly in syntax, but the internal structure of their representations is very similar to what I am proposing here.

A question that naturally arises at this point is one of ontology. Why does the syntax of the first phase decompose into exactly these three projections under this view? What does it follow from, and is it logically possible to have further subevental decomposition? If not, why not?

One part of the answer is sheer empirical expediency: the argument is that these projections are the ones necessary to express all and only the generalizations about verb meaning and verb flexibility that we find in natural language. So, in one sense, the data drive our choice of primitives, which, though abstract and minimal, simply have to be stipulated. If they are on the right track and give a simple explanatory account of a wide range of data, as claimed, then a natural further step is to inquire what principles (if any) they follow from. The rest of this book is an attempt to provide some evidence for the explanatory power of this particular syntactic decomposition, i.e. to justify the hypothesis that these are the primitives involved.

There is perhaps another way of looking at the primitives espoused here in terms of the part–whole structure of events, which might serve to ground the intuition behind what is being proposed. If we think of a core dynamic event as representing the topological equivalent of a path, then the proposal here amounts to the claim that a verb must represent a single coherent path which can be assembled from a dynamic portion *proc* with or without endpoint *res* and beginning point *init*. The flanking state eventualities can be integrated with a process portion to form a coherent single event, by specifying its initial and final positions, but no *distinct* dynamic portion is possible without giving rise to a separate event path. *This* is the intuition that either must be stipulated or made to follow from something deeper.

The process projection is thus the heart of the dynamic verbal event (much like the nucleus in syllable structure). The bounding eventualities of 'initiation' and 'result' are related states: the former being a source, initiational or conditioning state of affairs that gives rise to the process; the latter being the end result of the process. While it is relatively easy to see that the result of a process is a 'state', it has not (to my knowledge) been claimed that the causing subevent is a state. It is not clear what the evidence for this position would be from a simple inspection of the semantics of causative verbs, since the process and the initiation/causation of an event are difficult to tease apart. However, I will assume this position in what follows, partly because it gives a simpler ontology, and also because it allows a simpler analysis of stative verbs. Any hypothesis about event-structure decomposition must be evaluated on the basis of the general theory it gives rise to. In what follows, I will assume the causing subevent to be a state but leave it open whether further investigation of the data might require relaxing this position to admit any eventuality more generally.

3.1   The semantic interpretation of structure

An important aspect of this proposal is the claim that there is a general combinatorial semantics that interprets this syntactic structure in a regular and predictable way. Thus the semantics of event structure and event participants is read directly off the structure, and not directly off information encoded by lexical items.

The semantic approach taken here will share the intuition of the neo-Davidsonian position (Parsons 1990, Higginbotham 1985, after Davidson 1967) that event variables are a crucial element in the logical representation of sentences, and that participant roles involve separate relations between that event and each participant. Here I have taken this a little further in assuming that the event position classically taken to be associated with a single lexical item may actually be internally complex. For the semantic interpretation of this first-phase syntax, I therefore adopt a post-Davidsonian[1] semantics which interprets the verbal heads within the syntax in a regular and systematic way.

More concretely, let us examine the first relation between events argued to be important – the relation of 'causation/initiation'. The event position corresponding to a transitive verb such as *eat* can be decomposed into two subevents related by causation, where e_1 is the causing or instigating force and e_2 is the event of something being consumed (I follow the notation of Hale and Keyser 1993 in using → to represent the relationship between the subevents in (2)).

---

[1] I use the term 'post-Davidsonian' to describe a syntacticized neo-Davidsonian view whereby verbal heads in the decomposition are eventuality descriptions with a single open position for a predicational subject (one subevent per predicational position).

(2)   eating (e) *where* e = (e$_1$ → e$_2$: [cause-eat(e$_1$) & process-eat(e$_2$)])

The second important semantic relation between events is that of the addition of a particular attained result, sometimes called telic augmentation. Once again, following much recent work (see Parsons 1990, Higginbotham 2001, Levin and Rappaport 1998), I assume that accomplishment predicates (in the Vendler 1967 sense) contain two subevents of process and telos in their representation (independent of whether initiational information is also present or not), to create a complex event such that the process 'leads to' the result state. In (3) I show the representation of the subevents of process (e$_1$) and result state (e$_2$) as based on the notation of Higginbotham (2001) for a verbal predicate such as *defuse the bomb*. In Higginbotham's notation an event pair in angled brackets is used to abbreviate what he calls an 'accomplishment event structure', or a 'telic pair' (see also Pustejovsky 1991).

(3)   'defuse the bomb'(e) *where* e = <e$_1$, e$_2$>:[process-defuse(e$_1$) & result-of-defusing(e$_2$)]

I will propose some modifications to this well-known system. Because of the abstract similarity of the 'leads-to' relation to the one invoked in attaching the causing subevent, I will claim that the same semantic combinatoric process is involved and use the same notation for telic augmentation as I use for linking the causational subevent to the combination. Thus, since a verbal predication like *defuse the bomb* also encodes a causational or initiational element, the decomposition actually encodes not just two, but three subevents, as shown in (4) below.

(4)   'defuse-the-bomb'(e) *where* e = e$_1$ → (e$_2$ → e$_3$) :[initiate-defuse(e$_1$) & process-defuse(e$_2$) & result-of-defusing(e$_3$)]

A number of further comments are in order. The causal embedding '⟶' relation is the only primitive of the event combinatorial system which can be used to create complex events of the same logical type – the hierarchical order of the embedding gives rise to the difference between causational semantics or resultative semantics. The simplest assumption is that subevents themselves are not of a different ontological type from macro-events – out of combination they are of the same sort as simple processes or states. The macro-event corresponding to a predication is just an event which happens to have subparts. For some linguistic purposes (anchoring to tense, certain types of adverbs and intersentential effects) this event is the only event variable manipulated or 'seen' by the logical relations. However, the evidence from aspectual semantics and internal morphology of verbs indicates that eventive substructure is linguistically real and follows certain strict syntactic and semantic generalizations.

For concreteness, I lay out here how the general semantic combinatorial system works to interpret this kind of syntactic structure. I take particular nodes in the first-phase syntax tree to denote relations between properties of events and properties of events, constructing more and more complex event descriptions. Under this more 'constructionist' view, neither events nor individual entities are arguments of the lexical item itself, but of the predicates introduced by the semantic interpretation of particular categorial nodes; however, like the neo-Davidsonian position, events and individuals are never all co-arguments of the same predicate, and they are discharged in different ways.

To reiterate, there is a basic primitive rule of event composition in this system, the 'leads to' relation:

(5)   *Event Composition Rule*
       $e = e1 \rightarrow e2$: e consists of two subevents, e1, e2 such that e1 causally implicates e2
       (cf. Hale and Keyser 1993)

There are two general primitive predicates over events corresponding to the basic subevent types as follows:

(6)   (a) State(e) : e is a state
       (b) Process(e): e is an eventuality that contains internal change

I am assuming that both the initiational eventuality and the result eventuality are states, and that their interpretation as causational or resultative respectively comes from their position in the hierarchical structure. In particular, in the *init* position, the state introduced by that head is interpreted as causally implicating the process; in the *res* position, the state introduced by that head is interpreted as being causally implicated by the process. We can therefore define two derived predicates over events based on the event-composition rules.

(7)   IF $\exists e_1, e_2[\text{State}(e_1) \& \text{Process}(e_2) \& e_1 \rightarrow e_2]$, then by definition Initiation(e_1)

(8)   IF $\exists e_1, e_2[\text{State}(e_1) \& \text{Process}(e_2) \& e_2 \rightarrow e_1]$ then by definition Result(e_1)

Further, the objects of particular event types are interpreted according to the primitive role types defined as the relations between objects and events below:

(9)   (a) Subject (x, e) and Initiation(e) entails that x is the INITIATOR of e.

(b) Subject (x, e) and Process(e) entails that x is the UNDERGOER of the process.

(c) Subject (x, e) and Result(e) entails that x is the RESULTEE.

Using lambda notation for convenience, I spell out the denotations of the different pieces of structure, showing how they can be made to combine systematically to produce the required interpretations. The important point here is not the denotations in terms of lambda notation, but the idea that this dimension of skeletal semantics can be built up independently merely from the specification of the interpretation of pure labelled structure, *in the absence of lexical-encyclopedic information*.

The *res* head in the first-phase syntax is interpreted as building a state description that has a particular 'holder' in its specifier position. Its semantic interpretation is given below:[2]

(10) $[[res]] = \lambda P \lambda x \lambda e[P(e) \ \& \ res'(e) \ \& \ \text{State}(e) \ \& \ \text{Subject} \ (x,e)]$

When the *res*P is selected by a process-introducing head, *proc*, the holder of the state is then the holder of a 'result'. I have labelled this special type of holder RESULTEE. The interpretation of the process-introducing head *proc* is given below. It takes an argument in its specifier position that is interpreted as the UNDERGOER of the process, and a state description in its complement position that is interpreted as the result state (by (11)):

(11) $[[proc]] = \lambda P \lambda x \lambda e \exists e_1, e_2[P(e_2) \ \& \ proc'(e_1) \ \& \ \text{Process}(e_1) \ \& \ e = (e_1 \rightarrow e_2) \ \& \ \text{Subject} \ (x,e_1)]$

Finally, once the whole *proc*P is formed, the highest verbal head *init* is interpreted as an initiating event which leads to the (possibly complex) event constructed by the lower structure that it combines with. The specifier position of this projection is interpreted as the INITIATOR of the subevent:

(12) $[[init]] = \lambda P \lambda x \lambda e \exists e_1, e_2[P(e_2) \ \& \ init'(e_1) \ \& \ \text{State}(e_1) \ \& \ e = e_1 \rightarrow e_2 \ \& \ \text{Subject} \ (x,e_1)]$

---

[2] In the formulas that follow, *res'*, *proc'* and *init'* stand in for the lexical-encyclopedic content contributed by the result, process and initiation heads respectively depending on the particular lexical item that projects. This is the equivalent to the contribution of CONSTANTS in the lexical decompositional system of Levin and Rappaport Hovav (1995). The association to lexical content is discussed in section 3.2.

3.1.1   *Rhematic material*

Now we must turn to RHEMES as discussed in the previous chapter and where they fit in this event-structural semantics. We have seen that certain aspectually relevant arguments are related in a one-to-one fashion to the projections corresponding to each subevent – they are the 'subjects' or 'specifiers' of those projections. Rhematic material, by definition, will never occur in the specifier position of an eventive head; it will always occur in complement position to an eventive head. RHEMES, and as an important subcase PATHS, do not describe elements that are referentially individuated and predicated over within an event topology, but those that actually construct the specific predicational property (static or dynamic) that the 'subject' is asserted to have. In an extension of the terms of Talmy (1978), for example, the specifiers are 'Figures' and complements are 'Grounds' in an asymmetrical predicational relation.

The proposal is the following. While the *proc* head can combine felicitously with a whole *res*P to create a telic pair, it can also take a simple PP or DP in its complement position. In that case, the PP or DP does not determine its own independent subevent, but acts as a further modifier or descriptor of the *proc* event. In the terms of Higginbotham (2001), *res*Ps combine with the *proc* head by 'telic pair formation' while DPs and PPs will combine by event 'identification', to further describe the properties of the relevant subevent.[3]

The structures at issue here are those that have the form as in (13) below.

(13)

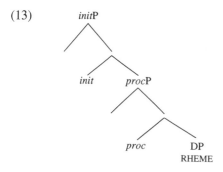

In this case, there is no separate event introduced, but the rhematic material further describes the event already introduced by the process head. The rhematic relation however, is not completely open or vague; certain wellformedness conditions on event–event correspondences must hold if an XP RHEME is

---

[3] In this sense, the DPs I am interpreting as RHEMES are similar in spirit to the 'predicate modifiers' of de Hoop 1992.

to be interpreted as being 'identified' with a particular event. My proposal for
RHEMES of process builds on the formalism and intuitions regarding PATHS
and the material objects of creation/consumption verbs. The intuition is that a
rhematic projection (in complement position) must unify with the topological
properties of the event: if the event head is dynamic *proc*, the complement must
also provide a topologically extended structure. In the case of directed paths
that can be measured, the measure of the PATH increases monotonically with
the change expressed by the verb; in the case of (complement) RHEMES to stative projections, that RHEME must crucially *not* involve a path structure. More
specifically, DP/NP RHEMES must provide structure in terms of the part/whole-
structure of their material constituency when combined with a dynamic event.
Of course, rhematic elements are not just NPs, they can also be PPs and APs.
In each case, however, the rhematic projection denotes an entity whose essential properties determine a scale which can be measured. PP RHEMES represent
locational paths which are mapped onto the dynamic event (Zwarts 2003), and
AP RHEMES provide a gradable property scale which functions as the mapping
to the event-change path (see Wechsler 2001 for a claim along these lines). My
claim is that the complement position of a process head is associated with the
semantic relation of structural homomorphism, regardless of the category of that
complement. The homomorphism has been noted before in different domains,
and given formal representation. Here, I wish to offer a characterization that
unifies the different cases that have been noted in the literature.

Let us take the cases in turn. With the well-known class of cre-
ation/consumption verbs, Krifka (1987) introduced two basic principles,
Mapping-to-Objects and Mapping-to-Events, which enforced a homomorphism
between the part structure of the object and the part structure of the event. This
mapping ensured that quantized objects gave rise to bounded events, for example. It corresponds to the intuition of the object providing a 'measure' of the
event. For Krifka, not every thematic relation between verb and object satisfied
those mapping properties, i.e. they were properties of certain thematic relations
only. In our case, we are claiming that the relation holds with DPs in complement position of the process head, and not of UNDERGOERS more generally.
Examples of this kind of relation include verbs like *eat*, or *draw* or *build* where
the quantization effect can be seen.

(14)   (a) Michael ate porridge for ten minutes/??in ten minutes.
        (b) Michael ate the apple for ten minutes/in ten minutes.

However, as Krifka points out, it is not always all parts of the object that are
relevant.

> As an example, consider *eat the apple* and *peel the apple*; in the first case, all the parts of the apple are involved, whereas in the second case, only the surface parts are. Another example is *read the book* and *burn the book*; surely there are parts of the book which are relevant in the second case (e.g. the cover of the book) which do not count as parts of the book in the first case. To handle these phenomena, we may assume that the verb selects specific *aspects* of an object (e.g. only its surface).   (Krifka 1987: 45)

Because of this variability, I will not formalize the mapping relation as directly mapping between the mereological part structure of the event and the mereological part structure of the object. Instead, the mapping must be between the part–whole structure of the event and a set of 'measures' of a particular property which is monotonic with respect to the part–whole structure of the object. Schwarzschild (2002) makes this distinction as well in his study of the measure phrases possible with nominals – a measure can take a DP complement mediated by the preposition *of* only if it measures a property that is monotonic with respect to the part–whole structure of the object.

(15)   (a) Two gallons of water/*twenty degrees of water
        (b) Twenty grams of gold/*twenty carats of gold

This is determined strongly by the part–whole structure of the nominal itself in some essential way, but can also be affected by context. Thus, in the context of measuring for a recipe, *15 grams of breadcrumbs* is grammatical and measures weight, but in the context of Hansel and Gretel leaving a trail, *3 miles of breadcrumbs* also works and measures length. The important thing is that the property be monotonic in the relevant sense.

> Now while all measurement systems mirror the degree to which an entity has the property in question, some but not all mirror as well the intuitive part structure of the stuff being measured. For example, if a quantity of oil has a certain volume, then every proper subpart of it will have a lower volume and superparts will have larger volumes. On the other hand, if the oil has a certain temperature, there is no reason to expect that proper parts of it will have lower temperatures. We will call a property **monotonic** if it tracks part–whole relations.   (Schwarzschild 2002: 2)

We need also to unify this case with the more spatially straightforward cases of paths, where PPs create a path homomorphic with the process of change described by the verb. The boundedness of the PP path in this case gives rise to a temporally bounded event.

(16)   (a) Karena walked to the pool in ten minutes/*for ten minutes.
        (b) Karena walked towards the pool *in ten minutes/for ten minutes.

The exact relationship between the preposition and the denotation of the object of that preposition in constructing a path is not at issue here (but see Zwarts 2003 for details). The important thing is that a PP denotes a path which can either be bounded or unbounded (noncumulative vs. cumulative respectively, according to Zwarts 2003), and there is a relation between it and the verb which is homomorphic.

(17)   *Isomorphism*
       An isomorphism between two systems is a one–one correspondence between their elements and a one–one correspondence between their operations and relations which satisfies the following conditions:
       1. If a relation R holds between two elements of A, the corresponding relation R′ holds between the corresponding elements of B; if R does not hold between two elements of A, R′ does not hold between the corresponding elements of B.
       2. Whenever corresponding operations are performed on corresponding elements, the results are corresponding elements.
       Homomorphism is a correspondence with all the properties of an isomorphism except that the mapping from A to B may be many-to-one; the set B may be smaller than the set A.   (Partee and Wall 1990)

In this particular case, the path structure of the PP is mapped onto the temporal path structure of the time line of the event – the two relations R and R′ would be spatial ordering and temporal ordering respectively. In Zwarts's terms this homomorphism is expressed by means of a trace function of an event which tracks its spatial location.

(18) $[[V\ PP]] = [\ e \in [[V]]: Trace(e) \in [[PP]]\ ]$

However, if we wish to unify the spatial paths with the objectual paths, the Trace function is not sufficiently general. Rather, to unify the cases, I will exploit an idea that was necessary in Schwarzschild's analysis of measures.

   A system of measurement is one in which elements of an ordered set of measurements, a scale, are assigned to a domain of entities, based on some property. The goal is for the ordering of the measurements to reflect the extent to which entities in the domain have the property in question.   (Schwarzschild 2002)

The idea here is that monotonicity is an important linguistic constraint on certain linguistic relations. Generally, a relation between two structured domains is said to be monotonic if it preserves the ordering from one domain to the other.

(19)   *Monotonicity*
        Let f:P → Q
        be a function between two sets P and Q where each set carries a partial
        order (both of which we denote by ≤, for convenience). The function
        f is monotone if, whenever x ≤ y, f(x) ≤ f(y)   (Wikipedia)

Nominals or PPs do not themselves denote a scale, though they do give
rise to one. We need to assume a function which takes us from the denotation
of the NP/PP to some scale which bears a monotonic relation to the part–
whole structure of the NP/PP in question. In the cases of PP paths, that scale
is something like 'distance from an initial point'; in the case of an NP, it might
be 'volume' or 'degree of completedness' in the case of a created object. Let us
assume that this property is determined by pragmatic selectional restrictions,
the only constraint on it being that it is monotonic in Schwarzschild's sense
(extending his notion to paths, as materially extended locational entities). In
the case of adjectives, the null Prop function is not required since, plausibly,
adjectives denote properties directly.

(20) $\Pi_C(x)$ is the property determined by x and the selectional context C,
        which is monotonic on x.

Now, we need to determine a related set of measures, d, based on $\Pi_C(x)$,
which are all the possible measurements of the property in question based on
the part–whole structure of the entity, given by the relation notated here as ⊂.

(21)   Let μ be a function which gives a measure of Π.
        Let $D = \{ d \in \mu(\Pi(x)): \forall x' \subseteq x \, \mu(\Pi(x')) = d \}$
        Let ≤ be a relation that determines a linear order on D, such that if
        $\mu(\Pi(x1)) = d1$ and $\mu(\Pi(x2)) = d2$, $d1 \leq d2$, iff $x1 \subseteq x2$.

μ and ≤ will exist if the property in question really is monotonic with respect
to the part–whole structure of the entity. Let us call a set of ordered measures in
this sense for an entity, x, D_x (where entities include both objects and extended
locations).

We are now ready to define the relation between this set of measures and
the verbal event, when the rhematic/complement relation holds. We define a
thematic role PATH, which is the relation that holds between an entity and an
event, if a monotonic property of that entity is monotonic with respect to the
part–whole structure of the event as well. I will express this formally, in the
spirit of Krifka (1987), as 'Measure-to-Event Mapping' and 'Event-to-Measure
Mapping'.

(22) $\text{PATH}(x, e) =_{def} \exists R \exists D_x [\; \forall e,d,d'[R(e,d) \; \& \; d' \leq d \rightarrow \exists e'[e' \subseteq e \; \&$
$R(e',d')]$ (mapping to measures) $\& \; \forall e,e',d[R(e,d) \; \& \; e' \subseteq e \rightarrow \exists d'[d'$
$\leq d \; \& \; R(e',d')]$ (mapping to events)

In the case of adjectival phrases in rhematic position, the adjective denotes a property directly,[4] and the measure is the degree to which the property holds. We will see in the next chapter that the difference between closed scale or open scale gradable adjectives corresponds to resultativity in certain constructions (after Wechsler 2005). This will lead us to assume that the path relation also applies to APs in rhematic position.

Thus, in the case of the *proc* head combining with an entity (either an individual, a spatial path, or a property), instead of with a predicate of events, the interpretation is as follows.

(23) $[[proc]] = \lambda y \lambda x \lambda e [\text{Path}(y,e) \; \& \; proc\,'(e) \; \& \; \text{Process}(e) \; \& \; \text{Subject}(x,e)].$

In the case of the *result* head itself, we can also have rhematic elements. But because the *result* head denotes an event without any part–whole structure (it is a state), rhematic complements of *res* will be constrained to be 'place' locations rather than 'path' locations, single nongradable properties, or a single entity where no part–whole structure is relevant. Here the DP will have to give rise to an unchanging property as determined by its denotation, selectional restrictions and context.

The structures being proposed here embody a primitive difference between the combinatoric semantics of the specifier position with the head, as opposed to the complement position and the head. Put in informal terms, the specifier syntactic position always introduces a 'Figure' or 'Theme' related to the subevent denoted by the head; the complement position is never a 'Figure', but rather the 'Ground' or 'Rheme' of a particular subevent. With respect to properties which are homomorphic to the part–whole structure of the event, rhematic DP objects are related by properties which are also homomorphic to their own part–whole structure. Arguments in specifier position are also related to the event, but via the relation of predication, and the property that they are ascribed by virtue of predication is never constrained to be monotonic with respect to their part–whole structure.

I summarize the basic argument relations given by the primitives of this system including the composite roles that will be derived by Move, together with

---

[4] I follow Chierchia and Turner (1988) in assuming primitive ontological status for properties, too, as a type of entity.

some illustrative examples (a detailed discussion of different verb types can be found in chapter 4).

INITIATORS are the individuated entities that possess the property denoted by the initiational subeventuality, which leads to the process coming into being.

(24) (a) *The key* opened the lock.   PURE INITIATORS
      (b) *The rock* broke the window.
      (c) *John* persuaded Mary.
      (d) *Karena* drove the car.

The differences among the different initiators in the sentences above are due to the different lexical-encyclopedic content of the verbs in question, and to the referential/animacy properties of the DP argument. By hypothesis, they are not related to structural position.

UNDERGOERS are individuated entities whose position/state or motion/change is homomorphically related to some PATH. UNDERGOERS are 'subjects' of process, while PATHS are complements of process.

(25) (a) Karena drove *the car.*   PURE UNDERGOERS
      (b) Michael dried *the coffee beans.*
      (c) *The ball* rolled.
      (d) *The apple* reddened.

(26) (a) Katherine walked *the trail.*   PATHS
      (b) Ariel ate *the mango.*
      (c) Kayleigh drew *a circle.*
      (d) Michael ran *to the store.*

RESULTEES (Figures of result) are the individuated entities whose state is described with respect to the resultative property/Ground.

(27) (a) Katherine ran *her shoes* ragged.   PURE RESULTEES
      (b) Alex handed *her homework* in.
      (c) Michael threw *the dog* out.

GROUNDS of Result possess an inherent nongradable property which describes the result state.

(28) (a) Karena entered *the room.*   GROUND OF RESULT
      (b) Kayleigh arrived *at the station.*

UNDERGOER–INITIATOR is a composite role which arises when the same argument is the holder of initiational state *and* holder of a changing property homomorphic with the event trace of the *proc* event. (This is represented using the copy theory of movement.)

(29)   (a) *Karena* ran to the tree.   UNDERGOER–INITIATORS
       (b) *The diamond* sparkled.
       (c) *Ariel* ate the mango.
       (d) *Kayleigh* danced.

The example (29b) represents Levin and Rappaport-Hovav's class of internally caused verbs, the (a) example is a motion verb which classically exhibits mixed behaviour with respect to unaccusativity diagnostics. The (c) example deserves special mention because it is a case where the INITIATOR of the eating event is also somehow experientially affected by the process in a way that is only possible with animate/sentient causes. Because of this, we will see that the class of UNDERGOER–INITIATORS includes many cases of so called Actors or volitional Agents in the literature (see the next subsection for further discussion). RESULTEE–UNDERGOER is a composite role which arises when the same argument is the holder of a changing property homomorphic with the event trace of the *proc* event, *and* the holder of the result state.

(30)   (a) Michael pushed *the cart* to the store.   RESULTEE–UNDERGOERS
       (b) Katherine broke *the stick*.
       (c) Ariel painted *the house* red.

I have assumed that a composite role comprising of a rhematic position and a role in specifier position is not attested. This is an empirical issue, and in the discussion of verbs and argument types in chapter 4 I do not make use of such a possibility. For the moment, then, I have assumed they do not exist in my classification of role types. However, I leave it open that such movements might be possible in special circumstances. In part, this will also bear on what constraints one wishes to place on these thematic movements. It would be interesting if some compatibility principle of participant role unification rules them out, if they can be shown really not to exist.

3.1.2   Agents and experiencers: the special case of mental states
So far, I have been describing participant relations in terms of objectively observable causes, changes and effects where intuitions seem more secure. However, initiation, process and result are claimed to be the abstract structuring

principles behind all eventive predications and are intended to cover changes and effects in more subjective domains as well. Traditional thematic role systems often make a special case of Volitional Agents and Experiencers (Butt 1995, Belletti and Rizzi 1988), and the feature of mental state is one of the primitives used by Reinhart (2002) in her lexicalist theory of argument structure ([+m]). Crosslinguistically, animacy hierarchies play an important role in the syntactic realization of participant relations (see Ritter and Rosen 1998), and there is general cognitive evidence that humans interpret causational and affective relations differently when there are participants who possess sentience and will involved. I do not wish to deny the reality of these effects, but I propose to account for them without introducing additional heads or 'flavours' of initiational projections. Rather, I will argue that humans reason about sentient participants differently from the way they reason about inanimate objects and that this allows sentient creatures to participate in a wide variety of 'Subject' roles for subevents by virtue of their internal/psychological causes and effects, i.e. they don't have to be physical effects.

Often, the entailments of a particular participant differ systematically according to whether an animate or inanimate DP is in argument position, without any obvious change in the syntactic form of the verb phrase. In (31), the rock is a pure 'cause' or 'instrument', but John can be a volitional agent. In (32), the lever undergoes a physical change of orientation, while John is affected purely psychologically. In the latter case, the lexical-encyclopedic content of the verb *depress* must be consistent both with physical and psychological motion 'downward' as a part of a pervasive analogy between physical and mental effects.

(31)   (a) The rock broke the window (*deliberately).
        (b) John broke the window (deliberately).

(32)   (a) Mary depressed the lever.
        (b) The weather depressed John.

The point here is that animate/human-referring DPs have the option of being interpreted as volitional causers, as wilful controllers of a process and as experiencers of static or changing mental states. For every subpredication type and role type in specifier position that I have discussed in this section, I speculate that there is an analogue in the psychological domain. For the stative subevents, it is clear what those interpretational inferences are: psych INITIATORS are 'intentional'; psych RESULTEES are experientially affected.

The case of the process projection is an interesting one. I have claimed that the UNDERGOER is the individuated entity who possesses/experiences a varying property that runs homomorphic with the run time of the event. In the case of someone sentient, this could be their continuous experiencing of the process in a relevant way. I will claim that psychological involvement in a process such as that of continuous experience is also one way of being an UNDERGOER. Basically, the difference between pure 'Causes' and actual 'Actors' will be that an 'Actor' is related to both initiation and process (which may or may not lead to a result), whereas 'Cause' is a pure specifier of INITIATION. The psychological version of a pure cause is an 'intentional initiator', the psychological version of 'actor' is a volitional agent with continuous experiential involvement in the process.

Thus, in this system I do not make use of 'flavours' of the initiational head in a feature-based sense (as in Folli and Harley 2006), nor do I separate a causational head from an agent introducing one (as in the system of Pylkkä-nen 1999) to account for the different types of 'subject'. There are two distinct dimensions for accounting for differences in the entailment properties of different subject types: the first involves the difference between pure INITIATORS and UNDERGOER–INITIATORS, the latter of which are continually involved in the process and are represented as such; the second dimension is that of encyclopedic content either via the verb's own lexical-encyclopedic information or through the perception of the referential properties of the DP participant (animate vs. inanimate).

3.1.3 Stative predications

Finally, a word about stative verbs is in order here. The way the system is being built up so far, a stative verb cannot have any *proc* element in its first-phase syntax, or any UNDERGOER argument, but only RHEMATIC or nonaspectual internal arguments. I will assume that stative verbs therefore consist simply of an *init* projection, with rhematic material projected as the complement of *init* instead of a full processual *proc*P. Since the *init* does not have *proc*P as its complement in this case, it is not interpreted as causational, but simply as a state. If there is an internal argument, it is in complement position and serves to further describe the state (without any path structure). The subject of *init*P is then straightforwardly interpreted as the holder of the state. Thus, a sentence such as the following (33) would correspond to the first-phase syntax as shown in (34).

(33) Katherine fears nightmares.

(34)

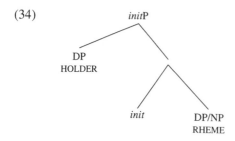

Notating the first-phase syntax of statives as '*init*' is not strictly necessary, since we could simply assume an independent verbal head corresponding to an autonomous state. However, I have unified the ontology because of the similarities in behaviour between verbal statives and verbal dynamic verbs. Specifically, if we assume (as in one popular current view) that *init* (or rather, its analogue, *v*) is the locus for the assignment of accusative case as well as the licensing of an external argument (as per Burzio's generalization), then statives are clearly verbal in this sense and have the equivalent of a little *v* head in their first-phase syntax.[5] Representing statives in this way also utilizes the ontology proposed here to the full – all possible combinations of heads and complements are attested and give rise to the different verb types we find in natural language. In particular, the phenomenon of *Rheme* nominal complements to V heads (in complementary distribution to RPs) exists side by side with *Rheme* nominal complements to *init* heads (in complementary distribution to *proc*Ps).

To summarize, given the semantics of the various categories proposed here, if the structures are not built up in the correct order, the derivation will at best converge as gibberish. Given the existence of a functional sequence, then, whose order is forced by the semantic interpretation rules, we can assume that the syntactic structures are freely built up by Merge, but as we will see in the next section, they will have to be licensed by the presence of specific lexical items.

---

[5] Here I leave open the issue of where one needs to distinguish 'unergative' from 'unaccusative' states, or whether that might correlate with the property in question being internally determined by the 'holder' (an individual-level property) or simply an accidental or contingent property of that 'holder' (stage-level). It may well be that these differences also need to be structurally represented, but a detailed investigation is beyond the scope of this book.

3.2   Integrating the verbal lexical item

What has not yet been discussed is the relationship between the abstract functional structure of the first phase and the actual lexical items which instantiate it. In being explicit about this part of the theory, a number of choices have to be made concerning 'insertion' vs. 'projection', and the nature of the features that the lexical items carry. Insertion models assert that the lexical item inserts under a particular terminal node (presumably according to the lexical item's category specification), and other features on the item must perform the job of 'selection' if the broader context of insertion is to be sensitive to that particular item. A projection model (such as Chomsky 1995) does not make a distinction between a terminal node and a lexical item that it dominates, but assumes that the lexical item itself becomes a 'terminal' of the syntactic representation if it is the minimal element on a projection line which bears that category feature. In the latter kind of model, the lexical items derive the syntactic structures by their projection properties. As with lexical insertion, a mechanism is still needed to ensure that the generalizations about certain selectional properties are to be met. Implementing a system of ensuring 'selectional' properties are met is the most difficult part of the current enterprise, and the problem is equally difficult whether one uses an insertion or a projection model. The difficulty is twofold: establishing which selectional properties of verbs should really be built in as part of the computation; establishing a mechanism to implement selection which does not involve serious departures from the mechanisms already admitted into the theory for independent reasons. Adger (2003) implements syntactic selection of a complement type XP by ascribing an uninterpretable category feature X to the selecting head which then has to be checked by first Merge. In the system described here which uses an articulated functional sequence whose ordering is determined, some of the syntactic selectional work already resides in that ordering of projections. Another difference between standard models is that the category label for Verb has been decomposed into *init, proc* and *res* and it is no longer clear what the position of Merge (or insertion) should be. However, because these categories have a systematic semantic interpretation, many of the differences among verb types that seem linguistically potent are directly correlated with the existence or nonexistence of these projections in the first phase. Taking the event structure and argument types discussed earlier as the fundamental natural classes gives a more pared down and abstract set of selectional properties than the traditional thematic role labels. It means that much of the selectional burden can fall on category features themselves, provided that we ensure that certain lexical items project certain particular subsets of these features. If selection can reduce to feature checking of category labels (cf. Svenonius 1994a) then we do not need to invoke an independent selectional mechanism for the purpose. The hope is that the patterns usually captured by syntactic selection can be accounted for by specifying a list of category features in the verbal item's lexical entry which will determine what kind of first phase it will be able to build/identify. The further hope is that semantic selectional facts either reduce to the semantic correlates of the functional sequence, or to felicity conditions based on the encyclopedic properties of the lexical items.

The categorial features we need for the first-phase syntax proposed above are the category features of the three eventive functional heads (*init, proc, res*). They are in principle *interpretable*, since they are the features that trigger the semantics of event composition, and are required for the proper interpretation of the first-phase syntactic structure, which I assume is simply the domain of event building.

What we know about the lexicon is that each lexical item is a bundle of information in radically different modalities (phonological, articulatory, syntactic, conceptual and even personal/associational) in some kind of memorized association. In terms of meaning, the lexical item contributes a huge store of conceptual and encyclopedic content, but it is the syntactic feature information that allows that content to be accessed and deployed within a linguistic computational system. But instead of seeing the lexical item as a structured syntactic entity that projects its information unambiguously to create syntactic representations (the structured lexicon view), I have proposed a view by which the syntax with a basic templatic semantics is built up autonomously, as one tier or dimension of meaning (a constructionalist view),with the association to lexical content providing the other tier or dimension of meaning. Encoding the structure in the syntax means that the only syntactic encoding necessary on the lexical item will be the category features themselves. Note that unlike the radically constructionalist views of Marantz (1997b), Borer (2005), the lexical item is not devoid of syntactic information, and it does not appear at the bottom of the syntactic tree. I will assume that the lexical item contains category features, and that this performs the 'selectional' work that gives the verb its partial rigidities of usage. Specifically, a lexical item with a *res* feature can project the *res* feature to form a *res*P predication, but it also carries lexical-encyclopedic content which can identify the content of the state in question; a lexical item with a *proc* feature can Merge as *proc* and has the nature of the process specified by its encylopedic content; a lexical item with an *init* feature can Merge as *init* and identify the nature of initiational conditions involved. From this discussion, it should be clear that a particular lexical item can carry more than one of these features in any particular case.

Thus, the first-phase syntax is freely built up by Merge, subject to the interpretational principles at the interface. Merge of syntactic features in the wrong order will create gibberish at the interface. To make 'selection' work, lexical items must carry a particular bundle of categorial label tags which allow particular first-phase configurations to be built. The idea is that the category labels or 'tags' on lexical items are the only information necessary to regulate their use, and moreover the minimal nature of the syntactically relevant information they have will be part of the solution to 'flexible' lexical use within a language. Since the lexical item may carry more than one category tag, it must therefore multiply associate to different syntactic heads (within the same phase) (cf. Larson 1988, Déchaine 2003). This seems to call for some equivalent of head movement, although head movement does not actually capture the intuition that the verb is a single lexical item that can project more than one category label. In addition, there are well-known technical issues with head movement in current minimalist theorizing (violation of the Extension Condition (Chomsky 2000) being the most obvious). Instead of pursuing a technical solution, I will simply drop the assumption that lexical items 'insert' under a single terminal node (see also Starke 2001), or that the initial Merge position is somehow privileged. Instead, elements may Merge and project and then Remerge in the sense of Starke (2001) at a later stage of the derivation. Basically, if the Merge of two elements is conceived of as set formation, then nothing prevents a particular item from being a member of more than one set. Remerge simply takes that idea seriously by creating a new association line without going through the redundant step of making a copy. Sometimes in what follows I will represent Remerge using copies, since it represents the same relationships more perspicuously, even though I do not actually believe that copies are necessary. This general idea has also been pursued for independent reasons in syntax, as in Ackema, Neeleman, and Weerman (1993), Koeneman (2000) and Bury (2003). Remerge of 'heads', as argued for by those authors, becomes a necessity in this system because lexical items have more than one category label. Intuitively, this is the technique by which a a single item can be associated to more than one position simultaneously.[6]

---

[6] Using a principle like Remerge (or Copy Theory) immediately gives rise to the question of the linearization of the elements that are in more than one 'position'. For the purposes of the data examined at this level of the clause, it seems enough to say that the spell out of an item corresponds to its 'highest' position in the syntactic representation. However, this may need to be complicated for higher levels of the clause.

If all that is specified by the lexical item are the category labels, how are the number and nature of arguments established? Perhaps very little needs to be said explicitly about this, in fact. As we have seen, specifier positions are interpreted systematically by the general semantic component as: INITIATOR, UNDERGOER and RESULTEE respectively. There are thus no thematic roles in this system, only three universal semantic rules triggered by syntactic structure. Another major departure this proposal makes from other systems is that these specifier positions are not claimed to be mutually exclusive. In other words, it is possible for a single argument to be in more than one of these positions simultaneously (or have them linked together in an A-chain). The simplest assumption is that all the projections of the first phase require a filled specifier (in other words, the information about who is the holder of the result state, who is the UNDERGOER of change and who is the INITIATOR need to be specified whenever *res*P, *proc*P or *init*P exist, respectively). In this way, the existence of a particular category will force the existence of the relevant specifying participant.

However, because of the possibility of filling those positions by either Merge, or Remerge (Move), one further condition needs to be stated: lexical items appear to impose a requirement concerning whether the specifier positions made available by the subeventual heads are filled by distinct nominal projections, or by the same nominal projection. This amounts to stipulating for each category label *init*, *proc* or *res*, whether it is a *raising* head or not. We will see when we examine the different verbal types in English that this possibility is something that seems to be related to the lexical item itself. Although it is possible that this information is part of real-world knowledge and not something that needs to be specified in addition to the category information, I will assume for now that this also has to be stipulated. I will notate this possibility by coindexing the category labels on the lexical items in question, as a way of indicating that the specifier positions of the two projections are filled by the 'same' DP. This is a weakening of the position that the only thing that needs to be present on the lexical item is category label features, but as I see it so far, an unavoidable one.

To make this discussion more concrete, I illustrate a sample derivation of a verb like *push* below. I assume that *push* is a verb which is specified as [*init*, *proc*]. In other words, it has lexical-encyclopedic content that identifies a process/transition as well as conditions of initiation. The *push* verb will Merge with a DP in its specifier and project its *proc* label. Since it also has an *init* feature, *push* can now be Remerged with *proc*P, which now projects the *init* label. This new syntactic object now Merges with the specifier to project an *init*P. The semantic computational rules at the interface will interpret this as a process of change characterized by translational motion of which DP_2 is the

UNDERGOER, and DP$_1$ is the INITIATOR, specified as possessing the physical force properties to put such translational motion in train.

(35)

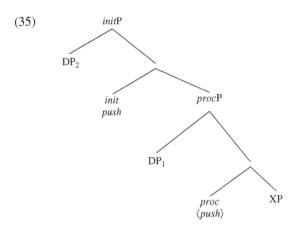

In this example, there is no PATH overtly specified, so I assume that the complement of the process head is filled in by a contextual variable (let us call this Y$_c$ for concreteness). In addition, the lexical encyclopedic content of *push* fills in the content for the process event.

(36)   [[$\overline{proc}$]] = $\lambda y \lambda x \lambda e$[Path(y,e) & *push*(e) & Process(e) & Subject(x,e)].(Y$_c$) = $\lambda x \lambda e$[Path(Y$_c$,e) & *push*(e) & Process(e) & Subject(x,e)]

The DP argument in the specifier now Merges with $\overline{proc}$ to form a *proc*P, giving:

(37)   [[*proc*P]] = $\lambda x \lambda e$[Path(Y$_c$,e) & *push*(e) & Process(e) & Subject(x,e)] ([[DP$_1$]]) = λe[Path(Y$_c$,e) & *push*(e) & Process(e) & Subject(DP$'_1$,e)]

Finally, once the whole *proc*P is formed, the highest verbal head *init* is interpreted as an initiating event and the lexical verb Remerges to identify the content of the initiational subevent.

(38)   [[*init*]] ([[*proc*P]]) = $\lambda P \lambda x \lambda e \exists e_1,e_2$[P(e$_2$) & *push'*(e$_1$) & State(e$_1$) & e = e$_1 \rightarrow$ e$_2$ & Subject (x,e$_1$)] (λe[Path(Y$_c$,e) & *push*(e) & Process(e) & Subject(DP$'_1$,e)]) = $\lambda x \lambda e \exists e_1,e_2$[Path(Y$_c$,e$_2$) & *push*(e$_2$) & Process(e$_2$) & Subject(DP$'_1$,e$_2$)] & *push*(e$_1$) & State(e$_1$) & e = e$_1 \rightarrow$ e$_2$ & Subject (x,e$_1$)]

DP$_2$ now Merges as the specifier of the initiation phrase to create a fully formed *init*P, which is a predicate of events (with internal complexity).

(39) $[[initP]] = \lambda x \lambda e \exists e_1, e_2[\text{Path}(Y_c, e_2)$ & *push*(e_2) & $\text{Process}(e_2)$ & $\text{Subject}(DP_1', e_2)]$ & *push*(e_1) & $\text{State}(e_1)$ & $e = e_1 \rightarrow e_2$ & Subject $(x, e_1)]([[DP_2]]) = \lambda e \exists e_1, e_2[\text{Path}(Y_c, e_2)$ & *push*(e_2) & $\text{Process}(e_2)$ & $\text{Subject}(DP_1', e_2)]$ & *push*(e_1) & $\text{State}(e_1)$ & $e = e_1 \rightarrow e_2$ & Subject $(DP_2, e_1)]$

We will consider a range of verbs of other types from English in the next chapter.

Another important constraint on the syntactic expression of participant relations that I will assume here without much comment is Case Theory. I assume that Case is an important component of the grammar, probably checked after the first phase of the syntax is complete, but providing a constraint on that first-phase syntax, since I will assume that only two arguments can be licensed by structural case in natural language. I will assume that *init* is the head that is responsible for the assignment of internal structural case, and that the I inflectional head (or some decomposed element of it) is responsible for the assignment of nominative. Thus, in the descriptions of the verb types in English that follow in the next section, there will never be more than two arguments licensed in specifier positions, even though there are in theory (at least) three positions made available by the event-structure template I have assumed. The phenomenon of the double object construction is a separate one, and will be dealt with in the next chapter.

4   Deriving verb classes

Given the outlines of the system presented so far, we can use the primitives at
our disposal to discuss the different natural classes of verb that emerge from
this kind of syntactic organization. I wish to emphasize that this chapter is not
intended primarily as a detailed investigation of any one set of phenomena. The
purpose is to explore the ways in which this system can be used to analyse
different possible verb types – the emphasis will be on the flexibilities and
constraints on the system itself. In each case I indicate what verb types are
possible and how they might be instantiated in English. I describe what the
most natural mode of analysis would be for many common verb classes in
English that have received treatment in the literature, pointing out where the
system forces one to make choices between various analytical options. In all
cases, the particular structures proposed here are intended to be starting points
for more detailed research. In chapters 5 and 6, I take up the issues of path
construction and causative formation respectively in more detail, and attempt
to make some more substantive proposals.

   In general, by taking seriously the event-structure participanthood of arguments, I aim to show that a somewhat different classification of verb types
emerges. In addition, the system I am arguing for will allow flexibility in a
verb's syntactic behaviour, within a system of constraints. Importantly, some
of the previous principles of mapping between lexical information and syntax
assumed in the literature will be abandoned. One important difference is the
assumption of 'multi-attachment' for verbal roots (i.e. the idea that verbs are not
inserted under a single syntactic node). Also, because this is a constructional
system, the wide variety of different verb types and role types will be derived
from the different combinatoric possibilities of the syntax.

4.1   Initiation–process verbs

In this section, I examine the argument structure of verbs which have an initiation component as well as a process component. Because they already contain

a representation of causation, they do not causativize in English; because they contain no result phrase, they do not possess an obligatory final transition. However, within these limits, there are still a number of different possibilities offered by the system. First of all, we must distinguish verbs in which the INITIATOR and UNDERGOER are distinct, from ones in which the INITIATOR and UNDER-GOER are filled by the same DP constituent. Secondly, we need to distinguish genuine UNDERGOER arguments from those which are 'rhematic' PATHS within the process phrase.

4.1.1   Transitives

Verb phrases built from verbs like *push*, *drive*, *dry* (transitive), *melt* (transitive) and *redden* (transitive) each contain some DP which is conceived of as the initiator of a dynamic event, where the second DP is commonly represented as undergoing a change. In the case of *push* and *drive*, the DP object undergoes a change of location. In the case of *melt* or *redden* the change is that of some (noninherent) property of the object. In each case, the lexical-encyclopedic content of the verb identifies the initiational transition as well as the process and thus is listed as an [init, proc] verb. Notice that a number of superficially different verbs are classed under the same heading here. The claim is that the notion of a caused process whereby a distinct initiator instigates a process undergone by another participant isolates an important linguistically relevant grouping. The internal differences among these verbs, e.g. whether the process in question is position along a spatial path or degree of attainment of a property, are part of the lexical-encyclopedic properties of the root that identifies the process, and are not directly encoded in the syntax.

With respect to UNDERGOER arguments, the event path predicates some varying property of the argument in spec, *proc*P. This property is not inherent to the object, and does not have to be monotonic with respect to its part–whole structure. Rather, it is a property that the object is asserted to possess (possibly incrementally), purely by virtue of participation in the event. By homomorphism, the endpoint of event is identified with final stage on the property or spatial path achieved by the object. Examples of verbs hypothesized to have UNDERGOER objects are shown in (1) below, and given a phrase-structural representation in (2).

(1)   (a) John pushed the cart.
         (b) Mary drove the car.
         (c) Michael dried the cocoa beans.

(d) The sun melted the ice.

(e) The clown reddened his cheeks.

(2)

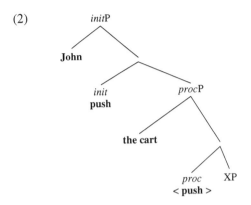

    There are, in addition, some transitives in this category whose direct objects
are not UNDERGOERS, but PATHS. While there is still a relation between the
process and a DP PATH, the difference lies in whether the DP is construed as
definitional of the process itself, or whether it is simply a 'traveller' or 'trajector'
of the path. As discussed in chapters 2 and 3, the PATH object is the kind of direct
object that has sometimes been called 'incremental theme' in the literature.
So, in the case of UNDERGOER DP, we have the relationship to the event path
being established by predication. In the case of the PATH, the property that is
mapped onto the process is inherent to the DP and does not itself change; the
homomorphism to the process of the event is established via the scalar structure
of that inherent property. Thus, the process is defined by its progress through
the scale contributed by the PATH object. In the case of UNDERGOERS, the DP's
existence is independently established and it possesses varying degrees of a
property as a result of the event. As discussed before, the class of verbs having
PATHS of process includes the classic consumption verbs such as *eat* and *drink*.
Because these objects are PATHS and because the path that is homomorphic
to the process is correlated with the material extent or degree of coverage of
the object, quantization effects occur and the boundedness of the direct object
translates directly into temporal boundedness of the process (cf. Krifka 1989,
1992).

    Thus, the semantic generalization concerning PATHS is that the event path is
homomorphic with some monotonic property of the entity denoted by the DP

(where a monotonic property is defined as in Schwarzschild (2002) as tracking the part–whole structure of the entity). Examples of verbs with PATH DP objects are shown in (3), and given phrase-structural representation in (4).

(3)   (a) John read the article.
       (b) Mary ate the mango.
       (c) Michael walked the trail.

(4)

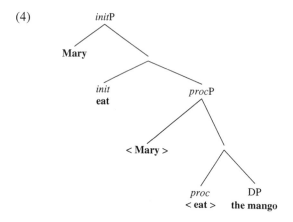

Note that here we have to assume that the UNDERGOER position in the specifier of *proc* is not itself filled by the direct object DP. Given the discussion in the previous chapter concerning sentient agents, it could be that the DP argument 'Mary' itself fills the UNDERGOER position in addition to the INITIATOR position, because of her status as continuous experiencer of the process. We will see in the chapter on causativization that certain subjects of 'ingestive' verbs in Hindi/Urdu show very clearly that they class as 'affected' in addition to being initiational. The alternative for English would be to relax the requirement that all specifiers of subevental projections be filled at some stage of the derivation. Such a relaxation would require further specification on the roots (e.g. a specification which forces the nonprojection of a specifier). In the interests of theoretical parsimony, I will tentatively assume that for these verbs in English with rhematic objects, the subject argument is always an UNDERGOER–INITIATOR.

This predicts that rhematic object verbs will require 'actors' (sentient or otherwise) but never allow pure 'causes'. There is some suggestive evidence that this might be the case. See also Folli and Harley (2004) for the first discussion that I am aware of of these kinds of contrasts.

(5)   (a) John ate the apple.
        (b) *Rust ate the drainpipe.
        (c) Rust ate (away) at the drainpipe.

The (c) example above is fine, suggesting that the conative construction has a rather different structure, although I leave a detailed analysis to further research.

As further evidence for the rhematic/complement status of a certain class of DP objects, McIntyre (2002) points out that direct objects and PP rhemes do not co-occur for many verbs. This is when the DP in question is itself rhematic and occupies the same position as a PP path. As McIntyre puts it, the existence of an 'event path' disrupts the ability of the normally selected DP object to be linked, in certain cases. This is predicted under the present system where both DP rhemes and PP paths occur in the complement position of the process head (examples from McIntyre 2002).

(6)   (a) I read through the book.
        (b) I saw (*Mary) into the window.
        (c) I rang (*the number) through to her.

(7)

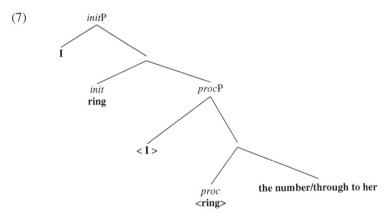

However, this is not the case with all verbs that take PP 'event paths'. In cases where PP paths do co-occur with direct objects, the direct object is an UNDERGOER and the PP is interpreted as the path travelled by that UNDERGOER.[1] Thus,

[1] We will see that the PP path can either simply be a rhematic PP complement to *proc*, or more deeply embedded within a result projection, depending on whether it describes the trajectory of the UNDERGOER or whether it names its final location. I will ignore these differences here, but take them up again in chapter 5.

co-occurrence with PP paths is an important test for the difference between
UNDERGOER and PATH DP objects.

(8)   (a) John pushed the cart to the store.
        (b) The sun dried the leaves to a crisp.

(9)

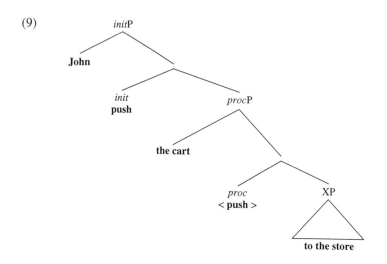

The class of creation verbs is interesting to examine here because phrases
like *bake DP*, or *paint DP* seem to be systematically ambiguous between a
reading in which the verb describes the process of an individuated UNDERGOER
argument (the (b) examples below) and a completive reading where the DP
object that comes into being describes the result (the (a) examples).

(10)   (a) John baked the cake from scratch (in two hours).
        (b) John baked the potato (for two hours).

(11)   (a) John painted a picture (from memory).
        (b) John painted a wall (with beautiful designs).

In the (a) examples above, the creation event is defined by the process of
'baking' or 'painting' and is complete when the DP in question comes into
being. In the (b) examples, the dynamic process expresses a change that the DP
(already in existence) undergoes. Thus, in the former cases the DP is a PATH
of process (12) with 'John' experiencing the process, but in the latter it is a
specifier (UNDERGOER) of process (13).

(12)

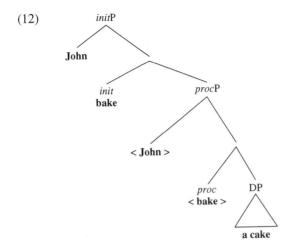

(13)

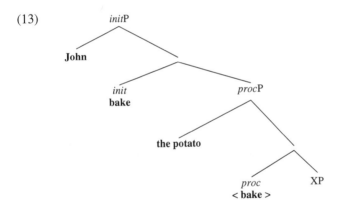

The entailments in the two cases are different. DP UNDERGOERS allow resultative secondary predication, while DP RHEMES do not.

(14)   (a) *John painted a picture red.
         (b) John painted a wall red.

In English, the addition of benefactives (constrained in English to 'creation' verbs (cf. Levin 1993)) is felicitous only under the 'creation' (PATH) interpretation of the DP, not an UNDERGOER interpretation.

(15)   (a) John painted me a picture.
         (b) ??John painted me a wall.

Certain adverbials like *a little* go well with UNDERGOER objects, but are strange with PATH objects.[2]

(16)   (a) ??John painted the picture a little.
        (b) John painted the wall a little.

What we can see about the verbs in this class is that there is considerable flexibility in the syntactic frames in which the verbs can occur (DP vs. PP rheme; DP undergoer vs. XP rheme). Thus, these verbs should be specified with respect to the elements in the functional sequence they can identify, and not with subcategorization frames per se. On the creation reading, the quantization of the DP rhematic object gives rise to a bounded interpretation of the event, much like in consumption verbs.

Turning now to processual verbs in the domain of motion, the example of *push* is instructive.

(17)   Lexical entry for *push*: [init, proc]

Because the lexical verb is associated with the identification of both the initiation head and the process head, it contributes lexical-encyclopedic content to both: it gives information about the kinds of actions required to initiate a pushing event (some sort of initiating impulse) as well as what constitutes undergoing a pushing (translational motion, not of own accord). Note that if these semantic selectional restrictions of the root are not met, the result is infelicity, i.e. the event cannot be described as a 'pushing'. If John causes the cart to undergo translational motion by forcing Mary to shove it then we cannot describe that as 'John pushed the cart'. If a small minor earthquake dislodged the cart from its resting place and caused it to move down the hill, (18a) is similarly infelicitous. If (18b) is to work, the stone needs to be already conceived of as rolling or moving of its own accord, not pushed or guided by something/somebody else.

(18)   (a) ?? The earth tremor pushed the cart down the hill.
        (b) ?The stone pushed the cart over the bridge.

General abstract causers are indeed possible in subject position for many verbs in English, depending on the lexical verb. I take the strong semantic selection restrictions on the subject position of *push* here to be an indication of

---

[2] These data are pointed out for Spanish in Batsiukova (2003), who also points out that the same constraint seems to apply to the Russian attenuative/semelfactive suffix *nu*.

the fact that *push* lexically encyclopedically identifies the initiation component, and does not merely specify the nature of the process. This is the same position as the one taken by Hale and Keyser (1993) in analysing the difference between *splash* and *smear*. For them, it is the existence of a manner of initiation component of meaning in *smear* that correlates with the fact that it does not appear in an intransitive version (see (19), their examples).

(19)   (a) Mud splashed on the walls.
        (b) ??Mud smeared on the walls.

In my terms, only *smear* is an [init, proc] verb; *splash* is a [proc] verb which can transitivize by the addition of a null [init] morphemic head with fairly impoverished lexical-encyclopedic content. I will discuss transitivization briefly later in this chapter, and again in more detail in chapter 6.

4.1.2   *Intransitives*

Within the group of verbs that identify both initiation and process, we also find some intransitives. This is a logical possibility of the system, whereby participant relations can be composite. Recall that different 'thematic roles' are not completely distinct monolithic entities but arise because they are constituted differently from the different syntactic positions in a relational structure and composed via Move. In this particular case, an intransitive [init, proc] can arise when a single DP occupies both UNDERGOER and INITIATOR position. These verbs have a single DP argument which undergoes change, but which is also self-initiating. A large class of motion verbs in English conform to this description.

(20)   (a) Alex ran.
        (b) Katherine danced.
        (c) The soldiers marched.
        (d) Michael swam.
        (e) Karena jogged.

The INITIATOR component of these verbs can be identified by the fact that they do not causativize (21).[3]

---

[3] As we will see in the next chapter, a distinct direct object is indeed possible with these verbs, but only when an additional position is made available by extra predicational information corresponding to 'result' or 'path'.

(21)   (a) *Michael ran Karena.
        (b) *Alex danced Ariel.
        (c) *The lieutenant marched the soldiers.
        (d) *Karena swam Kayleigh.

While a transitive version containing separate INITIATOR and UNDERGOER is not possible with these verbs, PATH objects are in principle possible and are perfectly grammatical, indicating once again the difference between UNDERGOERS and PATHS both structurally and semantically.

(22)   (a) Michael ran the race.
        (b) Ariel danced a waltz.
        (c) Kayleigh swam her way into history.

Crucially, the subject argument preserves the entailments of UNDERGOER as well as INITIATOR because the DP in question undergoes a change in position/location as a consequence of the activity. When a path phrase is added, the subject DP is the one that is asserted to travel along that path (23).

(23)   (a) Karena jogged to the coconut tree.
        (b) The soldiers marched around the block.
        (c) Katherine danced around the room.

(24)

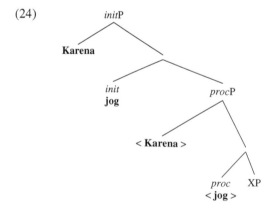

Thus, these verbs differ from *push* in that the DP that fills the specifier of the process projection is the same as the DP that fills the specifier of the initiation projection – in derivational terms, the higher specifier projection is filled via

Move, not first Merge. Once again, it is unclear to what extent this needs to be expressed directly in the lexical entry of the verbs in question. In principle, it could be real-world knowledge that tells us that 'walking' is the kind of activity that is self-initiated. If the lexical encyclopedic constraints are relaxed, by convention, the requirement that the INITIATOR and the UNDERGOER be identical can be suspended as in (25a,b).

(25)   (a) Katherine walked the dog.
       (b) Michael ran the water/the meeting/Mary's life.

Note that the possibility of composite roles has so far been restricted to adjacent specifier positions. If we consider a verb like *walk* which can also occur with a PATH direct object, as in (26), we might ask the question whether an intransitive version of *walk* is possible whereby the PATH roles and the UNDERGOER-INITIATOR roles are unified. An attempt to construct such a VP, as shown in (27), yields an ungrammatical sentence.

(26)   Karena walked the trail.

(27)   *The trail walked.

It may be that there is a basic incompatibility in the semantics here preventing unification of the PATH with UNDERGOER and INITIATOR roles. PATH objects are not frozen in place, as evidenced by the fact that they can appear as subjects in the passive versions of verbs like this. There could also be a more general prohibition against movement from the complement position to the specifier of the very same projection. For the moment, since I do not know whether such cases actually exist or not, I leave the matter open.

As noted before, there also seems to be a deep difference between the way in which we conceptualize animates, and particularly humans, in describing events and assessing causation. The fact of having a sentient initiator seems to be an important semantic selectional restriction for many lexical verbs. As we have seen, the fact of having intentions and desires is a salient causational factor in events. In particular, animates can be 'subjects' of process just in virtue of the fact that they are experientially continuously affected by it. It may be that considerations such as animacy and real-world knowledge are sufficient to constrain the various role-composition possibilities here. If, on the other hand, we were to take these restrictions on role composition/conflation seriously and wish to notate them in the verb's lexical entry, then we would need an extra diacritic to distinguish the intransitive verbs in this section from the transitive ones where INITIATOR and UNDERGOER are distinct. For convenience, I will use subscripting to indicate the difference between these two possibilities – the lexical entry for verbs of the *run* type will have the [init] and [proc] features co-subscripted to indicate identity of specifiers, while still leaving it open that this might not have to be explicitly present in the system.

(28)   Lexical entry for *run*: [init$_i$, proc$_i$].

The syntactic decomposition proposed here also has repercussions for subsequent anchoring to tense, although importantly I am assuming that no tense variables are present at this level of composition. The event-topological requirements for building macro-events from subsituations seem to be fairly strict: the initiation subsituation and the process must be related temporally, up to a tolerance of complete overlap; process and result must also temporally overlap at the transition point, although here the result state must also at least partially follow the process. This internal topology will be relevant once we consider the embedding of the complex event within a system of temporal interpretation. We will see that the nature of the lexical identification of the different subevents can give rise to different temporal entailments for the same event hierarchies within this general set of constraints. The important point at this stage is that time is a variable that is logically distinct from the event variables and their causational relationships, and that it is an empirical issue how the one should be embedded within the other.

4.2   Initiation–process–result verbs

There are a number of verbs in English that seem independently able to identify the result state of a process. I will argue that these include the transitives such as *break, throw, find, explode, enter*, and intransitives such as *arrive, disappear*.

4.2.1   Transitives

Taking the transitives first, the idea is that the transitive verb *break* encodes both a causational initiation by a DP subject (the 'breaking') as well as a final result of the DP object becoming 'broken'. For this kind of verb, the DP object is the UNDERGOER of the process as well as the RESULTEE, and the verb identifies the content of all three causationally related subevents. This is shown in (29) below.

(29)   Katherine broke the stick.

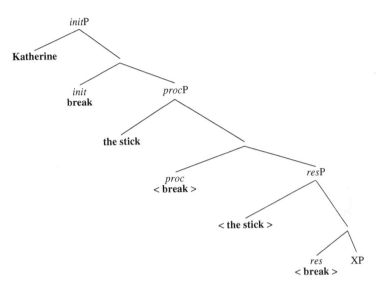

The verbs in this class encode a *res*P, which we can diagnose by the fact that they can take simple locational state prepositions as the rhematic complement of *res*, to describe the final result (30).

(30)   (a) Katherine broke the stick in pieces.
           (b) Ariel threw the ball on the ground.
           (c) Alex stuck the picture on the wall.

In each case the DP object undergoes the verbal process to end up in the final state or location as described by the locative PP – e.g. the 'ball' in (b) gets 'thrown' and ends up 'on the ground'. By the homomorphism requirement on rhemes discussed in chapter 3, we expect that PPs denoting extended paths should be able to appear as the complement of *proc* (a dynamic projection), while PPs denoting static locations should be able to appear in the complement of *res* (a stative projection). Because the result subevent is the state that the process subevent 'leads to', the result projection and its stative complement describe the final location of RESULTEE–UNDERGOER in a dynamic event. The possibility of a nondynamic, purely locative phrase describing the result of the action is dependent on the existence of the *res* head whose semantics ensures that this is the way the property or state is connected to the rest of the eventuality. Note that this contrasts minimally with the process verbs in the previous section, which consistently allow path PPs with directional prepositions (31a), but are not grammatical with simple locatives if we wish to express result (31b). I will take up these cases in more detail in the next chapter.

(31)   (a) *Kayleigh pounded the metal in pieces.
        (b) Kayleigh pounded the metal into pieces.

Verbs like *find* and *enter* are a little bit different in that their DP objects are not undergoers of the process or holders of any result state, but are rhematic DPs describing the final result. When Ariel 'enters the room', it is 'Ariel' who is the INITIATOR of a process which she herself is the UNDERGOER of, and where she bears the RESULTEE role of attaining the final location described by the GROUND DP, 'the room' in (32).

(32)   Ariel entered the room.

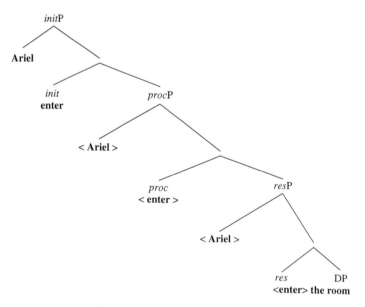

This latter type does not form explicit resultatives because the rhematic position is already filled by the DP object, but they are like the previous [init, proc, res] class in that they are incompatible with 'for an hour' in English (33).[4]

---

[4] In running this test, we must abstract away from the repetitive reading of *hit* in (33b), and the measuring of the duration of the result state in (33d). The ungrammaticality of the *for*-phrase in these examples is under the reading where the *for*-phrase measures the temporal duration of the process portion of the event.

(33) (a) *Katherine broke the stick for two minutes.
     (b) *Michael hit the stick for two minutes.
     (c) *Alex exploded the balloon for two minutes.
     (d) *Ariel entered the room for two minutes.
     (e) *Kayleigh found the gold for two minutes.

One other important diagnostic for the presence of *res* in the lexical specification of a single verbal item is the way that the event structure is subsequently anchored to tense. I have hypothesized that a verb that identifies an initiation transition as well as process seems to impose an overlap requirement on the initiational subpart of the eventuality with the process portion. When a single lexical item identifies both *proc* and *res*, as in the verbs seen above, the event expressed is punctual. I claim that this is because when a single tense-carrying verb identifies both an initiational state and the result state, all three subevents must be interpreted as overlapping. This means in turn that the process portion is reduced to a single instantaneous change.

The classification that is emerging here bears some resemblance to, but is distinct from, many of the aktionsart features and classifications in the literature. It is important therefore to be explicit about the ways in which this system differs from others, while still capturing the basic intuitions of previous work in this area. One of the points to note about this system is that it makes a principled distinction between the event-building portion of the clause, and the temporal interpretational portion of the functional sequence. At the event-building (lowest) portion of the clause, causational and predicational structures are built up, independent of tense. The verbs that contain [init, proc] could be seen as the ones that have traditionally been described as 'activities' in the terms of Vendler (1967), or [+continuous] [−bounded] in terms of aspectual features (Verkuyl 1993). While the traditional 'activity' verbs do indeed belong to my class of [init, proc] verbs, there are however [init, proc] verbs which would traditionally be called accomplishments. In fact, all of the accomplishments − the ones which embody duration as well as boundedness − are [init, proc] verbs. This is because temporal boundedness in my system can arise from bounded paths in the complement position of the *proc* head, or can even arise from real-world knowledge in the case of the degree achievements of Hay, Kennedy and Levin (1999). In other words, *res*P is not necessary for boundedness in the temporal sense; it is an element of causational substructure and gives rise to its own predicational entailments and is not the locus of telicity.

On the other hand, the [init, proc, res] verbs are classic punctual verbs, or achievements in Vendler's terms. Duration is an emergent feature in the decomposition described here: verbs which identify a nonpunctual process (whether bounded or not) have to be those which do not simultaneously identify process and result. Conversely, an 'achievement' interpretation is achieved when a lexical verb identifies both process and result.[5] However, the presence of all three subevents *init*, *proc* and *res* does not in and of itself necessitate that the resulting predication should be an achievement. I will claim that punctuality only emerges when a *single* lexical item carries all three features, with only one tense specification.

4.2.2   Intransitives

As with the previous class, intransitives also exist in the group of [init, proc, res] verbs despite the three specifier positions made available by the event-building substructure. This is because, as we have seen, roles can be composite. In this subclass of verbs are punctual achievements such as *arrive* and *fall*. Even though these verbs have traditionally been considered to be 'unaccusative', this is because of their obligatory telic character and their monotransitivity. I see no English-internal reason for ascribing a verb like *arrive* to the class of verbs that has no initiation component.[6] Because of the punctuality facts and the lack

---

[5] An alternative would be to allow the possibility that one stative projection can directly embed another and let the compositional semantics 'read in' the idea of transition via the 'leads to' relation. Another possibility is that the *proc* head could come in different flavours depending on whether it was [± duration]. I will stay away from both these possibilities here, since they represent a substantial increase in power for the system.

[6] I am assuming that the *there*-insertion test in English is not a diagnostic for unaccusativity, but rather is related to independent constraints related to locative existential predications. The possibilities of passive participle attribution likewise give unclear results: compare *the arrived train* with *the recently arrived train*, whereas *the melted butter* and *the broken stick* require no such modification. Since they don't always pick out the same natural class of verbs, unaccusativity diagnostics are notoriously problematic in the absence of a clear definition of what we are calling an unaccusative. For concreteness, I will use the term unaccusative to refer to the verbs in this system which do not have an [init] feature. (As we will see later, this means in effect that I am taking the core cases of unaccusative verbs in English to be the ones that alternate in transitivity. This is also the position taken in Hale and Keyser 2000). I will assume that being an UNDERGOER or RESULTEE is a necessary condition for passive participial prenominal modification in English. However, I tentatively assume that if the argument in question is *also* an INITIATOR, the construction is seriously degraded and modification related to the initiation portion of the event is required. The single argument of an *arrive* verb is RESULTEE, UNDERGOER *and* INITIATOR, which is why it does not pattern cleanly with the true unaccusatives.

of causativization, I will analyse a verb like *arrive* as containing a single DP argument which initiates its own transition to a final locational state – it is simultaneously the INITIATOR, UNDERGOER and RESULTEE. Moreover, because the verb identifies all three heads in this functional decomposition, the resulting predication is punctual (34).

(34)   Michael arrived.

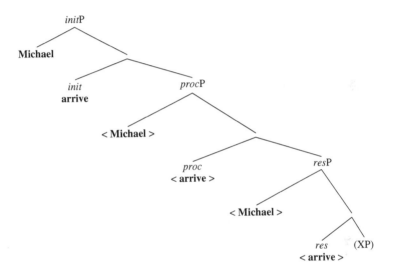

The class of 'semelfactives' as isolated in the literature by Smith (1991) also fall into this category. These are the punctual intransitives such as *jump*, *hiccup* and *trip*. The INITIATOR of the activity is also the UNDERGOER, and moreover, there is also particular final transition achieved by that argument, so it is also a RESULTEE. We can see that a locative (place) PP can indeed get a result interpretation with these verbs, showing that *res* is licensed by this verb.

(35)   Katherine jumped in the lake/on the table.

Therefore, in the absence of an explicit place PP, the result of a semelfactive of motion must be the covering or a particular distance to a final location, by jumping. Seen in this way, the single argument of *jump* must also be in RESULTEE position.

(36)   Katherine jumped in the lake.

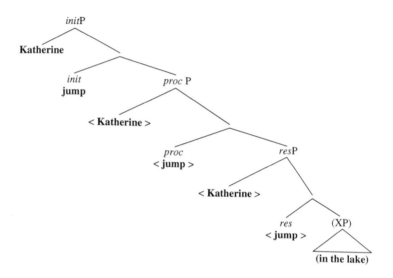

  Since the verb *jump* identifies both *proc* and *res* means that it, just like achievements and verbs like *break*, will be punctual. On the other hand, the defining fact about semelfactives is that they also systematically give rise to a durative, indefinitely iterated reading, in which case they are atelic. While Smith (1991) argues that semelfactives should be treated as a separate class, that of 'atelic achievements', this position has been criticized by Rothstein (2004), who argues that semelfactives are basically telic punctual events which are joined via 'S-summing' to give the durative, indefinitely repeated version.

  The definition of S-summing is given in terms of a system of event mereology represented as a lattice as in Link (1983). S-summing is simply the join of individual events to form a larger one. However, the most important fact about S-summing is independent of the lattice algebra used: the operation is only defined when the event atoms are such that the start point and the final point are identical (see also Kamp 1980 for this idea). This property allows events to be S-summed 'seamlessly' without any temporal or spatial gaps. Crucially, other kinds of event concatenation, like habituals or iteratives proper, do not have this property, and this is what makes the semelfactives special.

I will therefore assume that the basic first-phase syntax of semelfactive verbs is as shown in (36) above. One possible analysis is that the durative reading is a result of S-summing which is effected by a higher aspectual operator outside the first phase. This analysis is the one that is most congruent with the one given in Rothstein (2004), if we were to give her semantic S-summing operator a position in the syntax.[7] The disadvantage of this is that it obscures the difference between genuine iterativity (which is possible for all dynamic events and is blind to the internal structure of the first phase) and this special class of semelfactives whose durative reading seems intuitively just as basic and uncoerced as the punctual one. The former case, the one of genuine iterativity, is one that I would argue should be represented by an aspectual head outside the first phase proper. I am more uncertain about what should be done about S-summing in the sense of Rothstein (2004).

Pending further investigation, I tentatively assume that the special status of semelfactives is something noted in its lexical entry, i.e. that they are the only verbs we have seen so far which are ambiguous between being [init, proc, res] and [init, proc]. On the [init, proc, res] version, the verb so built will have to be punctual, and the lexical-encyclopedic content of *jump* will have to describe the nature of the transition. On the [init, proc] version, the lexical-encyclopedic content of *jump* purely describes a process – the facts we know about jumping activity. The idea here is that the Kamp/Rothstein intuition about the special conditions on S-summing is essentially correct, but that they are not conditions on the applicability of an operator in the syntax, but diagnostic conditions for a lexical item that could be ambiguous between being a process verb and a process–result verb.

Thus, when a verb like *jump* is used in its activity reading, it is compatible with Path PPs just like other motion verbs (37a) and not with locative Place PPs (37b). The activity reading of (37a) is represented in (38).

(37)   (a) Katherine jumped into the field. (*with directed motion: activity reading possible*)

         (b) Katherine jumped in the field. (*with directed motion: only punctual reading possible*)

---

[7] Although it is not clear whether Rothstein herself would sanction such a move.

(38)

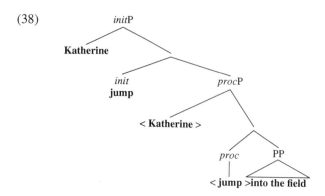

4.3   Transitivity alternations

So far, I have not considered verbs which do not contain an [init] feature at all. In other words, the intransitives I have considered have been those that arise because of composite roles, not because of the lack of initiational predicational structure. Although there have been various different definitions of 'unaccusativity' in the literature, I will call the verb class which lacks an initiational functional head in the eventive decomposition the 'unaccusative' type.[8] Does this latter type exist, and how do we distinguish them from other intransitives? Also, what distinguishes the classes of alternating verbs from those which do not alternate?

There has been a lively debate surrounding the causative–inchoative alternation as found in English (and Romance) where a major point of contention has been the direction (if any) of lexical derivation for the alternation. Levin and Rappaport Hovav (1995); henceforth L&RH) distinguish between two types of intransitive verb: (i) those which embody *internal causation* and (ii) those which involve *external causation*. The externally caused verbs include *break*

---

[8] The general intuition behind unaccusativity is that the single argument of the verb shares crucial properties of 'objects' of transitives. Because roles are composite in this system, this could be captured by the fact that verbs like *run* have a single argument that is both INITIATOR *and* UNDERGOER (i.e. sharing something with transitive subjects which can be pure INITIATORS), while others might be pure UNDERGOERS if the initiational subcomponent is missing. The correlation of unaccusativity with telicity that has been claimed in the literature is not systematic under this system, correctly so, I believe, since there are unaccusatives such as Hay, Kennedy and Levin's (1999) degree achievements which are not obligatorily telic despite conforming to unaccusative diagnostics in many languages.

and *open* and other verbs that participate in the causative inchoative alternation in English. According to L&RH, these verbs have essentially dyadic lexical templates, which under certain circumstances can be realized as monadic predicates in the syntax, expressing only the internal argument. The internally caused verbs include *laugh, run, glow* and *sparkle*. These have essentially monadic lexical templates and only rarely appear as transitive predicates in the syntax. Thus, L&RH agree with Chierchia (2004) and Reinhart (2002) in deriving the causative–inchoative alternation from a fundamentally transitive frame. The process by which the dyadic template comes to be associated with monadic syntactic structure in a verb like *break* is a lexical 'binding' at a level that changes the argument structure. According to L&RH, this process is available when the events can be conceptually conceived of as 'occurring spontaneously', when the root does not 'directly specify the nature of the causing event'. The argument for 'anticausativization' in this sense is bolstered by the morphological evidence from languages like Romance where the inchoative version of a verb transparently contains the verb itself plus a piece of 'reflexivizing' morphology (e.g. *si* in Italian, *se* in French, *sja* in Russian). However, a typological study of the morphology associated with causative alternations shows that languages vary considerably in the direction of morphological complexity, with many languages showing a preference for causativizing as opposed to anticausativizing morphology. The strongly causativizing languages in this group include Indonesian, Japanese, Salish and all the languages of the Indian subcontinent, and many other languages show some causativizing morphology in at least a subset of their verb classes (see Haspelmath 1993).[9] Thus, the argument from morphology is equivocal at best. The safest position from the point of view of morphology would be that the derivation can potentially go in either direction. L&RH seem to believe that the anticausativization story is also compelling on conceptual and empirical grounds, although I think that those arguments go through only on a particular conception of the lexical module and its relation to syntax and semantics.

L&RH's central conceptual argument comes from certain patterns they find in the selectional restrictions on subjects and objects of alternating verbs.

---

[9] There is also a class of 'labile' or equipollent alternations, where either both verbal forms seem to be morphologically derived from the same root (language), or where no explicit morphology can be found on either alternant (English). These languages do not constitute a direct argument for anticausativization, and once they are removed from the picture the languages with anticausativizing morphology look like an interesting minority, rather than an argument for a universal principle of directionality.

Specifically, they point out that in many cases the idiomatic interpretations of a verb that exist with special direct objects in the transitive version are ungrammatical with those same objects expressed in subject position of the intransitive counterpart (39).

(39)   (a) John broke his promise.
        (b) John broke the world record.
        (c) *His promise broke.
        (d) *The world record broke.

Because the range of semantically internal arguments is more constrained in the intransitive version than in the transitive, this is supposed to argue for a derivation in the direction of transitive to intransitive. There are, however, some cases that go in the opposite direction: in (40) the idiomatic interpretation is available in the intransitive but impossible in the transitive counterpart of the same verb.

(40)   (a) The tent collapsed.
        (b) Mary collapsed.
        (c) Sue collapsed the tent.
        (d) *Sue collapsed Mary.

But even if the generalization that L&RH appeal to is the dominant pattern, it is not clear that the argument goes through. The idea seems to be that any semantic content that is not predictable has to be listed together with the lexical item, and moreover that verbal meaning itself wholly resides in the lexical item. For the lexicalist, semantic content can easily be subtracted from a memorized specification via a straightforward rule; conversely, adding lexical content via a rule does not give a simple predictive system unless the added content is exactly the same for every alternation. Thus, in a *lexical* system, idiosyncratic/idiomatic transitive versions are a problem for any additive rule that is supposed to generalize. However, once one accepts that idiom formation is not restricted to 'the word' or single lexical item, but can be associated with larger structures (cf. Marantz 1997a), as in the constructivist framework more generally, then this argument goes away. In other words, it is perfectly possible for an intransitive root to be built up further via a causational head into a transitive version, which then is associated via the encyclopedia to a specific, idiomatic or conventionalized interpretation. Moreover, for the constructivist, the intransitive to transitive derivation does not need to be stipulated as a rule at all, but is predicted as the outcome of structure building during the course of the derivation. Under a structure-building system like the one defended more generally in this book, one actually expects transitivization to be more regular and transparent than detransitivization. It is not my purpose here to argue that the intransitive-to-transitive direction of derivation is the only conceptually attractive option, I mean only to deny the opposite claim. The claims of the conceptual and empirical superiority of the transitive-to-intransitive direction of derivation (as in Levin and Rappaport Hovav 1995, Reinhart 2002, Chierchia 2004) in fact prejudge the issue because they are based on specific assumptions about the existence of the lexicon and its role in expressing selectional restrictions.

In the present system, there is no mechanism of argument identification per se, but its equivalent can be found in the creation of composite roles instead of filling each specifier position with a distinct DP. So far, there is no equivalent of argument suppression, but a logically possible analogue would be the non-projection of category features of the root. In either case, it would be important to constrain these mechanisms if they are to be part of the system and deployed to create intransitive alternants from transitives.

Looking first from the perspective of 'detransitivization', considering the verbs analysed as belonging to the [init, proc] and [init, proc, res] classes, we can see that there are transitives in both classes that have intransitive variants, side by side with transitives that do not. So, for example, in (41), we see an [init, proc] transitive that has an inchoative version, while in (42) we see an [init, proc] transitive that does not.

(41)   (a) Karena melted the butter.
         (b) The butter melted.

(42)   (a) Karena hammered the metal.
         (b) *The metal hammered.

Similarly, in the [init, proc, res] class of transitives, some verbs such as *break* have an intransitive alternant (43), but others such as *enter* or *throw* do not (44).

(43)   (a) Alex broke the stick.
         (b) The stick broke.

(44)   (a) Ariel threw the ball.
         (b) *The ball threw.

One question is whether these alternations, when they occur, represent a conflation of INITIATOR and UNDERGOER roles (something allowed in this system and exploited for motion intransitives such as *run* and *dance*), or whether the initiation component is entirely missing, pointing to a kind of suppression. Either way, some diacritic in addition to the feature composition of the lexical entry would be necessary to register whether detransitivization is possible in any particular case. This is especially so, if, as I have argued, *break* vs. *throw* and *melt* vs. *hammer* cannot be distinguished by their category features or the aktionsart properties that derive from them.

However, if we look at the alternation as being causativization as opposed to detransitivization, a potentially simpler system emerges. The intransitives that I have argued to contain an initiation component in the previous sections, i.e. those arising from role composition, are precisely the ones that do not causativize (45).

(45)   (a) *Michael ran Karena.
        (b) *Kayleigh arrived Katherine.

If we now assume causativization to be a general process in English, as a result of automatic structure building, and allowed because of the presence of a default null *init* head, then the verbs that causativize will have to be those which do not contain [init] in their lexical specification. Thus, contrary to what I assumed earlier for the simplicity of exposition, *melt* and *break* are actually listed as [proc] verbs and [proc, res] verbs respectively. English has a null *init* head which can be built on top of those structures. The transitive versions of *melt* and *break* should always contain a null *init* head with the semantics of general causation (shown below in (46) for *melt*).

(46)

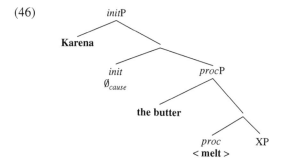

In the intransitive version, *melt* would occur on its own, allowing just [proc] to be identified.

(47)

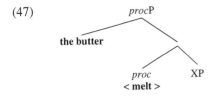

Similarly, the representation for *Katherine broke the stick* would not be as assumed in the previous sections, but instead involves transitive *break* being morphologically complex, containing a null causative suffix in the *init* head position (48).

(48)   Katherine broke the stick.

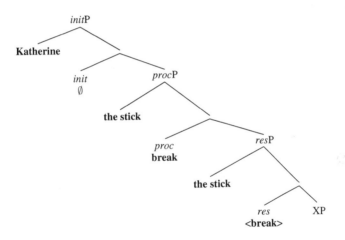

The advantage of the causativizing approach to the alternation is that no additional mechanism or diacritic is necessary to isolate the relevant alternating class other than the listing of category features already assumed by the system. Very simply, the verbs which alternate are those which do *not* contain an [init] feature in their lexical entry; the transitive version is always available because of the presence of a null lexical item (the causative 'suffix') in English. Many languages do indeed possess explicit causative suffixes on roots (see chapter 6 for further discussion) which mediate transitivity alternations. The disadvantage of this analysis is that it forces the postulation of a null causative head, although because of the robustness of the alternation in English, its existence would plausibly be very salient to the learner.

The alternative to the null causative head would be to claim that some verbs like transitive *break* or transitive *melt* are listed as [(init), proc, res] and [(init), proc] respectively, with an optional initiation portion, while verbs like *throw* are [init, proc, res] and do not offer such optionality. As far as possible, I wish to pursue an approach whereby this kind of optionality is restricted to certain semantically well-understood subcases, as in the semelfactive verbs discussed in the previous section. The system also does not allow any 'reduction rules' in the lexicon – these are simply not statable under current assumptions. On the other hand, given a constructionist approach, alternations based on legitimate structure building are the most natural ones to state. In the particular case of English, causativization by means of structure building in this system is a logically possible option. Moreover, allowing it via a null *init* head would make for a simpler set of mechanisms for capturing the distributional restrictions on the process.

Since English does not provide us with any overt morphological indicator of derivational complexity, the other factor to consider would be whether any evidence can be gleaned from semantic selectional restrictions. In fact, as has been pointed out in the literature (Hale and Keyser 2002), the selectional restrictions on the subject position of alternating transitive verbs are far less stringent than on the nonalternating verbs. Thus, in English, transitive *break* and *melt* seem to admit a wider range of general causes in subject position (49) than nonalternating verbs like *throw* (50) or *pound*.

(49)   (a) The sudden change in temperature broke the glass.
      (b) The storm broke the glass.
      (c) Michael broke the glass.
      (d) The sun melted the butter.
      (e) Rising salaries artificially increased store prices.
      (g) Age yellowed the pages of the book.

(50)   (a) ??The sudden change in wind direction threw the towel over the fence.
      (b) ??The storm threw the towel over the fence.
      (c) Michael threw the towel over the fence.
      (d) ??The traffic pounded the pavements.
      (e) ??The storm smeared mud on the walls.

Under the null causative head analysis, this is understandable: the nonalternating verbs are lexical entries that identify *init* and will impose specific lexical-encyclopedic requirements on their INITIATORS; the alternating verbs have a null cause head identifying *init* in their transitive versions and the requirements are more abstract, constrained only by general causational semantics.

For these reasons, I will assume a causational analysis of alternating verbs, via a null lexical cause head in English.[10]

One other point that should be addressed at this point is the systematic difference between 'unaccusative' alternants of such verbs and productive processes like passive which also create non-INITIATOR predications. The general wisdom concerning passive is that, while the 'agent' is absent, it is somehow still semantically present and can control purpose clauses, and license certain agentive adverbial phrases not possible with real unaccusative verbs (compare (51) and (52)).

(51)   (a) The ball was thrown to annoy Alex.
        (b) The ball was thrown by Kayleigh.
        (c) The ball was thrown deliberately.

(52)   (a) *The stick broke to annoy Alex.
        (b) *The stick broke by Kayleigh.
        (c) *The stick broke deliberately.

I assume that with passive, the transitive verb still retains and projects its [init] feature, although the passive morphology existentially binds off the actual INITIATOR position.[11] Many recent accounts have proposed that passive is a particular 'flavour' of the little *v* head, analogous to my *init*. Under the system being explored in this book, that analysis cannot be correct, because it would leave mysterious why passives of unaccusatives are impossible. Rather, passive is composed of a number of different mechanisms, perhaps the most crucial of which is the binding off of an argument in INITIATOR position, and does not apply when *init* is not projected and identified. This is different from the analysis offered here for unaccusatives, where no *init* head is present.

4.3.1 Degree achievements

Before leaving alternating verbs, I wish to address, briefly, the issue of degree achievements, whose aspectual properties have been subject to much recent

---

[10] I will take up cases of causativization in more detail in chapter 6, where I will examine a language with explicit causative morphology.

[11] I leave it open at this point whether this is done by a functional head embedding *init*P, or via some actor null pronominal in the INITIATOR position. See Ramchand and Svenonius (2004) for discussion and a proposal.

interesting work (Hay, Kennedy and Levin 1999, Rothstein 2004). I can scarcely do justice to the complexity and subtlety of the semantic data within this class of verbs in the context of this short monograph (as indeed with so many of these verb types), but the system laid out here comes along with a particular analysis for these verbs. Recall that degree achievements are classically (i) alternating in transitivity, (ii) ambiguous between a telic and atelic reading, and (iii) often 'deadjectival'. I follow Hay, Kennedy and Levin (1999) in analysing these verbs as a special kind of process verb where the degree of verbal change is mapped onto a property scale of some sort (derived from a basic adjectival meaning). Thus, in their intransitive use, they are classic *proc* verbs, with the single argument being an UNDERGOER.

(53)   (a) Waiting times at the NHS lengthened steadily for five years.
         (b) The cocoa beans dried in the sun for two hours.

(54)

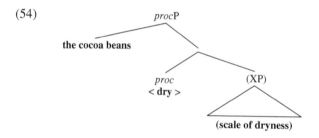

I further follow Hay, Kennedy and Levin (1999) in assuming that the fact that these verbs can also be interpreted telically does *not* arise from them identifying a *res* subevent, but is a contextual effect. Recall that in the case of motion verbs (also [proc] verbs), a telic reading could be obtained if the XP in complement position to *proc* denoted a bounded path. In the case of degree-achievement verbs, the complement position is filled implicitly by the property scale denoted by the corresponding adjective. If that property scale is contextually bounded then the verb will be telic.

(55)   (a) The tailor lengthened the trousers in just twenty minutes.
         (b) My hair dried in just ten minutes in that weather.

Note that this behaviour is predicted by the homomorphic unity proposal for rhematic complements, if we assume that the complement of the degree achievement is actually an implicit property scale. In addition, in this system, if the degree-achievement verb were to (optionally) also identify *res*, then on that reading it would have to be punctual. I am inclined to agree with Kearns (2006) that such cases exist alongside the bounded-path reading for the adjectival scale.

(56)   (a) The gap widened (suddenly).

         (b) John froze (in his tracks).

If such cases can be argued for, then we would have another subclass of verbs that was ambiguous between being [proc] purely and [proc, res]. It is relevant in this regard to point out that Rothstein (2004) actually explicitly makes a connection between semelfactives and degree achievements with respect to S-summing. She argues that degree achievements are of the right type to undergo S-summing because an indefinite change along a property scale can always be the starting point of another indefinite change along the same property scale, and thus the atomic changes of state denoted by the degree achievement can be S-summed seamlessly to form a derived process. I concede that there is something interesting in common with these two classes of verbs, but my intuition is that there is an important difference: while the activity reading of semelfactives can be *derived* from the punctual by S-summing, with the degree achievements it is not clear to me that the telic reading found in cases such as (55) above really is an atomic subpart of the readings in (53). For this kind of alternation, then, I think that the telicity arises from the bounding of the property path in the complement position of *proc*. On the other hand, if genuinely punctual readings of degree achievements (as perhaps in (56)) exist, then the description of that alternation should be unified with the semelfactive alternation. For concreteness, I will assume that degree achievements, like semelfactives, can be ambiguous between being [proc] and [proc, res] because they meet the conditions on S-summing. In addition to the telic punctual reading that they get as [proc, res], however, they also get a telic accomplishment reading as [proc] under circumstances where the adjectival path is bounded. (The existence of these two distinct types of telic reading for degree achievements is essentially the one taken in Kearns 2006.)

Degree achievements nearly always have transitive versions. I assume that this is true simply because they are [proc] verbs, and are thus input to the structure-building processes that would create derived causatives, as in the general case discussed in this section.

4.4   Conflation verbs

In the lexical decompositional system of Hale and Keyser (1993) and subsequent work, a good deal of emphasis is placed on 'conflation'-type verbs (denominal and deadjectival verbs) where it is claimed that the verb is derived by abstract incorporation into the head of the verbal projection from complement position, subject to principles of syntactic movement.

Under the system I am proposing here, the complement position of a verbal head is filled by RHEMES (either RHEMES of process or RHEMES of result). An example of a syntactic structure showing the rhematic PATH object 'a mile' is given in (57) below.

(57)

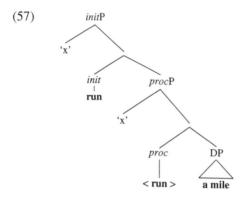

Conflation verbs seem to arise from rhematic material being incorporated from complement position into the head. In Hale and Keyser (1993), the verb *dance* is covertly transitive: the nominal 'dance' can be thought of as the complement of the generalized *do* process, which then conflates into the verbal head.

(58)

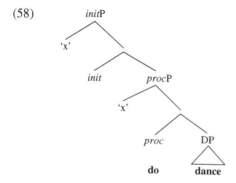

In the case of the location verbs, the nominal in question is the complement of the PP (what I would call RHEME of result, further describing the result state achieved by the undergoer of translational motion). In the case of locatum verbs, the RHEME of result is the possessional PP '*with saddle*'. So, once again, the nominal '*saddle*' is within the rhematic material of the clause, and incorporating it would be an (unproblematic) case of incorporation from a complement position.

(59)

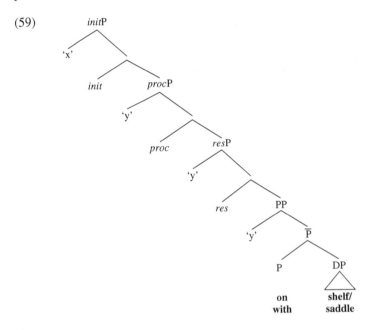

In the case of deadjectival verbs, once again the incorporation seems to be from the AP rhematic complement of the *res* head.

(60)

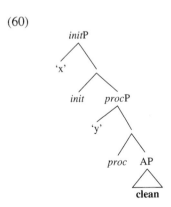

So far, I differ from Hale and Keyser only in that I have a more articulated decomposition than they do, in particular, making a distinction between RHEMES of process (which further describe the process by expressing manner or path) and RHEMES of result (which further describe the final state or location). Thus the crucial distinction is not between deadjectivals and denominals, or between location verbs and manner verbs, but between conflation into the *res* head vs. conflation into the *proc* head.

The intuition behind Hale and Keyser's account is that the correlation with selection (which determines the complement) and 'conflation' reflects a real syntactic generalization. In Hale and Keyser (2000), however, a distinction is made between conflation and genuine syntactic incorporation (which is assumed to be constrained by 'government'). The problem is that 'conflation' verbs are compatible with an overt DP in complement position.

(61)   (a) They are dancing a Sligo jig.
        (b) They shelved the books on the windowsill.   (Hale and Keyser
            2000: 49)

Hale and Keyser (2000) end up rejecting an incorporation analysis of denominal verbs. On the other hand, the generalization relating rhematic content to recognizable morphological properties of the verb does not seem to be an accident. Hale and Keyser's solution is to claim that there is a special binding relation between the content of a head and the interpretation of its selected complement. They define 'conflation' as in (62) below. It allows the transference of the p-signature (roughly speaking, the phonological content) of the selected complement to the head, as a concomitant of Merge.

(62)   *Conflation*
            Conflation consists in the process of copying the p-signature of
            the complement into the p-signature of the head, where the latter
            is 'defective'.   (Hale and Keyser 2000: 63)

There is also potentially a distinction between verbs that take 'cognate objects' (where the form of the noun and the verb are the same) and those that also allow hyponymous objects (objects whose denotation bears a subset to superset relation to the nominal concept encoded in the verb). The following examples from Hale and Keyser illustrate the two types: cognate objects (63a, b) and hyponymous objects (63c, d).

(63)   (a) She slept the sleep of the just.
        (b) He laughed his last laugh.

(c) He danced a jig.

(d) He bagged the potatoes in a gunnysack. (Hale and Keyser 2000: 71)

Hale and Keyser (2000) argue that the cognate objects are a true case of conflation, but where two copies of the p-signature are produced. Conflation is possible because they assume that the selectional relationship is not disrupted by functional elements of the extended projection of the head; both p-signatures are necessary because English prohibits the stranding of determiners. They leave it open whether the verbs with hyponymous objects should be given the same treatment or not.

Consider again the kind of decomposition I have been assuming for predicational structures: embedded situational descriptors with a predicational asymmetry between specifier ('theme') and complement ('rheme'). This structure is recursive, but not in practice infinite. At some point, the structures must 'bottom out' and contain a nonbranching, missing, or implicit rhematic position. With verbs this is possible when the lexical-encyclopedic content is in principle rich enough to identify the nature of the subevent without any explicit complement material. One way of thinking of this is to see the rhematic material as being implicit. Thus, another possibility for analysing 'conflation' verbs is to see them as having implicit RHEMES, licensed by the lexical-encyclopedic content of the root. This, as I read it, is the intuitive condition underlying the relationship between the phonologically defective verbal head in Hale and Keyser's analysis and the nominal complement whose content is specifically selected.

(64)

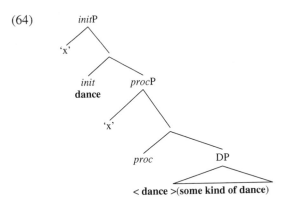

However, there are reasons to find this way of thinking of things unsatisfactory. The process of conflation as described in Hale and Keyser (2000) seems somewhat mysterious, as does the appeal to 'implicit' rhemes. Fortunately, in the system being developed in this book, another possibility is open to us. Since lexical items come with a clutch of category labels, and since the system abandons the assumption that lexical items are inserted under a single terminal node, it is possible to endow a lexical item like *sleep* or *dance* with a nominal feature in addition to its verbal features. Recall that multiple association/Remerge is designed to take the place of 'selection' in this system, and the features that are possible in any single lexical chunk are constrained only by adjacency under complementation. The conditions for conflation are precisely those of direct complementation. Consider the representation below: if a root like *dance* is endowed with [init, proc, N] category features, it will be able to identify the subtree indicated, providing lexical-encyclopedic content for not only the process but also the rhematic material of the process event. (I assume that since in this case the verb doesn't introduce a true referential argument, the complement of *proc* is actually an NP.)[12]

(65)

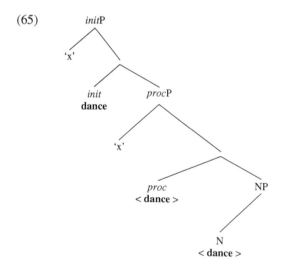

---

[12] I notate the feature on the verb *dance* as N, abstracting away from the fact that the categorial decomposition of a nominal projection probably involves more category heads than just N and D. The point is merely that in a complex predication of this type, the nominal complement contains less syntactic functional structure and is less obviously referential than when a nominal projection stands in an argument position. Moreover, if a certain level of structure in the nominal extended projection determines a phase, the nominal complement of the verbal head will have to be at least smaller than *that*.

Under the view where lexical items have multiple category features and lexicalize chunks of trees, the usual constraints on insertion have to be reconfigured. In particular, I will assume what is essentially a 'superset principle' which states that a lexical item may insert to spell out a sequence of heads if its category signature is a superset of the sequence to be spelled out. The 'superset principle' terminology is due to Michal Starke,[13] who also assumes a system where lexical items spell out chunks of tree structure. It can be shown that the superset principle essentially replaces the 'subset principle' of theories like distributed morphology (Halle and Marantz 1993, Marantz 2001, Embick and Noyer 2001) to express 'the elsewhere condition' (Kiparsky 1973, 1982) in a system that does not assume insertion under terminal nodes (see Caha 2007 for data and discussion). Use of a lexical item that bears a superset of the category features it actually spells out in the structure is what I will call 'underassociation'. Underassociation is allowed in this system and will be exploited further in chapters 5 and 6 in the discussion of complex predications of various types. The reason it is introduced now is because it is potentially important in understanding the behaviour of denominal verbs. The idea is that the structure in (65) above is not the only way to build a tree using the lexical item *dance*. In principle, the nominal feature of *dance* can underassociate, and an independent DP structure can be merged in the complement position (where the underassociated N feature on *dance* is shown in brackets).

(66)

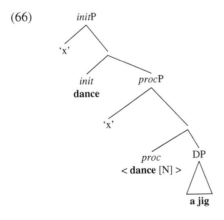

---

13 Nanosyntax Seminar, University of Tromsø .

Underassociation however is not free, but is only possible under a set of specific conditions. I will tentatively assume the following constraint on underassociation, which I believe is sufficient to prevent overgeneration but still allow the situations that we will analyse in chapters 5 and 6.

(67)   *Underassociation*
         If a lexical item contains an underassociated category feature,
         (i) that feature must be independently identified within the phase and linked to the underassociated feature, by Agree;
         (ii) the two category features so linked must unify their lexical-encyclopedic content.

In the case at hand, denominal verbs, we must fill the complement with a projection that will identify N, and in addition, the information about the rheme provided by the conceptual content of the root (i.e. that the person is performing a 'dance') must be unified with the conceptual content of the DP complement. This will be successful if *dance* and the denotation of the DP stand in a hyponymous relation.

In the case of true 'cognate' objects with verbs like *sleep*, or *laugh*, I assume that the only difference is that for these roots there are no ready-made lexical hyponyms. In other words, a *chuckle* isn't really a subtype of *laugh*, they are separate, possibly overlapping things. Similarly, a *nap* is not a subtype of *sleep* in our conceptual lexicon. The only way to create DP complements that will successfully unify with the lexical-encyclopedic content of the verbal item in these cases will be precisifications of the nominals *sleep* and *laugh* themselves, via modification.[14]

Assuming that items such as *dance* and *sleep* are endowed with both so-called verbal and nominal features allows us to make sense of the curious property of English whereby the same form can be used as either a noun or a verb with no overt derivational morphology. It is this pervasive property of English that has contributed to the plausibility of the 'naked roots' view of the lexicon, as found in Borer (2005) and Marantz (2001), for example (see chapter 1 for discussion). However, the position I will take in this book is that English is special in this regard. Its specialness can be reduced to a fact about large

---

[14] Hale and Keyser (2000) point out that the examples with *sleep* and *laugh* with hyponymous objects improve on repetition, something that one might expect if some accommodation concerning the relationships among concepts is possible.

chunks of its lexical inventory which contains items with both nominal and verbal features. This fact, together with the superset principle, means that a given lexical item in English can be used in both nominal and verbal environments provided its underassociated features can be otherwise satisfied. Thus, in a complex predicate, if the light verb *do* inserts to identify process, then *dance* may underassociate to identify just the nominal complement part of the structure. Here, the underassociated [init, proc] features of *dance* will have to unify with the information about process and initiation provided by *do*. This immediately accounts for why the structure is only possible when the verbal identifier (here *do*) is fairly underspecified for conceptual content, what we generally call a 'light' verb.

(68)

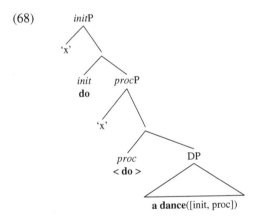

Of course, this by itself is not enough to account for the use of *dance* in a full-fledged phasal DP in an argument position, since there, no intraphasal dependency with an [init, proc] set of features is possible. I speculate that this possibility is mediated by higher nominal functional structure which is able to bind these purely verbal features (via some kind of intensionalized closure operation) when they appear in full DP structures. The claim of this analysis is that such usages are *possible* in the first place only because the relevant items in English bear both nominal and verbal categorial features. A detailed examination of this hypothesis is beyond the scope of this short book, but the issue of complex predications will come up again in chapters 5 and 6.

4.5   Double object verbs

In this section, I lay out how a certain plausible view of the dative alternation can be represented in the system I am exploring in this book. While Larson (1988) argues for a transformational account of the alternation, essentially deriving the double object version via a kind of internal passivization of the dative alternant, subsequent work by Pesetsky (1995), Hale and Keyser (2000) and Harley (2002) argued for a base generation account. The base generation account takes seriously the facts in Oehrle (1976) and Jackendoff (1990) which show that the semantic predicational relations for the two structures are actually subtly different. To illustrate, the contrast in (69) described by Oehrle (1976) shows that there is an animacy requirement on the first object of a double object construction which does not carry over to the complement of *to* in the dative alternant.

(69)   (a) The editor sent the article to Sue.
         (b) The editor sent the article to Philadelphia.
         (c) The editor sent Sue the article.
         (d) ??The editor sent Philadelphia the article. (from Harley 2002: 37)

Conversely, there are examples that are good in the double object construction but not in the dative alternant version.

(70)   (a) Bill threw Mary a glance.
         (b) *Bill threw a glance to Mary.
         (c) The war years gave Mailer a book.
         (d) *the war years gave a book to Mailer.   (from Harley 2002: 41)

The difference in semantic roles justifies a difference in base-generated predications, since the UTAH (Uniformity of Theta Assignment Hypothesis) (Baker 1988) would now not be violated. Pesetsky (1995) proposes that the difference in predications flows from the different prepositional heads mediating the relationship between the DPs in each case. According to Pesetsky (1995), in the dative version, the THEME is the specifier of a predicational relationship to the GOAL that is headed by *to*; in the double object version, the GOAL is the specifier of a predicational relationship headed by what he calls G. Harley (2002) takes this further and claims that *G* is in fact the possessional preposition P_{have}, thus unifying the predicational substructure in the double object construction

with other possessional constructions. Harley's (2002) structures for the two
versions are given below.

(71)

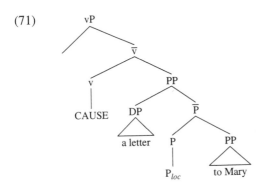

(72)

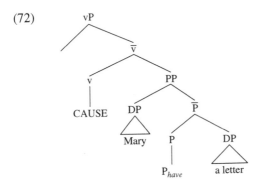

(from Harley 2002: 34)

In the system proposed in this book, flexibility with respect to the insertion
possibilities of a particular lexical root such as *give* is built in, given structure building. I will essentially adopt Harley's (2002) analysis, but modify
it to the particular decompositional structures I have been arguing for more
generally.

The first difference between the two proposals is that the decompositions I
have provided here have a *proc* head in addition to the little *v* causational head
assumed by Harley. Secondly, I also have a *res* head in the decomposition which
gives rise to a resulting final predication. I am assuming that *give* contains a *res*
feature in its lexical entry since it gives rise to a punctual verb with a definite

result. I further assume that the directional preposition *to* in English is special in that it contains a *res* feature in *its* lexical entry. Because of underassociation, *give* can combine with *to*, satisfying *give*'s *res* feature by Agree and unification. Since an independent lexical item is identifying result, it is potentially possible for the time at which the result state holds to be nonadjacent to the giving event, and even for it to not actually transpire (since the result phrase is not directly linked to a time variable).

(73)   Alex gave the ball to Ariel.

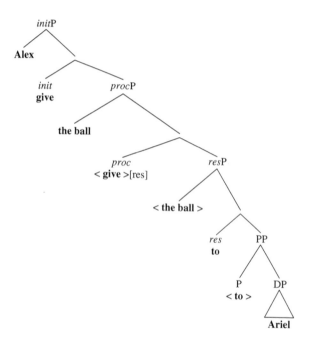

In the double object version, the verb *give* itself identifies *res* and therefore must take a stative PP complement. This is the Harleyan PP consisting of the null possessional P head and a DP complement. Note that in this case, the result of giving is cotemporaneous with the giving, since the verb is identifying both *proc* and *res*. This is the source of the intuition reported in the literature that the double object version actually does entail a final result (cf. Oehrle 1976, Larson 1988).

(74)   Alex gave Ariel the ball.

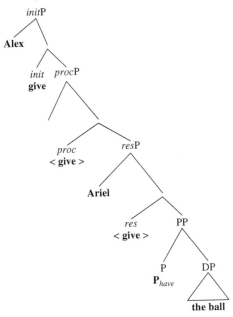

The structures above capture the same intuition as Harley (2002) and Pesetsky (1995) in that they give different predicational structures for the two versions, and thus can also account, in principle, for the difference in entailments noted by Oehrle (1976). It also agrees with them in identifying one of the predicators as an abstract possessional head. I differ from Harley's account in having a slightly more decomposed structure, and also in claiming that the division of labour between the *give* verb and its co-predicator is different in the two cases: in the double object version, it is the *give* verb that identifies the result, whereas in the dative alternant it is the preposition *to*. The claim that *to* in English bears a *res* feature will have implications for the data on motion verbs and resultatives in chapter 5.

One other important difference between the *res*P structure and the dative alternant is that while 'Ariel' is the RESULTEE, it is not at all clear that the semantics are consistent with 'Ariel' being the UNDERGOER.[15] It is well known

---

[15] For case reasons, the expression of a distinct UNDERGOER is impossible, so it must remain implicit. If there is a notional UNDERGOER, it would have to be 'the ball' itself, although that particular relation is not, I assume, represented directly in the double object structure.

that there are differences in the behaviour of the two 'objects' in the double object construction, and also that there is a difference between the direct object in the dative version and the 'first' object of the double object version. This difference would be surprising under an account where the only thing that varied was the predicational content of the 'small clause' complement to the verb. Under the account I am suggesting here, the 'first' object of the double object version is a RESULTEE but not an UNDERGOER, while the direct object of the dative version is both RESULTEE and UNDERGOER.

One important asymmetry between true UNDERGOER objects and the RESULTEE objects of double object verbs is that secondary depictives can always go with the former, but not the latter. Even in the double object construction, the nonrecipient argument, which isn't even the syntactic (passivizable) direct object, can support depictives (75) (Bowers 1993, Hale and Keyser 2000).

(75)   (a) Karena gave the baby the bottle full.
        (b) Karena gave the bottle to the baby full.
        (c) Karena gave the baby the bottle crying.
        (d) Karena gave the bottle to the baby crying.

It is not clear how these facts can be made to fall out of the structures I am assuming here. One could assume that depictives attach either to *initP* as adjuncts, or to *procP*. In the former case, they modify the INITIATOR argument, but in the latter, they target the UNDERGOER argument. This explains the interpretational possibilities of (b), (c) and (d): in (b) either 'Karena' or 'the bottle' can be full; in (c) only 'Karena' can be 'crying'; in (d) either 'Karena' or 'the bottle' can be 'crying', although the latter is discounted for real-world knowledge reasons. The only mystery is the fact that (a) allows an interpretation whereby the bottle is full, even though under this account, 'the bottle' is in the rhematic position of the result possessional head. It is possible that there is an implicit UNDERGOER here, whose content is identified by 'the bottle'. In that case, the *procP* adjunct position might be controlled by the implicit UNDERGOER (since we know already that 'control' by implicit arguments is possible). Control would therefore not be by the element in the complement of *res* directly, although it indirectly gets its reference from it. This is not an entirely satisfactory solution, but in the absence of a deeper understanding of the structure of depictives, I put the problem aside for now.

Given the possibilities of verbal decomposition, and, crucially, the existence in English of the null prepositional possessional head, we predict that any dynamic predicate that identifies *res* should be augmentable with a DP, provided its encyclopedic semantics are compatible with a final abstract 'possession'.

Many verbs of directed motion also participate in the alternation. As Levin (2006) points out, verbs of directed motion undergo the double object construction, but they differ from *give* verbs in that they also give rise to a spatial goal interpretation in their *to* alternants. The exact nature of the result asserted in these predications comes from a unification of the lexical-encyclopedic content of the verbal *res* with the prepositional *to*'s *res* feature. In the case of verbs of motion this will allow a change of location reading; in the case of nonmotional verbs like *give* this will result in only a possessional reading. Verbs of continuous accompanied motion do not typically allow the double object version (see Pesetsky 1995, Pinker 1989 for discussion), and I assume that this is because they do not identify a *res* portion of the clause (since they are nonpunctual).

4.5.1 *Applicatives more generally*

Applicatives have been the subject of much recent work on argument-structure-changing operations (Baker 1988, 1996, Pylkkänen 1999) and are an important locus of crosslinguistic variation. There seems to be some consensus that there are at least two types of applicatives in language – the 'inner' ones which are more lexically restricted, and which crucially rely on an internal predicational relationship with the initial direct object; 'outer' ones which are more productive and which create a relationship between the applied argument and the whole event (see Pylkkänen 1999). Pylkkänen argues that the inner applicatives involve a special inner applicative head that occurs between the verbal categorial head and the root, while the outer ones involve a head that occurs between little *v* and the root. The inner applicative heads in this sense are the ones that I believe are part of the verbal decomposition being proposed in this book, and the possessional result head that I am assuming for the English double object construction is one lexical instantiation of what Pylkkänen calls the lower applicative head. It is this head, which mediates a predicational relationship between the original direct object and an applied argument, which is equivalent to the P*poss* I have been assuming. While possessional lexical heads are common crosslinguistically, I assume others to be in principle possible with different, or more abstract, lexical content, depending on the lexical inventories of the languages in question. High applicative heads, however, I assume are outside the remit of the core verbal decomposition and relate more directly to the event as a whole. I assume that such heads, when allowed, introduce predicational relationships between an applied argument and the whole constructed *init*P. This is somewhat at odds with Pylkkänen's technical assumptions since she places the higher applicative head lower than little *v* (presumably the closest analogue to my *init*). However, the reasons for placing it there as opposed to outside the little *v*P altogether are not to my mind overwhelming: the semantic facts dictate that the complement of the higher applicative head should denote the whole event, and the only reason it is placed lower in Pylkkänen's account is to allow the highest argument to be eventually attracted to the clausal subject position. If we assume that the 'applied' argument gets its own form of prepositional case and is invisible for attraction to the Spec, TP position to become the subject, then it can be generated outside *init*P without sacrificing the subject properties of the clause.

This brief discussion scarcely does justice to the vast literature on double objects and applicatives crosslinguistically. As in practically every other topic treated in this chapter, I leave a detailed investigation and analysis to later work, but indicate merely how the research programme being defended in this book would apply to various important empirical domains in the literature.

4.6   Statives

Stative verbs are different in an important way from the other verb types considered so far in this chapter, most importantly in not containing a *proc* projection, the hallmark of dynamicity. I assume that stative verbs arise when an *init* head selects rhematic material instead of a 'process' complement. The rhematic material in question can be either a DP as in (76a), an AP (76b) or a PP (76c). It is also possible for *init* to be filled with the encyclopedically impoverished verb *be*, in which case the existence of rhematic material is almost forced in order to fully describe the state (77).

(76)   (a) Katherine fears nightmares.
        (b) Ariel looks tired.
        (c) The two rivers meet at the end of the field.

(77)   (a) Katherine is in bed.
        (b) Alex is happy.
        (c) ?Ariel IS.

(78)   **State:** *x fears y*

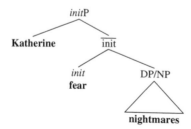

I am assuming that it is the *init* head that is at issue here because it shares some salient properties with the *init* head in dynamic predications. First of all, the DP argument in its specifier is the entity whose properties are the cause or grounds for the stative eventuality to obtain, for example, it is because of Katherine's personality that the state of her fearing nightmares arises. Secondly, stative verbs are able to assign accusative case to their objects, a characteristic we have been assuming applies to the *init* head generally in dynamic predications as well.

4.7   Summary

Although there are potentially many issues left to discuss, I close this chapter with the idea that the many different types of verbs and verb classes can be put together with a relatively impoverished set of primitives, and that the different possibilities for verbal event-structure meanings/behaviours can be predicted by syntactic form, and some general principles of lexical association.

The internal eventive/causational structure of a verbal predication maximally decomposes in this system as follows.

(79)

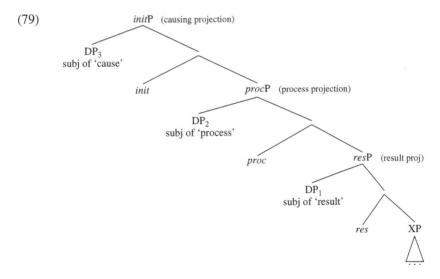

In the above structures, the embedding of subevental descriptions is interpreted via a causing, or leads-to relation; non-event-denoting complements must co-describe the eventuality identified by the head. In the latter case, they must denote a scale (or derived scale) that can unify with that head via a homomorphism. Specifier positions represent the thematic participants related to individual subevents.

Also, as we have seen, identification of syntactic structure is subject to a superset, and not a subset principle (Caha 2007). This means that any particular lexical item can underassociate its particular category features provided those features are independently identified within the phase, and provided the lexical-encyclopedic content of two 'Agreeing' features can unify without infelicity.

Thematic relations are determined by their configuration within the system above. In principle, the thematic participants available are: INITIATOR, UNDER-GOER, RESULTEE, PATH, RESULT–RHEME. However, many more than these are possible because of the availability of composite thematic relations related by movement. A summary of the lexical verb types found in English and discussed in this chapter is given below in (80).

(80)				
		[init, proc]		
	I	Transitive	INITIATOR, UNDERGOER	*drive, push, paint*
		Transitive	INITIATOR, PATH	*eat, read, paint*
	II	Intransitive	INITIATOR$_i$, UNDERGOER$_i$	*run*
		[init, proc, res]		
	III	Transitive	INITIATOR, UNDERGOER$_i$, RESULTEE$_i$	*throw, defuse*
		Transitive	INITIATOR$_i$, UNDERGOER$_i$, RESULT-RHEME	*enter*
	IV	Intransitive	INITIATOR$_i$, UNDERGOER$_i$, RESULTEE$_i$	*arrive, jump*
	V	Ditransitive	INITIATOR, UNDERGOER RESULTEE	*give, throw*
		[proc]		
	VI	Intransitive	UNDERGOER	*melt, roll, freeze*
		[proc, res]		
	VII	Intransitive	UNDERGOER$_i$, RESULTEE$_i$	*break, tear*
		[init, proc, N]		
	VIII	N-conflation	INITIATOR$_i$, UNDERGOER$_i$	*dance, sleep*
		[init, proc, A]		
	IX	A-conflation	UNDERGOER	*dry, clear*

Unaccusatives are verbs in this system which independently identify no *init* subevent, but which are augmentable via the null default *init* head in English.

Unergatives have a single argument that is an INITIATOR (whether or not it also carries other participant entailments).

As far as the connection to traditional aspectual classes goes, the following appears to be the case: 'activities' correspond to either [init, proc] or [proc] verbs; 'accomplishments' are [init, proc] verbs with incremental theme or PATH complements; 'achievements' are [init, proc, res], or [proc, res]; semelfactives are verbs ambiguous between [proc] and [proc, res]; degree achievements are [proc] verbs with a property-scale path. Deadjectival and denominal verbs exist because verbs in English can also come with an A or N category feature respectively, which they lexically encyclopedically identify in the functional sequence line determined by complementation. The distributional facts in the table indicate that deadjectival verbs tend to be unaccusative, while denominal ones tend to be unergative. While I have no explanation for this at this time, I speculate along with Hale and Keyser (1993) that having a nominal feature is equivalent in some sense to having a direct internal argument and thus the pattern basically conforms to Burzio's generalization (Burzio 1986), and these verbs require an INITIATOR.

There is no single projection in this system which carries a [+telic] feature. Rather, telicity emerges from a number of different interacting factors. In the absence of secondary aspectual modification, however, the existence of *res*P does give rise to telicity. Classes III, IV, V and VII are default telic and are also punctual. Class I is telic when the PATH argument is bounded, class VI, when there is an endpoint on the scale of change implied (as in Hay, Kennedy and Levin 1999).

5 *Paths and results*

5.1 PPs: paths and places

In order to investigate the interaction between full prepositional phrases and resultative formation, we need first to be more explicit about the internal structure of prepositional phrases. Following Jackendoff (1983) in the conceptual domain, we need to make a distinction between PATH and PLACE prepositions. Recent work on the syntactic behaviour of PPs has converged on the idea that the P head must be decomposed into Path and Place, with the Path head embedding the PlaceP in the structure (van Riemsdijk and Huybregts 2002, Koopman 2000, van Riemsdijk 1990, Svenonius 2004b, Kracht 2002).

(1)

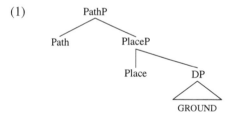

This decomposition also corresponds to the semantics: Zwarts (2005) and Zwarts and Winter (2000) argue that paths are constructed from place denotations in a compositional fashion. In languages where distinctive morphology is found, the place morpheme is always closer to the root than path morphology (cf. Svenonius 2004b, Kracht 2002). In addition, there is an analogue to telicity/boundedness in the domain of PPs which, according to Zwarts (2005), can be characterized as cumulativity under path concatenation. Thus, PathPs can be bounded (noncumulative) or unbounded (cumulative). They can also be distinguished according to the role that the embedded PlaceP plays in defining the path: Path heads can be at least TO, FROM and VIA (according to Svenonius 2004b). Some straightforward examples are shown in (2) below.

(2) (a) *in the house* is a PlaceP.
     (b) *into the house* is a bounded TO PathP.
     (c) *toward the house* is an unbounded TO PathP.
     (d) *under the bridge* is ambiguous between being a PlaceP or a bounded VIA/TO PathP.

According to the system being proposed in this book, PathPs can be the complement of a *proc* head in the verbal decomposition. Just as a quantized DP path object gives rise to a bounded event with creation/consumption verbs, so a bounded PathP complement will give rise to a bounded event with a dynamic motion verb. For a verb like *dance* in English, this is straightforward, with goal-of-motion readings arising with bounded PathPs (3a, b), but not with unbounded PathPs (3c), or with PlacePs (3d).

(3) (a) Mary danced to the store.   *goal of motion*
     (b) Mary danced into the room.   *goal of motion*
     (c) Mary danced towards the bridge.   *directed path*
     (d) Mary danced in the park.   *location of motion*

The first important consequence of this view is that we do not want to conflate goal-of-motion constructions with the existence of *res*P: a bounded reading will arise with a PathP complement of *proc* as long as that PathP has a bounded denotation.

However, it is possible for a 'goal' interpretation to arise, even with a purely locative (Place) preposition, provided the verb is chosen carefully. Consider the pattern with the English verb *jump* below (4).

(4) (a) Mary jumped to the store.   *goal of motion*
     (b) Mary jumped into the room.   *goal of motion*
     (c) Mary jumped toward the bridge.   *directed path*
     (d) Mary jumped in the water.   *goal of motion; location of motion*

Notice that while *jump* is ambiguous between a punctual and repeated activity reading, only the former licenses the goal-of-motion interpretation in (d) above. Specifically, verbs in English that are obligatorily telic (punctual readings of semelfactive verbs, for example) allow a purely locative PP (*in the water*) to name a *final* location, while activity process verbs like *dance* do not.[1]

Indeed, in a crosslinguistic survey of languages as diverse as Spanish, Icelandic, Korean and Finnish, we find this pattern repeated. In each case, the language in question allows a subset of verb types to appear with locative PPs to express goal of motion, and in each case the punctual/telic verbs seem to fall into this class (The data and generalizations in this area come directly from the results of the *Moving Right Along* seminar on Adpositions led by Peter Svenonius, at the University of Tromsø in autumn 2005 and spring 2006, the results of which can be accessed at the following URL:www.hum.uit. no/mra/).

To illustrate the pattern in detail, I present the findings from Son (2006) for Korean. The table in (5) shows the way different types of preposition are used to express location and goal meanings in Korean, with a further division according to whether they combine with static eventualities or dynamic ones, and a systematic distinction between animate and inanimate (although we will be ignoring the latter distinction here).

(5) | *Location (in/at/on)* | *Goal Path (to)* |
|---|---|
| Static (BE AT): *-eykey* [animate]/*ey*[inanimate] | |
| Dynamic (HAPPEN AT): *-eyse* [inanimate] | *-kkaci/-(u)lo-* 'until/to' |

In (6), we see a PlaceP in the complement of a stative verb, and in (7), we see one modifying an activity (a *proc* verb).

---

[1] There is an intermediate class of verbs, such as *run*, *walk* or *crawl*, which seem to show variable behaviour across dialects of English. For the author, those verbs pattern with *dance*, while for other speakers they pattern more like *jump* in allowing final locations to be named by locative PlacePs. However, even for these speakers, the possibility seems to be dependent on the availability of a 'threshold-crossing' interpretation of the event. In (i) below, the final location interpretation is more difficult to get than in (ii). And even the author accepts the final location reading in (iii).

　　(i) Mary walked in the park.
　　(ii) Mary walked in the room.
　　(iii) Mary walked in the door.

One possibility is that the availability of this reading is systematically correlated with an interpretation of the predicate as licensing a *res* head in the decomposition. The other is that there is a null Path head licensed in these structures in English with the default semantics of 'phase transition' of some sort. I remain agnostic about which of these two possibilities is correct, and will abstract away from speaker differences here, concentrating on the core cases of my own British dialect.

(6) Sean-i   pang-*ey*   iss-ta
     Sean-NOM   room-LOC   be-DEC
     'Sean is in the room.'

(7) John-i   atul-kwa   kongwon-*eyse*   nal-ass-ta
     John-NOM   son-with   park-LOC   play-PAST-DEC
     'John played with his son in the park.'

In (8), a goal preposition, a PathP in this system, combines with a *proc* verb to give a goal interpretation.

(8) Inho-ka   kichayek-*ulo*   kuphakey   ttwi-ess-ta
     Inho-NOM   train.station-DIR   in. a. hurry   run-PAST-DEC
     'Inho ran to the train station in a hurry.'

The striking fact is that in Korean, the purely locative series can also give rise to goal interpretations when embedded under punctual directed motion verbs (9). In this case, the goal PP option is ungrammatical (10).

(9) John-i   patak-*ey*   ssuleci-ess-ta
     John-NOM   floor-LOC   fell.down-PAST-DEC
     'John fell down on the floor.'

(10) *John-i   patak-*ulo*   ssuleci-ess-ta
      John-NOM   floor-LOC   fell.down-PAST-DEC
      'John fell down on the floor.'

The straightforward claim is that verbs that contain *res*Ps in their representation can combine with PlacePs by event-complement composition. The semantics of the *res* head will straightforwardly give rise to the 'goal' interpretation of that location.[2]

(11)

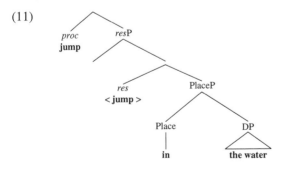

---

[2] The actual analysis proposed here using Ramchandian decomposition trees is very similar in detail to the one argued for in Son (2006), although we reached our conclusions independently.

On the other hand, verbs that only contain *proc*Ps in their representation must combine with PathPs to get a directed motion interpretation. If that PathP is bounded, it will give rise to a 'goal' interpretation via event-path homomorphic unity.

(12)

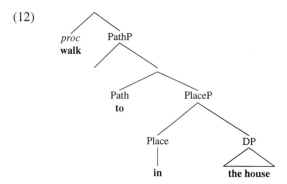

Interestingly, a few verbs, like 'go' and 'come', in Korean allow both PlacePs and PathPs interpreted as goals. These are verbs that, by hypothesis, have both *res*P and non-*res*P versions. There is a subtle meaning difference, however: in the *proc* + Path version, the undergoer does not actually have to reach the final location (13); in the *res* + Place version the final state interpretation is unavoidable (14).[3]

(13)   Mary-ka   cip-*ulo*   ttwi-e   ka-ss-ta
        Mary-NOM   house-DIR   run-LINKER   go-PAST-DEC
        'Mary ran to the house.'
        (Undergoer of the motion does not have to reach the Ground final
        location)

(14)   Mary-ka   cip-*ey*   ttwi-e   ka-ss-ta
        Mary-NOM   house-LOC   run-LINKER   go-PAST-DEC
        'Mary ran to the house.'
        (Implies that the undergoer of motion reaches the final location
        expressed by Ground DP)

The idea that the goal interpretation of locatives is dependent on the *res* projection gets confirmation from the fact that when these verbs are used with

---

[3] Zubizarretta and Oh (2006) argue that the *ulo*-PP in a sentence like (13) is actually an adjunct. However, Son (2006) shows, using the *do so* substitution test, that these PPs, like the locatives, are inside the vP.

an aspectual form (the perfect) that explicitly requires a target state, only the locative PP is grammatical.

(15) Inho-ka   samwusil -*ey* ka-a   iss-ta
      Inho-NOM   office-LOC   go-LINKER   be-DEC
      'Inho has gone to the office (and is still there).'

(16) *Inho-ka   samwusil-*lo*   ka-a   iss-ta
      Inho-NOM   office-DIR   go-LINKER   be-DEC
      'Inho has gone to the office (and is still there).'

Thus, the data from English and Korean show that genuine PlaceP goal of motion is indeed possible, but only when the verb itself independently licenses a *res* projection. Thus, for English, verbs under a punctual interpretation allow a simple locative preposition to name a final location (17a). On the other hand, locative prepositional phrases are ungrammatical with pure process verbs, under a goal-of-motion reading (17b).

(17) (a) Michael pushed the car in the ditch.
      (b) *Michael danced Karena in the room.

In contrast to Place prepositions, PathP phrases are grammatical with process verbs and can express both bounded paths (a) as well as unbounded paths (b).[4]

(18) (a) Michael drove the car under the bridge.
      (b) Michael drove the car towards Edinburgh.

More surprisingly, there are also cases of PathPs introducing 'unselected' objects with pure process verbs, and once again this is independent of whether the PathP in question is bounded (a) or unbounded (b).

(19) (a) Alex danced the puppet over the bridge.
      (b) Kayleigh walked Ariel round and round the room.

Cases like (19b) above show most clearly that no *res*P in my sense need be involved to license the 'unselected' object since the resulting predication is

---

[4] I am assuming that the purely locative prepositions are *in* and *on*; that prepositions like *under* and *over* (and indeed many others) are ambiguous between a place interpretation and a path interpretation (see also Higginbotham 2001). Zwarts (2005) also claims that *under* and *over* are VIA paths in their path interpretation, but that they are bounded, i.e. noncumulative, giving rise to telicity effects. I will put aside the prepositions including the morpheme *to* for the time being, since I think they also have a *res* feature.

atelic. To my knowledge this type of sentence was first explicitly noticed and analysed in Folli and Harley (2006).

(20)   *PP unbounded path, with unselected object*
     (a) Bill waltzed Mary round the campfire.
     (b) *Bill waltzed Mary.

Under the first-phase syntactic principles being explored here, telicity can arise because of a bounded path in the complement of process. If this is the right analysis of motion verbs with PathP complements, then many cases of what have been called PP resultatives are actually of the non-*res*P type, even when they are telic and have unselected objects (as in (19a)).

Because of their role in licensing an 'extra' object, PathPs of all types should allow lower attachment as complements to a *proc* head, a legitimate option with regard to homomorphic unity. Thus, I will argue that the first-phase decompositions of sentences of the above type in (19) should be as in (21).

(21)

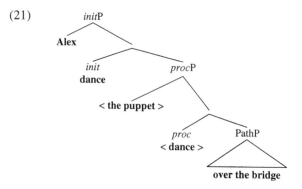

My claim about intransitives of motion has been that they represent a situation where the single DP argument possesses the composite role of INITIATOR and UNDERGOER.[5] I argue that the complex event formed from *proc* path homomorphism allows the relaxation of the requirement that the INITIATOR and UNDERGOER of a motion verb be identical. In other words, you cannot 'dance'

---

[5] Thus, the verbs in this class that are termed 'unergative' in the literature do not have DP subjects that are identical semantically to the subjects of transitives, but rather have semantic entailments in common with both 'external' arguments and 'internal' arguments in the traditional sense. This, I believe, is the reason why motion verbs exhibit ambiguous behaviour across languages, with different linguistic diagnostics being sensitive either to INITIATOR or UNDERGOER structural positions, giving rise to different options and a certain amount of Janus-like behaviour.

somebody because the instigation of dancing per se is something that is under the person's own direct control. However, 'dancing someone around the room' can be initiated by someone else because, in the absence of their instigation, the dancer's path of motion would have been different. This difference in lexical specification of the event via the PP path allows INITIATOR to be distinct from UNDERGOER and hence the illusion of an extra argument position. We have independent evidence that this requirement that INITIATOR and UNDERGOER be identical with motion verbs can be relaxed under particular circumstances, either when the UNDERGOER is a coercible animate in a conventionalized process as in (22), or when the lexical-encyclopedic requirements on the motion verb are relaxed/abstract enough to be applicable to inanimates as in (23). The situation of PathP complements is another way in which real-world knowledge intervenes to allow a single INITIATOR to affect someone else's motion.

(22)　　(a) Karena walked the dog.
　　　　(b) Michael jumped the horse.

(23)　　(a) Alex ran the bath water.
　　　　(b) Kayleigh ran the meeting.
　　　　(c) Karena ran Ariel's life.

Unselected objects can also emerge when a *res*P is added in the form of a *to* preposition. In this case, there are a number of options made available by the system which correspond to different interpretations for the participants involved. In (24a), the most natural interpretation is that Karena is also running, Michael accompanying her, and that Karena (at least) gets to the coconut tree – Karena is both UNDERGOER and RESULTEE. In (24b), the files do not 'walk', but they do end up at head office – 'the files' is a RESULTEE DP. In (24c), 'the puppet' may be interpreted most naturally as UNDERGOER, just like (21) above, but if we are in a situation where there is a magic puppet who will appear in the room to grant you a wish if you do a beautiful enough dance, then even though that may be an implausible scenario, (24c) can be used to describe the situation in which Alex managed to pull off that feat. In that latter situation, 'the puppet' is just a RESULTEE.

(24)　　(a) Michael ran Karena to the coconut tree.
　　　　(b) Michael walked the files to head office.
　　　　(c) Alex danced the puppet into the room.

The flexibilities of the system allow both kinds of structure to be built. In (25), I show a representation for (24a) where 'Karena' is also doing the running;

in (26) we see the tree for (24b), where 'the files' is just a RESULTEE. Notice that in both cases, the preposition *to* can identify both *res* and the 'place' head (presumably with the content of an abstract AT).

(25)

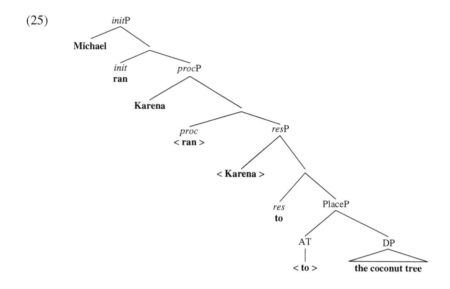

(26)

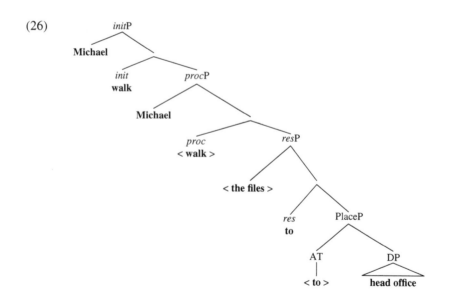

This analysis of *to* differs from most of the decompositional analyses of PPs known from the literature in saying that *to* is not a PATH head (among others, Jackendoff 1983, Zwarts 2005, Svenonius 2004b), but a head that obligatorily combines with a dynamic verbal extended projection, i.e. it has a *res* feature in addition to its specification for PLACE. The system being advocated in this book allows such category-straddling features on lexical items, although their choices of insertion are thereby limited to cases where the one head specifically takes the other as its complement, since Remerge will construct a hierarchically adjacent pair of heads. This is the case with *to*, which can be inserted whenever *res* takes a PlaceP complement with the meaning AT.

This view of *to* should carry over to the complex prepositions *into* and *onto*. The only difference being that with the complex versions, the *in* and *on* will fill the Place head, causing the *to* to underassociate (by the superset principle). Once again, the underassociated *place* feature of *to* is the most lexically vague place head one could imagine, and its content will unify unproblematically with *in* and *on*. This is plausibly the reason why we find *to* in these complex forms and not any other richer prepositional form. The tree for an *into*-PP sentence is given in (27).

(27)

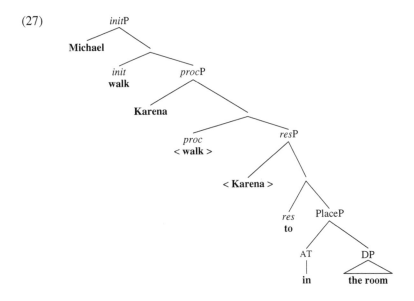

Although the *res* followed by *place* analysis of PPs containing *to* seems equivalent in some senses to an analysis in which it is a *path* head followed by *place*, there are some different predictions. Both analyses would allow *to*, *into* and *onto* to combine unproblematically with *proc* verbs, but only the *res place* analysis will allow *to*-containing PPs to combine with obligatory *res* verbs. A *res* verb should be incompatible with obligatory PathPs. The trick in testing the prediction is finding a preposition in English that is not ambiguous between Path and Place, and a verb which can be clearly distinguished as being pure *proc* or not. For an obligatory *path* preposition, I choose *towards*, and combine it with the verb *jump* which is a *res* verb under the 'single jump' interpretation. The prediction is that 'single jump' will be bad with *towards*, but good with *to/into/onto*. A further complication is then predicting the readings that arise. Recall that when a verb identifies both *proc* and *res* itself, a punctual reading results. If the *to* forms cause the verb to underassociate, it will give rise to the 'multiple jump' reading; if the verb identifies *res* and the *to* underassociates, then we can get a 'single jump' reading. Thus, the prediction is that pure location prepositions like *in/on* in English will get an obligatory 'single jump' reading with a goal-of-motion interpretation; *towards* will get a 'multiple jump' reading with goal-of-motion interpretation; *to*, *into*, *onto* will allow both multiple and single jumps for the goal-of-motion reading. Although the judgements are subtle, I think that this is the pattern we find.

(28)   *Goal-of-motion readings for 'jump'*
   (a) John jumped towards the fence. (only multiple jump reading)
   (b) John jumped in the lake. (only single jump reading)
   (c) John jumped into the house/to the window ledge. (either single or multiple jumps)

Of course, prepositions like *under* that are ambiguous between *path* and *place* will also allow both single and multiple jumps (the former on the *place* reading and the latter on the *path* reading. But these can be independently distinguished from the *to* forms by the fact that they can appear as the complement of a stative verb (29).

(29)   (a) John was under the bridge.
   (b) *John was into the woods.

The difference between the extended versions of *into* and *onto* and the fairly common transition readings are captured under this analysis by the two different structures proposed: when the verb identifies both *proc* and *res*, the event is punctual, the *to* underassociates and the *into*-PP expresses a punctual transition; when the verb underassociates to identify just *proc*, the *to* itself identifies *res*, but then the process and its result are not co-lexicalized and do not have to form a single transition and the temporal connection can be more extended.

It should be clear from this discussion that neither 'telicization' nor the possibility of 'causativizing' so-called unergative intransitives is correlated with a single kind of syntactic representation. An already punctual/telic verb can be augmented with a PlaceP as the complement of *res*; a process motion verb can have both bounded and unbounded PathPs in the complement position to *proc*. Argument structure flexibility is an important feature of the analyses proposed here: distinct INITIATOR and UNDERGOER are possible for motion verbs under these circumstances, giving the appearance of an extra argument, although the actual number of structural positions does not change. In fact, I have argued here that some of the cases that have been called PP resultatives do not involve an extra predicational structure in the first-phase decomposition at all: PlacePs and PathPs are complements of *res* and *proc* respectively, which are independently licensed by the particular motion verb. I have also argued that the morpheme *to* in English is special, carrying both *res* and *place* features, giving it and its cohorts (*into* and *onto*) a rather special distribution. In the next section, I turn to AP results and particle resultatives, where I examine further ways in which a *res* head can be identified in the absence of verbal specification.

5.2   APs: paths and results

AP resultatives are found with great productivity in English,[6] with both selected and unselected objects (Carrier and Randall 1992, McIntyre 2001, Wechsler 2005, inter alia).

(30)   *AP results with selected objects*
    (a) John hammered the metal flat.
    (b) Mary broke the safe open.
    (c) Bill painted the door red.

(31)   *AP results with unselected objects*
    (a) John ran his shoes ragged.
    (b) Mary sang the baby asleep.

---

[6] There are, of course, a host of constraints and restrictions as well, some having to do with real-world knowledge, and others, as I will discuss below, related to the semantic denotational possibilities of both adjective and verb (Wechsler 2005).

(c) Bill coughed himself hoarse.

(d) John wiped the table clean.

Wechsler (2001b) points out on the basis of a corpus study that in English AP results with selected objects are always formed from adjectives that are *gradable* and CLOSED SCALE (see Kennedy and McNally 2005). As I argued in chapter 3, gradable adjectives represent the property analogue of a scalar path (see also Hay, Kennedy and Levin 1999) which is equivalent to PathPs in the prepositional domain and incremental theme objects of consumption verbs. Wechsler's restriction would follow under the *homomorphic unity* requirement, from the assumption that AP resultatives of this type are actually the complement of the *proc* head directly, with no intervening *res* projection: the telicity of the resulting VP arises because the AP is *closed scale* and hence gives rise to a bounded path.

(32)

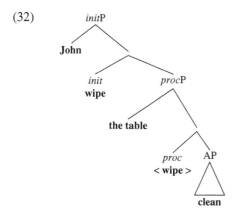

This structure is a natural possibility given the system being developed here, so it is a natural question to ask why this structure is not available in all languages. It is well known that languages like Italian are very restricted in their ability to form adjectival resultatives (Napoli 1992). In Italian, the resultative with the adjective *piatto* 'flat' is ungrammatical (33a). This may well be an independent fact about the possible denotations of simple adjectives in Italian, which may be like their simplex prepositions which obligatorily denote static situations with no internal path structure (Folli 2003). In fact, as Folli (2003) points out, when the adjective is doubled, as in (33b), modified with *too* or made comparative as in (33c), the resultatives are indeed possible.[7] It is plausible to assume that the existence of extra morphology is correlated with extra functional structure that allows property-scale denotations to be constructed from simple static properties in Italian.

(33)   (a) Gianni ha   martellato el   metalo piatto.
            John   has   hammered   the   metal   flat
            'John hammered the metal flat.'
        (b) Gianni ha martellato el metalo piatto piatto.
        (c) Gianni ha   stretto   i   lacci   più   stretti.
            John   has   tightened the   laces   more   tight
            'John has tightened the laces tighter.'

As Schwarzschild (2005) shows, in many languages unmodified adjectives are not modifiable by measure phrases, and in those languages where it *is* possible (English) the set of adjectives that allows it is restricted. Strikingly, no such restrictions seem to apply to comparatives or adjectives modified by *too*.

(34)   (a) *The car was driving 50 mph fast.
        (b) *The jacket was 50 pounds expensive.
        (c) The car was driving 15 mph too fast.
        (d) This car drives 15 mph faster than that one.
        (e) This jacket is 50 pounds too expensive.
        (f) That jacket is 50 pounds more expensive than this one.

I take these facts to indicate that comparative and *too* modification create phrases that have extended path-like structure quite generally. If adjectives in Italian cannot denote paths without the addition of this extra functional morphology, we would not expect to find them in the complement of *proc* verbs to create bounded predications.

There is another possibility in the system when it comes to building resultatives based on adjectives. Wechsler (2001b) further notes that there does *not* seem to be a clear homomorphism requirement in the case of the AP resultatives that have unselected objects. I speculate that this is due to the fact that the AP in question sits in the complement position of a distinct result-state subevent – i.e. it is a full small clause mediated by the *res* head itself. It is the semantics of the *res* head that creates the entailments of result and this makes the scalar structure of the adjective irrelevant as long as the adjective itself can refer to

---

[7] Original observation and data from R. Folli p.c.

a static property (35).[8] In these cases, there is a question about what identifies this *res* head in English, since adjectival resultatives with unselected objects can be constructed from verbs that are normally activities.

(35)

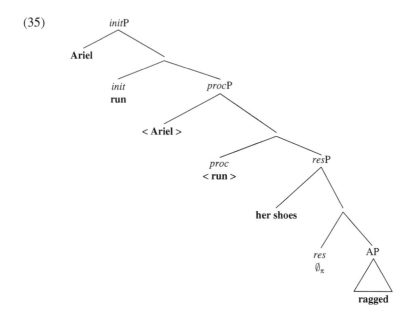

I also follow Hale and Keyser (2000) and Baker (2003) in assuming that APs do not independently license a specifier position (for Baker, this is one major thing that distinguishes them from verbal lexical items). Thus, the *res* head here is doubly necessary – it must license a specifier to host the RESULTEE, and it must provide the 'leads-to' semantics that will give a result interpretation. The null *res* head required for predication here must have very general semantics of 'property possession', where the 'shoes' in the sentence above come to possess the property of being 'ragged'. The claim here therefore is that

---

[8] Note that this analysis of adjectival resultatives, which insists on the existence of some structuring principle that constructs the 'result' or 'leads-to' relation, is very close in spirit to the intuition behind (Hoekstra 1988, 1992), who notes that APs could in principle express many different relationships to the event. Something extra is needed to enforce the resultative interpretation in these cases. In my analysis, the work is done by semantic composition rules that interpret embedded subevental descriptions as the 'leads-to' relation.

English must possess a null lexical item with the requisite semantics, but Italian does not.

In English, if a verb is consistent with the semantics of $\emptyset_\pi$, an AP *and* an extra predicational position will be licensed. AP results where no extra predicational position is introduced will always have to be the complement of a *proc* head directly, hence the correlation between homomorphism constraints on the adjective and the lack of unselected object, as noted by Wechsler (2001b).

5.3   Types of resultatives in the first phase

We have seen that verbs which contain both initiation and process can usually be systematically augmented in English by means of a secondary predicate (adjective or particle) which describes a final-result property or location arrived at by a thematic argument. This has been described in detail in the literature (Carrier and Randall 1992, Hoekstra 1988, Kaufmann and Wunderlich 1998, Levin and Rappaport Hovav 1995) and has received various labels: 'template augmentation' (Levin and Rappaport 1998), 'telic pair formation' (Higginbotham 2001), 'accomplishment formation' (Pustejovsky 1991, Parsons 1990).

As we have seen, in some cases of resultative augmentation, an extra, or 'unselected' object shows up which would not otherwise be licensed by the verb on its own. This is often correlated with the existence of additional predicational structure, given by the secondary predicate in the complement of *res*. But, as we have also seen, the existence of an 'extra' object does not necessarily mean that there is a *res*P in the structure, because of the existence of composite roles. On the other hand, we know that a resultative secondary predicate must be stative to be the complement of the *res* head directly, by homomorphic unity. In the case of AP result predications, this seems to be the case: the shoes come to be 'ragged'. These predications must be dependent on the lexical possibilities of the language for identifying *res*. In many cases when *res*P is present it is not identified by the root itself but by a null *res* head which takes the secondary predicative small clause as its complement. We saw one such *res* head already in English in our discussion of one type of adjectival resultative – the null property possessional head. Thus, in the case of adjectival results with unselected objects, I have assumed that this head mediates the predicational relation between the AP and its 'subject', which is then the RESULTEE of the predication. In the case of the preposition *to* in English, I also speculated that in addition to carrying a *place* feature, it carries a *res* feature that allows it to combine with any *proc* motion verb to create a goal-of-motion interpretation.

For some cases of result augmentation, the 'unselected' argument is a pure RESULTEE, and not an UNDERGOER of the process lexically identified by the verb. So, for example, the shoes in (35) do not 'run'. To be sure, the DP objects in question do undergo some process which results in them being 'ragged', but this is a matter of real-world knowledge. The semantic interpretations I have specified for these structures ensure that the specifier of the process must undergo the very process that is lexically/encyclopedically identified by the root verb.

However, the secondary predicate in question does form part of the event-building portion of the clause and hence creates a complex predicational structure rather than an adjunct structure. This can be seen immediately from the fact that (i) the object only becomes possible in the context of secondary predication, (ii) it is interpreted as being both the 'subject' of the secondary predicate and the holder of the result state, and (iii) it receives accusative case from the verb. In the case of *run*, the verb does not license a separate argument in UNDERGOER position at all. This is because the INITIATOR and UNDERGOER are coindexed for this verb in the normal case, so no distinct direct object is possible.

It is also possible to find a secondary predicate describing the result, where there does not seem to be an internal argument *added* – in these cases, the base verb already licenses an argument in UNDERGOER position. However, even here there is evidence of extra predicational structure, since the already existing object acquires new entailments because of the licensing and identification of the *res*P in the structure. I will assume therefore that the direct objects in (36) and (37) below are all RESULTEE – UNDERGOERS.

(36)   *AP result, no change in transitivity*
        (a) Karena hammered the metal flat.
        (b) Karena hammered the metal.

(37)   *Particle result, no change in transitivity*
        (a) Michael drove the car in.
        (b) Michael drove the car.

The system of composed thematic relations does the job for us here: the DP object in question is simultaneously the specifier of *proc* as before (UNDERGOER) as well as the specifier of the result projection (the RESULTEE) which is described by the AP or Particle phrase.

(38)

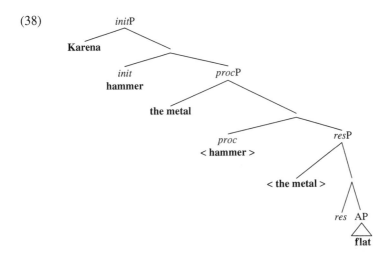

(39)

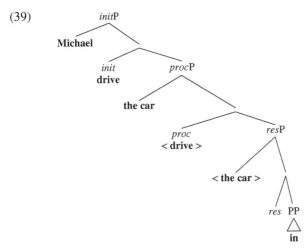

Given the flexibilities of event-building syntax, there is yet another logical possibility: since *res* exists for telic verbs even when there is no predicational complement for it, a secondary predicational structure can be added to verbs that already independently identify a result. In this case, all the secondary predicate does is further specify the final state expressed by *res* (in this case though, the secondary predicate must be nongradable/locational). All that changes here is that the result becomes more specific, and the direct object gains the entailments that result from being the subject of that embedded predicational structure, but the aktionsart of the event does not actually change. The cases that fall into this category are the ones shown in (40) below, and the first-phase representation would be as in (41).

(40)   (a) John broke the box open.
        (b) John broke the vase in pieces.

(41)

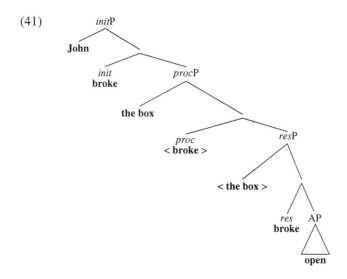

Further, given the Superset principle (i.e. the possibility for underassociation under certain constrained conditions), we can also build structures where two lexical identifiers for *res* are present but where one of the two 'underassociates'. We have seen this possibility before with *jump* and *to*, and we will see it again when we look at the interaction between certain verbs and particles.

Alongside true result augmentation, I have also argued that path phrases in complement position to the *proc* are also expected in this system. These path phrases are subject to a homomorphism or matching requirement with respect to the process head, and if they represent paths which have an implicit final bound, they give rise to telicity. This class of items includes directional PP complements to process verbs and path-homomorphic gradable adjectives as complements of process verbs. Crucially, these 'telicity' effects do not arise from the presence of *res*P and their distributional properties are different.

Thus, we can distinguish two clear types of what have been called resultative in the literature: those formed directly from a *proc* head unifying homomor-phically with a bounded path; those that are constructed from a *res* head with a static property predication in its complement. I will call the first type 'Path' resultatives and the second type 'Result' resultatives. Examples of the two types are repeated below in (42) and (43) respectively.

(42)   *'Path' resultatives*
      (a) Michael drove the car under the bridge. (bounded PP path)
      (b) Karena hammered the metal flat. (bounded AP property scale)

(43)   *'Result' resultatives*
      (a) Michael drove the car into the garage. (*res* identified by *to*)
      (b) Karena ran her shoes ragged. (null property possession *res* head)

In addition, 'Result' resultatives can differ from each other in whether the direct object is the RESULTEE – UNDERGOER or just RESULTEE, as we have seen.

There is another distinction that can be isolated, and that is important in this system. It is once again, a distinction *within* the class of 'result' resultatives. I take my starting point from a difference discussed by Levin and Rappaport-Hovav (1999), who propose the following distinction:

- A causative event structure consisting of two subevents formed from the conflation of temporally independent events
- A simple event structure formed from the conflation of two temporally dependent 'coidentified' events   (1999: 63)

I will call the first class the *indirect resultatives* and the second *direct resultatives*. However, in the terms being explored in this book, both types involve causationally dependent subevents, in involving a relation between the *proc* subevent and the *res* subevent.

Indirect resultatives
(44)   (a) John sang himself hoarse.
      (b) Mary sneezed the napkin off the table.

Direct resultatives
(45)   (a) The lake froze solid.
      (b) John's bottle broke open.
      (c) The mirror shattered to pieces.
      (d) John broke the bottle open.
      (e) The police shot the robber dead.

Superficially, it appears that resultative formation with unergatives and unselected objects gives rise to 'indirect' resultatives. Transitive verbs with selected objects and unaccusatives give rise to the 'direct' resultatives. This is not exactly the claim in Levin and Rappaport-Hovav (1999), who rely on independent entailment tests and synonymy judgements to isolate the two classes.

I believe that the distinction argued for in Levin and Rappaport-Hovav (1999) is real, and is important in the classification of resultatives, although it corresponds to a slightly different analytical set of options than they assume. It is important to bear in mind that the first-phase decompositions I have been exploring involve event variables, and no explicit reference to time at all. Thus, the classification of resultatives in terms of temporal dependence or independence cannot be a direct effect of these representations, but only an indirect one that arises when these complex events are mapped to a temporal time line.

Since the eventive composition is mediated by causational glue, and not mere temporal precedence, there should be no direct requirement that each subevent in a causational chain temporally precede the other. However, there *are* some coherence conditions that seem to be applicable. I propose the following two constraints on *init-proc* coherence and *proc-res* coherence respectively.

(46)   *Init-proc coherence*
Given a decomposition $e_1 \rightarrow (e_2 \rightarrow e_3)$, e_1 may temporally overlap e_2.

(47)   *Proc-res coherence*
Given a decomposition $e_1 \rightarrow (e_2 \rightarrow e_3)$, e_3 must *not* temporally overlap e_2.
(Although they may share a transition point.)

Since *init* leads to *proc* and *proc* is extended, *init* may either be a conditioning state that preexists the process, that coexists with the process, or is a continuous initiation homomorphic with it (see also Svenonius 2002). Since, intuitively, something that is conceived of as a result state does not preexist the process, the result state must *not* temporally overlap *proc*. However, if they are temporally dependent, then they abutt, giving rise to a transition point which links the end of the process with the beginning of the result state. With very general conditions in hand, we can now state the relationship between the eventive decompositions and the kind of temporal dependence isolated by Levin and Rappaport-Hovav. I will assume that temporal constraints exist over and above the general coherence conditions, and that they are affected by which lexical item(s) in the decomposition actually bear the tense feature. This idea has already been used centrally in the discussion of punctual verbs in English (which identify both *proc* and *res*. I state the condition more concretely here in (48).

(48)   *Temporal dependence and lexical identification*
        Temporal dependence is required for subevents identified by the *same* lexical content.

Thus, in the types of resultatives discussed above, the resultatives formed from process verbs with a null *res* head will be indirect, or temporally independent resultatives. Those where the main verb already independently identifies *res* will be the direct resultatives. In addition, bounded predications which arise from a PathP in the complement of *proc* will also be temporally dependent, since there is no independent *res* head, and *proc* and the PathP are identified by homomorphic unity.

5.4   The verb–particle construction

So far, I have been tacitly assuming that particles are simply P elements which happen not to have explicit complements. This is a view that has been defended in the literature, where 'particles' are simply intransitive versions of prepositions (Emonds 1976), ones which in the terms of Svenonius 1994b, 1996) have implicit or incorporated GROUND elements. Thus, resultative predication with particles is simply a subcase of the prepositional variety, with no overt complement of P present.

However, as is well known, the verb–particle construction has some interesting properties which set it apart from other kinds of result augmentation. Most famously, these constructions undergo the notorious 'particle shift'. While many different proposals exist in the literature for analysing these constructions, I will follow the analysis of Ramchand and Svenonius (2002), which builds on previous work of Svenonius (1994b, 1996). The difference between ordinary resultatives and the verb–particle construction is that the particle itself can identify the *res* head in the structure, giving rise to the V-prt order if the DP stays low in the embedded PP (49). In the particle construction, therefore, we have evidence for a PP-internal 'subject' position – the small clause subject of the prepositional phrase. I will assume this position more explicitly in the phrase-structure trees that follow, since its existence is crucial to the predicational argument and to the explanations of particle shift.

(49)

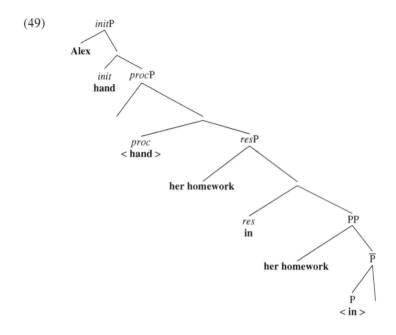

In what follows, I will actually assume that the particle moves *obligatorily* to *res*, and that the word-order variation results from whether the DP object is spelled out in its lowest or its highest predicational position.[9]

Thus, particles have a special status within the class of result augmentations more generally, in that they are (i) heads and (ii) have the requisite featural properties to identify the *res* head in a verbal decomposition. This is not a possibility for adjectives within an AP small clause which never give rise to shift, even when embedded under *res*, as is well known (50)(Svenonius (1994b)).[10]

(50)   (a) *Alex sang hoarse herself.
        (b) *Ariel ran ragged her shoes.

In Ramchand and Svenonius (2002) we argue that the first-phase decompositional account of the verb–particle construction makes sense of the otherwise

---

[9] This is different from what was argued in Ramchand and Svenonius (2002), where the different orders depended on whether head movement of the particle or DP movement of the internal argument to the specifier position was chosen as a way to license *res*P.

[10] Note also that a *to*-PP will not give rise to shift either, even though it identifies *res*, by hypothesis. This is because spelling out the FIGURE in the low position would disrupt the adjacency between the *to* and the DP it assigns Case to.

paradoxical properties of the construction. It resolves the debate between the small clause approach (Kayne 1985, Guéron 1987, Hoekstra 1988, den Dikken 1995) and the complex predicate approach (Johnson 1991, Neeleman 1994, Stiebels and Wunderlich 1994, Baker 1988, Koopman 1995, Zeller 1999) by representing the essential correctness of both positions. The small clause approach is correct because the particle is associated with additional predicational structure which thematically affects, and is sometimes even solely responsible for the presence of the direct object, which is essentially the 'subject' of that introduced small clause. On the other hand, the first-phase decomposition is in effect a complex (decomposed) predicate, where the subevents involved combine to create a singular (albeit internally articulated) event. This complex event is a unit for the purposes of case licensing and idiom formation.

Moreover, analysing particle shift as movement to license/identify the null *res* head avoids the claim that particle shift involves some kind of complex head formation in the syntax. In the analysis of Johnson (1991), V and Prt combine to form a complex morphological word, which then raises to a functional head above VP, μ. However, as pointed out by Svenonius (1994b), 1996), the complex head so formed would violate the RHR head rule in English and Scandinavian. Svenonius shows that the problem is particularly striking for Swedish, where particle shift in (51) contrasts with true incorporation in the 'passive' form in (52), which does give the expected right-headed structure.

(51) Det blev   hugget   ned   många träd.   *Swedish*
      it   became chopped   down   many   trees
      'Many trees got chopped down.'

(52) Det blev   många träd   nedhuggna.
      it   became many   trees down.chopped
      'Many trees got chopped down.'

The argument against either lexical word formation or head movement and incorporation is strengthened by the evidence that in Swedish and Norwegian, the movement of the main verb in V2 contexts can strand the particle, even after 'shift'. Indeed, the particle may never be moved along with the verb under V2 in these languages, demanding a rule of obligatory excorporation if the head movement account were correct (data below from Åfarli 1985).

(53) Kari sparka heldigvis   ut   hunden.   *Norwegian*
      Kari kicked fortunately out   the.dog
      'Kari fortunately kicked the dog out.'

(54)   *Kari   sparka   ut   heldigvis   hunden.
        Kari   kicked   out   fortunately   the.dog

The evidence shows that the verb–particle combination is not either a lexical word nor a complex head under a single syntactic terminal. Because of its effects on argument structure and aktionsart properties, the verb–particle construction in English and Scandinavian constitutes clear evidence that so-called 'lexical' properties of verbs cannot be confined to a lexical module. Rather, the different components of a complex event are part of a syntactic system which can be lexicalized through independent morphemes.

In the larger context of resultative formations more generally, particles are a special case because they can actually merge to identify *res*. The evidence for this is two-fold: firstly, unlike adverbs or even other kinds of resultative predicates, they can appear in a position that disrupts the continuity between verb and object (55).

(55)   (a) *John painted red the barn.
        (b) *John threw quickly the ball.
        (c) John threw out the dog.

Secondly, they can create resultative predications even when a normal locative PP will fail to do so with a particular verb (56).

(56)   (a) I opened the door, and Mary danced in. (result/goal reading)
        (b) Mary danced in the room. (only the locative reading)

In (56a) above, the verb *dance* cannot identify *res* on its own, and the null *res* head that English has for generalized property possession is not felicitous for locatives. The fact that (56b) is bad means that something independent must be going on in (56a). Therefore, I assume that, like *to*, particles themselves have a *res* feature as part of their lexical specification. In fact, we can also see particles co-occurring with PP complements which are in the complement of *res*. The analysis of (57) below would be that the particle identifies *res*, and that the PP is in the complement position. Note that the order here is rigid, as we would expect, and that *out of the rain* by itself is not sufficient to license a goal-of-motion reading with this verb which seems to be pure manner of motion.

(57)   (a) Mary danced in out of the rain.
        (b) *Mary danced out of the rain in.

(58)

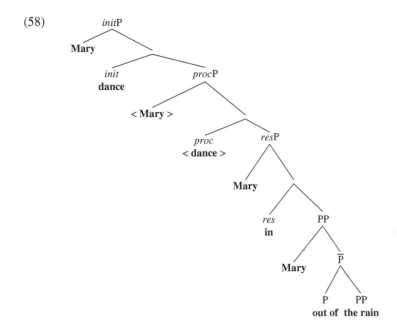

A question now arises concerning what happens when a particle co-occurs with a verb that *does* independently identify result, as in the English verb *break*. These constructions are perfectly grammatical.

(59)   (a) John broke the party up.
        (b) John broke up the party.

(60)   (a) John broke the handle off.
        (b) John broke off the handle.

We have already argued that PP predications can appear in the complement position of independently identified results. Under the proposal so far, the particle isn't just a complement of *res*, it *is* a *res*. In the case of *break* it appears that both verb and particle are competing for the same position. We do not want to say that *break* is simply ambiguous between being a *proc*, *res* verb and a *proc* verb because a pure process reading simply isn't available in the general case. Once again, we have a situation that gives evidence for the Superset principle (Caha 2007), and for underassociation of category features under the constrained conditions we have isolated previously. In fact, if we inspect the predicational semantics of these constructions, it appears that the direct object of *break* in (60) does not actually (necessarily) become 'broken', while it certainly becomes 'off'. It's harder to say with example (59) since the particle has such an abstract meaning, although perhaps because of its abstractness one might want to analyse it as a pure *res* head without any embedded specific predicational content at all. I have claimed earlier that a lexical item can underassociate its category feature(s) precisely when something else identifies that category within the same phase. I repeat the principle from chapter 4 in (61) below.

(61)   *Underassociation*

If a lexical item contains an underassociated category feature,

(i) that feature must be independently identified within the phase and linked to the underassociated feature, by Agree;

(ii) the two category features so linked must unify their lexical-encyclopedic content.

In other words, the category feature on a lexical item can be satisfied in two ways: by actually associating to a node of that category in the structure; or by not associating but agreeing with that feature locally. The other condition on underassociation is that the lexical-encyclopedic content of the so-Agreeing features must be able to unify conceptually. As we have seen in chapter 4, this forces at least one of the items to have fairly general and abstract semantics – to be 'light' – and this is plausibly one of the salient properties of particles in English.

This means that the examples in (60) above actually have the particle in *res*, while the *break* verb has an underassociated *res* feature which I assume can be licensed by some syntactic coindexation mechanism (possibly AGREE) because of the *res* head in the tree.

We can force a situation in which the particle really has to be in *res* by looking at cases where a particle co-occurs with a selected PP, as in the following well-known examples (adapted here from den Dikken 1995).

(62)   (a) Mary sent the schedules out to the shareholders.

(b) Mary sent out the schedules to the shareholders.

(c) I sent John up a drink.

(d) ?I sent up John a drink.

(e) *I sent John a drink up.

Here we find the particle interacting with a selected PP and the double object structure. Fortunately, the structures proposed here make fairly good predictions. Note that in (63), both *to* and *send* have underassociated Agreeing [res] features in the structure.

(63)

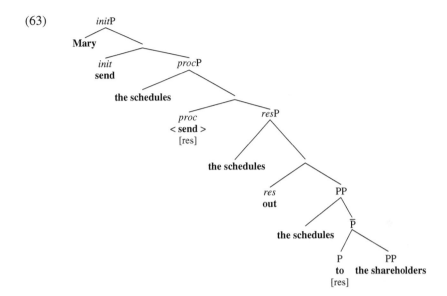

(64)

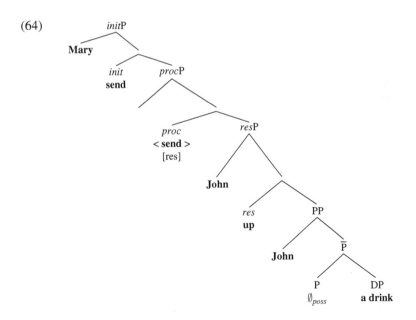

The particle in these cases doesn't actually shift, as discussed above. In fact the word order differences result from the direct object either being spelled out in its most deeply embedded predicational subject position, or in its highest landing site position.

Summarizing, apparent result augmentation occurs in English under a number of different circumstances. English possesses a $Ø_\pi$ head which is available with some verbs to license adjectival resultatives with no constraint on the semantic properties of the adjective at all, other than real-world 'felicity'. Some process verbs in this section also seem to be able to identify [*init, proc, res*], and the latter structures therefore license pure PP locational resultatives. In addition, English possesses a wide range of 'intransitive' prepositions (particles) which are independently able to license *res*, giving rise to a wide variety of different abstract results, and to the phenomenon of particle shift. The system also makes use of underassociation under restricted circumstances. Since underassociated features have to nevertheless be licensed in the same phase by Agree, this is not equivalent to free optionality of category features. Moreover, I have argued that Agreeing features need to be able to unify their lexical-encyclopedic content. This possibility is also what underlies 'light verb constructions' in a language like Bengali or Hindi/Urdu, as we will see in the final section of this chapter.

5.5   Russian lexical prefixes

What I have tried to argue in the previous chapters is that an articulation of 'first-phase syntax' allows a deeper understanding of the different verb classes and participant role types possible in natural language. In the next two sections, I pursue one important crosslinguistic consequence of the decompositional view: since verb meanings are compositional, there is no requirement (or indeed expectation) that 'first-phase' predications be monomorphemic. The claim is that the order of projections proposed and their interpretation expresses a generalization about articulation of events in natural language, and in particular predicts productive processes of result augmentation with great generality crosslinguistically, where their morphological consequences can be seen.

It has been long acknowledged in the Slavic linguistic tradition that prefixes are not all the same, but fall into a number of distinct classes. The broad classes that I will be concerned with here bear most resemblance to those of Isačenko (1960), as discussed and modified by Forsyth (1970). The class that I am interested in here is the class of 'lexical prefixes', which is opposed to the 'superlexical' ones (Smith 1995, Babko-Malaya 1999, Romanova 2006).

The 'lexical' prefixes in Russian are interesting because their meanings bear closest resemblance to their nonprefixal or prepositional counterparts (especially with motion verbs). Most prefixes in Russian have a corresponding homophonous prepositional form, but, like particles in Germanic, they seem to double as small-clause predicates in close conjunction with a verbal meaning (cf. Kayne 1985, Guéron 1987, Hoekstra 1988, Svenonius 1994b, den Dikken 1995). In other words, in many cases, the contribution of the prefix can be compositionally understood as bearing a predicational relation to the DP in object position.

(65)

v-bit'	'knock in'
vy-tyanut'	'pull out'
do-yti	'go as far as'
za-vernut'	'roll up'
s-letet'	'fly down'
u-brat'	'take away'

(66)

Boris vy-brosil sobaku.
Boris out-threw dog
'Boris threw out the dog.'

A small-clause analysis of constructions of this type sees 'the dog' in (66) above as undergoing the throwing event, as well as being the subject or the 'figure' (cf. Talmy 1985, Svenonius 1994b) of the small clause headed by the predicate 'out'. In other words, 'the dog' undergoes a 'throwing' and as a result becomes 'out'.

A detailed discussion of the effect of different lexical prefixes is beyond the scope of this book (but see Svenonius 2004a and Romanova 2006). It is important here to simply see the analytic similarity to the case of the Germanic particles. It is pervasively true of the lexical prefixes that they induce argument-structure changes on the verb that they attach to. In (67) we see a case where an object is added with the addition of the prefix, and in (68), the semantic participancy of the object is radically changed by the addition of the prefix (the patterns and generalizations here are taken from Romanova (2004b, 2004a).

(67)   (a) v-rezat' zamok v dverj   * rezat' zamok
into-cut[P] lock.ACC in door.ACC cut[I] lock.ACC
'insert a lock into a door'

(b) vy-bit'   glaz   * bit'   glaz
out-beat^P eye.ACC   beat^I eye.ACC
'hit an eye out'

(c) pro-gryzt'   dyru   * gryzt'   dyru
through-gnaw^P hole.ACC   gnaw^I hole.ACC
'gnaw a hole in something'

(68)   (a) Oni   stroili   garaži   na detskoj
They.NOM   built.IMP/3PL   garages.ACC   on children's.LOC
ploščadke.
ground.LOC
'They built garages on the children's playground.'

(b) Oni   zastroili detskuyu   ploščadku
They   za-built   children's   playground.ACC
(garažami)
(garages.INSTR)
'They built the children's playground up (with garages).'

If we extend the analysis of the verb–particle construction to the Russian lexical prefixes, we get a decomposition of the first phase in which the prefix occupies the *res* head in the structure. The 'object' of such a construction is simultaneously the RESULTEE and UNDERGOER of the decomposition. Thus, the representation of a Russian verb 'out-throw' in a sentence like (66) would be as in (69) below.

(69)

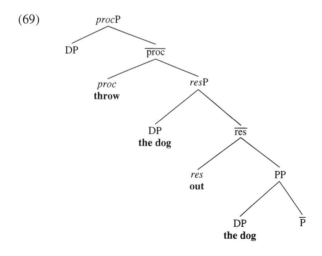

The only difference between the Russian case and the verb–particle construction is that head-to-head movement (or its implementational analogue) combines the *res* head with the main verb to give a prefixed morphological item. Further, as discussed by Romanova (2006), these prefixes nearly always require a PP *in addition* to the prefix on the verb. In Romanova (2006) it is assumed that the prefix occupies the head in a higher shell of the PP structure (her little *p*), from where it moves to identify *res*. I will assume for simplicity here that the prefix is generated directly in *res*, since nothing about the present line of argumentation depends on this choice.

There are a variety of particular properties of lexical prefixes which mirror the behaviour of the particles in Germanic. These are laid out clearly in Svenonius (2004a), from which I repeat the argument. In particular, the verb plus prefix combination can function with a more abstract (less overtly spatial) interpretation of the P element to give a more abstract result, while still retaining the same predicational structure.

(70) (a) vy-sušit'   out-dry ('to dry up')
      (b) do-nesti   up-carry ('to report')

These particle combinations are systematically subject to idiosyncratic interpretations and co-occurrence restrictions, as are verb-particle combinations in Germanic.

(71) (a) vo-plotit'   in-flesh ('to realize (a plan)')
      (b) vy-dumat'   out-think ('to invent')
      (c) raz-jest'   around-eat ('to corrode')

Under the assumption that the lexical syntactic level (in my terms, the first phase) is a phase for the assignment of idiosyncratic encyclopedic information (cf. Marantz 1997b), these facts are congruent with an account that places the prefix in a low position. The argument-structure-changing potential of these prefixes, the clear event-structural decomposition possible for them, and the potential for idiomatization, mark them out as elements of the first, event-building phase (see Svenonius 2004a for the argument that idiomatization does not straddle phase boundaries).

As we might expect from the addition of a *res*P to the structure, lexically prefixed verbal forms in Russian are always incompatible with 'for an hour' adverbials, showing that they do contain *res*Ps in their first-phase decomposition.

(72) Samoljot pere-letel   granicu (*čas).
      plane   across-flew border   hour
      'The plane flew across the border.'

(73)   Ona   iz-lila   mne   dušu   (*čas).
       She   out.of-poured   me   soul   hour
       'She poured out her soul to me.'   (Svenonius 2004)

Conversely, they *are* compatible with 'in an hour' adverbials, where the time frame adverbial indicates the time elapsed before the result state comes into being.

(74)   Samoljot   pere-letel   granicu   za   čas.
       plane   across-flew   border   in   an. hour
       'The plane flew across the border in an hour.'

(75)   Oni   zastroili detskuyu ploščadku   (garažami)   za
       They *za*-built children's playground.ACC (garages.INSTR)   in
       mesyats.
       a. month
       'They built the children's playground up (with garages) in a month.'

While there are many more details and subtleties that remain to be investigated here, I will assume that the Russian lexical prefixes are an example of the same kind of decomposition that we see in the English verb–particle construction, the interest being that the very same structures can be constructed at the analytic word level or at the morphological level.

5.6   Completive complex predicates in Indic

Pursuing the resultative structure further into the crosslinguistic jungle, we find a systematic class of constructions in the Indo-Aryan languages which are known as 'aspectual complex predicates' (Hook 1979, Masica 1991, Butt 1995). These complex predicates consist of two verbs – a main verb and a 'light' verb. The main verb is in nonfinite form and seems to carry the rich lexical content of the predication; the 'light' verb is inflected for tense and agreement and contributes to the meaning of the whole in more abstract ways. The type of V-V complex predicate I will be concerned with here is the 'completive' complex predicate, illustrated below from Bengali (76).

(76)   (a) ami   amṭa   kheye   phellam   *Bengali*
           I.NOM mango.CLASS   eat.PERFPART throw.PAST.1
           'I ate up the mango.'

(b) ami   amṭa   khelam
    I.NOM   mango.CLASS   eaten.PAST.1
    'I ate the mango.'

(77)   (a) ami   pathorṭa   thele   phellam   *Bengali*
            I.NOM   stone.CLASS   push.PERFPART   throw.PAST.1
            'I pushed (punctual) the stone/I gave the stone a push.'
        (b) ami   pathorṭa   thelam
            I.NOM   stone.CLASS   push.PAST.1
            'I pushed the stone.'

In each case, the main verb, which occurs first in the linear order, is the contentful predicate. The difference between the complex predicates in (a) and the corresponding simple verb forms in (b) is that the latter are aspectually ambiguous between an accomplishment and an activity reading, whereas the versions with the light verb are obligatorily resultative (cf. Singh 1994 for Hindi). The following examples show that the complex predicate version is incompatible with the Bengali equivalent of 'for an hour' and good with the 'in an hour' adverbial.

(78)   Ram ektu khoner moddhe ciṭhi-ṭa   lekhe   *Bengali*
        Ram in   a short time   letter-CLASS write.PERFPART
        phello
        throw.PAST.3
        'Ram wrote the letter in a short time.'

(79)   * Ram ektu khoner jonno ciṭhi-ṭa   lekhe   phello
        Ram in   a. short time letter-CLASS   write.PERFPART throw.PAST.3
        'Ram wrote the letter for a short time.'

Once again, despite the superficial differences between the Bengali construction and the verb–particle construction in English, the two share some important properties: (i) the 'meaning' of the predicate is distributed over two parts; (ii) the light verb and the particle are each in their own way very bleached and abstract meanings of simple motion, direction and transfer are used and are often strikingly parallel (compare Bengali light verbs 'rise', 'fall', 'give', 'take' with Germanic particles 'up', 'down', 'out', 'in'); (iii) the construction builds accomplishment meanings from more underspecified verbal forms.

The completive complex verbal construction is found throughout the Indo-Aryan languages with these same properties (Hook 1979). In Hindi/Urdu, it has been shown convincingly in Butt (1995) that the resultative light verb construction is monoclausal from the point of view of agreement, control and anaphora (see also Butt and Ramchand 2005). It is also true that the 'light' verb contributes to the argument structure of the whole, and changes the entailment properties of the arguments.

For example, in Hindi/Urdu, the choice of ergative case marking on the subject is determined by the light verb, not the main verb (cf. Butt 1995).

(80)   usnee/*voo   xat   likh-aa   *Hindi/Urdu*
        (s)he.ERG/(s)he.NOM   letter.M.NOM   write-PERF.M.SG
        'He wrote a letter.'

(81)   *usnee/voo   xat   likh   par-aa
        (s)he.ERG/(s)he.NOM   letter.M.NOM   write   fall-PERF.M.SG
        'He fell to writing a letter.'

(82)   usnee/*voo   xat   likh   lii-yaa
        (s)he.ERG/(s)he.NOM   letter.M.NOM   write   take-PERF.M.SG
        'He wrote a letter (completely).'

In some cases, the 'light' verb construction can even facilitate the addition of an unselected argument. In the examples below from Bengali and Hindi/Urdu, the light verb 'give' licenses the presence of a goal argument (83), (85), which would be impossible with the main verb alone (84), (86).

(83)   ami   ram-ke   cithi-ta   lekhe   dilam   *Bengali*
        I.NOM   ram-ACC   letter-CLASS write.PERFPART   give.PAST.1
        'I wrote up a letter for Ram.'

(84)   *ami   ram-ke   cithi-ta   likhlam
        I.NOM   ram-ACC   letter-CLASS write.PAST.1
        'I wrote a letter for Ram.'

(85)   naadyaa-ne   Saddaf-ko   makaan   banaa   *Hindi/Urdu*
        Nadya.F-ERG   Saddaf-DAT   house.M.NOM   make
        dii-yaa
        give-PERF.M.SG
        'Nadya built a house (completely) for Saddaf.'

(86)   *naadyaa-ne   Saddaf-ko   makaan   banaa-yaa
        Nadya.F-ERG   Saddaf-DAT   house.M.NOM   make-PERF.M.SG
        'Nadya built a house for Saddaf.'

Butt (1995) also shows convincingly that the main verb and light verb in Hindi/Urdu demonstrate an integrity which is not found with biclausal constructions, or with genuine auxiliary verb constructions, showing that the complex behaves like a single lexical verb with respect to diagnostics like scrambling and reduplication (see also Butt and Ramchand 2005).

In the following Bengali examples, I show that the complex predicate exhibits integrity with respect to scrambling. In (87) we see that the direct object of a simplex predicate may scramble to initial position.

(87) (a) ami   meye-ke   dekhlam   *Bengali*
          I.NOM   girl-ACC   see.PAST.1
          'I saw the girl.'
      (b) meye-ke   ami   dekhlam
          girl-ACC   I-NOM   see.PAST.1
          'The girl, I saw (her).'

In the biclausal construction in (88) the whole nonfinite verb plus its own argument may scramble.

(88) (a) ami   bari-te   jete   cai   na   *Bengali*
          I.NOM   house-to   go.INF   want.PRES.1   not
          'I don't want to go home.'
      (b) bari-te   jete   ami   cai   na
          house-to   go.INF   I.NOM   want.PRES.1   not
          'Going home, I don't want.'

However, in the completive complex predicate construction this is systematically impossible. The object *amṭa* 'mango' behaves like the direct object of the complex predicate as a whole and does not scramble together with its nonfinite verb. Adjacency between the two parts of the complex predicate cannot be disrupted by scrambling (89).

(89) (a) ami   amṭa   kheye   phellam   *Bengali*
          I.NOM   mango.CLASS   eaten.PERFPART   throw.PAST.1
          'I ate up the mango.'
      (b) *amṭa   kheye   ami   phellam
          mango.CLASS   eaten.PERFPART   I.NOM   throw.PAST.1

However, even though in both Bengali and Hindi/Urdu we find evidence of predicational integrity, in neither case can this integrity be understood as word (X^0) formation. For example, in Bengali and Hindi/Urdu, the light verb can be separated from its main verb by topic fronting.

(90) **so**   to   bacca   **ga-yaa**   *Hindi/Urdu*
      sleep   TOP   child.M.SG.NOM   go-PERF.M.SG
      'The child has gone to sleep.'

(91) **likh**   to   naadyaa   xat-ko   **l-e-g-ii**
      write   TOP   Nadya.F.NOM   letter.M-ACC   take-3.SG-FUT-F.SG
      'As for writing, Nadya will be able to write a letter.'

Thus, the very same paradoxes that arise with the verb–particle construction in English and Scandinavian arise here as well: the complex form acts like a single unit with respect to aktionsart and argument structure, but is not a single lexical word. This opens up the possibility of an analysis in terms of a first-phase decomposition as we have done for English, and again for Slavic above.

Bengali and Hindi/Urdu are descriptively SOV, and head-final more generally in all their projections. To extend the analysis to these languages, therefore, we predict that the process head should follow the result head (regardless of whether we choose to analyse this order in terms of base generation or movement). The predictions of the syntactic account are borne out. In our Indic resultative constructions, it is the first verb in the linear order that describes the final state achieved as a result of the event.

(92)   Naadyaa-nee   xat   likh   lii-yaa   *Hindi/Urdu*
       Nadya.F-ERG   letter.M.NOM   write   take-PERF.M.SG
       'Nadya wrote a letter (completely).'

In (92) a process occurs instigated by Nadya, as a result of which a letter comes to be written. If we take the semantics seriously, 'written' must end up under the *res* head in the first-phase syntax since it describes the final state. In a closely related language, Bengali, the morphology is clearer in that the first verb in the combination actually shows explicit perfect participle morphology (93), indicating the description of a result.

(93)   Ruma   cithi-ṭa   **lekh-e**   **phello**   *Bengali*
       Ruma   letter-CLASS   write-PERFPART   throw.PAST.3
       'Ruma wrote the letter completely.'

Note that analysing the first verb here as a *res* head is superficially at odds with the descriptive statement in the literature that the light verb in these constructions is what is responsible for adding the telicity (Hook 1979). However, the descriptive statement can easily be reconciled with the facts once we realize that it is the light verb that selects for a *res*P in this structure and thus in a way *is* responsible for the accomplishment reading, although the actual description of the final state achieved is the nonfinite verbal form. In fact, we can see that the crucial contribution of the tensed verb here is as the process descriptor, since it is this head that selects the *res*P.

If the participle describes the final state achieved, then the tensed verb must be responsible for instantiating the process head at least, and possibly the *init* head as well in the case of full transitive light verbs. It is not unusual in itself for a single lexical item to identify both *proc* and *init*, since under a decompositional account this is what main verbs do all the time. However, since the result of the process is given by the encyclopedic content of the participle, this forces the cause–process component of the meaning to be fairly abstract – light verbs like 'take', 'give' and 'go' found in this construction have fairly general meanings anyway.

The light verb phenomenon found so ubiquitously in the languages of South Asia is a direct consequence of the possibilities for underassociation argued for in this book. The light verb use of an item like 'take' or 'give' in Hindi/Urdu exists side by side with the full verb usage in the language, and has done stably for over a thousand years with the same lexical items (see Butt and Lahiri 2005 for a historical investigation of this phenomenon). Under this system, the light verb use of 'take' etc. is exactly the same lexical item as the full verb use, but with its *res* feature underassociated (identified instead by the perfect participle from a 'main verb', and agreeing with it). Moreover, the story also predicts that the verbs that can alternate productively in this way are ones where the lexical-encyclopedic content they contribute is very general and abstract, because they need to be able to conceptually unify with more specific lexical items. Thus, we find 'come', 'go', 'give', 'take' being used across the Indic languages as 'light verbs' but not 'destroy' or 'strangle' which have highly specific conceptual content.

The first-phase decomposition of the sentence in (92) would therefore look as in (94) (assuming a head-final phrase structure for these languages).

(94)

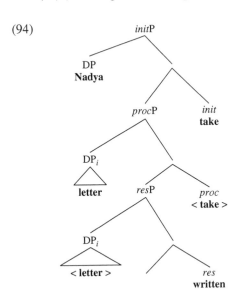

Under the view of compositional event roles outlined in the previous section, the internal argument must be base generated in Spec, *res*P, since it is the holder of the resulting state, but a copy is also merged in the specifier of *proc*P, since it is the entity undergoing the change. The word-order facts of the language also make it difficult to show exactly where the DP in question is spelled out, since in principle either location would be consistent with preverbal order. In general terms, however, it is striking that the structure of the first-phase syntax proposed makes exactly the right predictions for the order in which the subevents are instantiated, assuming head finality for this language.

This view of first-phase syntax accounts for the predicational unity of the complex predicate as well as their resultative semantics ((i) and (ii) above). Thus, aspectual light verb constructions manifest the same components of first-phase syntax (*init, proc, res*) as verb–particle constructions, but with different parts lexicalized.

The two language families are thus strikingly similar, but with a difference according to how rich the lexical-encyclopedic content of each part of the first-phase syntax is. In the case of the verb–particle construction, the main verb provides the bulk of the real-world content, and the particle representing the result is fairly abstract, or impoverished.

(95)   Rich *proc*, poor *res*:
        John ate the apple up.

This is not logically necessary, however, as it can be argued that even in English, the converse case can be detected, whereby a 'light' verb joins forces with a richly contentful final state to create a complex predication.

(96)   Rich *res*, poor *proc*:
        She got her boyfriend arrested.

In the descriptively head-final languages Hindi/Urdu and Bengali, this is also the case: the 'light verb' is the *proc* element which is descriptively quite abstract and impoverished, while the *res* head, the nonfinite perfective form, is full of encyclopedic content.

(97)   Poor *proc*, rich *res*:
        Ruma   ciṭhi-ṭa   **lekh-e**   **phello**.
        Ruma   the letter   written   threw

5.7   Conclusion

The purpose of this chapter has been to show that a theory that decomposes the simple verbal head to allow an embedded projection designated for resultant states makes good predictions for a variety of phenomena in natural language – namely those that involve what Levin and Rappaport (1998) call 'result augmentation'. Result augmentation is a pervasive phenomenon crosslinguistically. The argument I have been making in this book is that its effects should be handled not in the lexicon, or in some distinct semantic module, but in the narrow syn–sem computation itself. Accounting for the data in this way gives a more restrictive grammar, and allows us to capture generalizations across languages and lexical items. The first-phase decomposition allows us to see the commonality behind constructions such as the verb–particle construction, and lexical prefixation in Russian and Bengali complex predicates, with the very same mechanisms that also allow us to compositionally integrate PPs and APs into structured events. Syntactically decomposing the first phase also avoids the paradoxes these 'joint predications' give rise to if a purely lexical approach were adopted. From the point of view of the first phase, it is initially misleading to look at English, since its verbal forms are very often multi-valued for category features and give rise to 'synthetic' lexical items. Under the view that I have been proposing, there is no deep difference between languages like English, Russian and Bengali other than the differences between 'synthetic', 'agglutinative' and 'analytic' choices for lexicalizing the projections within the first phase. In the next chapter, I turn to the other domain in which the decomposition proposed here should have clear morphological and syntactic effects – causativization.

6   Causativization

6.1   Introduction

We have seen that causativization is one of the important factors underlying verb alternations in English, and one which I have argued is built in to the interpretation of verbal decompositional structure in a fundamental way. In this chapter, I look more closely at the morphology associated with causativization in one language, Hindi/Urdu, which productively constructs transitive verbs from simpler, usually intransitive bases. The argument here will be that in accounting for the regular morphology and its syntactic/semantic consequences, we can get some justification for the abstract system of primitives being argued for in this book. At the same time, the comparison between English and Hindi/Urdu will allow us to formulate some specific hypotheses about the nature of parametric variation in constructing verbal meaning. The larger picture will be, firstly, that there is explicit evidence for decomposition from morphological and analytical constructions, and secondly, once again, that languages vary only in the 'size' of their lexical items, not in the fundamental building blocks of eventive meaning.

In chapter 4, I discussed the debate in the literature concerning the direction of the causative–inchoative alternation. Recall that Levin and Rappaport Hovav (1995), Chierchia (2004) and Reinhart (2002) all agree in deriving the inchoative alternant from a lexically causative base. I argued in chapter 4 that the structure of the conceptual argument dissolves once one moves to a nonlexical, structure-building framework. While the morphological evidence from some languages where the inchoative version of a verb transparently contains the verb itself plus a piece of 'reflexivizing' morphology (e.g. *si* in Italian, *se* in French, *sja* in Russian) seems to support a detransitivization story, typological work shows that this is not generally the case across languages (Haspelmath 1993). The languages with overt 'causativizing/transitivizing' morphology include Indonesian, Japanese, Salish and all the languages of the Indian subcontinent, and many other languages show some causativizing morphology in at least a subset of their verb classes (cf. Haspelmath 1993). In this chapter, I examine productive causative morphology from Hindi/Urdu to argue further for the structure-building account.

The plot is to present an analysis of Hindi/Urdu causativization, and the difference between indirect and direct causation, in a framework that is syntactically decompositional, with no derivational processes operating in the lexicon. In fact, I will argue for exactly the opposite position from Levin and Rappaport-Hovav (1995): *break*-type verbs are basically monadic and can causativize because they embody no sense of causation in their intransitive version; *run*-type verbs contain both causational and processual components and therefore cannot add a distinct cause at the level of argument structure.

6.2   An analytic causative in Hindi/Urdu

The 'permissive' construction in Hindi/Urdu has been analysed extensively by Butt (1995) as a type of 'complex predicate' construction which has posed classical problems for frameworks which make a distinction between the 'lexicon' and the 'syntax'.[1]

In these constructions, the inflecting 'light' verb (using 'let' here as a typical case) combines with a main verb in the oblique inflectional form of the infinitive.[2]

(1)   kis-ne   kutte-ko   ghar ke   andar **aa-ne**
      who-OBL.ERG   dog-M.OBL.DAT   house GEN.OBL   inside come-INF.OBL
      diyaa?
      give.PERF.M.SG
      'Who let the dog come into the house?'   (Glassman 1976: 235)

One important fact about the above type of construction is that it can be shown from a wide variety of different diagnostics in the language that it seems to show properties of monoclausal as opposed to biclausal predication (like the completive complex predicates discussed in chapter 5). In particular, from the point of view of anaphor–antecedent relations, the possibility of control, and agreement phenomena, these constructions behave like a single clause with a single subject (see Butt and Ramchand 2005 for detailed argumentation).

---

[1] In the data, the following conventions are used in the romanized transcription: phonemic vowel length is represented by doubling; Ṽ represents a nasalized vowel; Ç is a retroflex consonant; the Ch digraph represents an aspirated consonant.

[2] The infinitive also functions as a verbal noun (cf. Butt 1995).

In earlier work, Butt and Ramchand (2005) argued that the permissive-type of complex predicate was built up with the 'light' verb appearing in the *init* position of the first-phase decomposition, and the main verb in the process portion. The 'light' verb is drawn from a reduced inventory of possible verbs (predominantly 'give' and 'take' in the case of the permissive), which can then combine with any main verb in the language productively to give a regular and predictable semantics. In particular, we consistently get the addition of a causer. Consider the examples below.

(2)   (a) naadyaa-ne   anjum-ko   nikal-ne   dii-yaa
           Nadya.F-ERG   Anjum.F-DAT emerge-INF.OBL   give-PERF.M.SG
           'Nadya let Anjum get out.'
       (b) anjum-ne   saddaf-ko   xat   likh-ne   dii-yaa
           Anjum.F-ERG Saddaf.F-DAT letter.M write-INF.OBL give-PERF.M.SG
           'Anjum let Saddaf write a letter.'

In all cases, the arguments related to the infinitival verb include everything but the subject. The subject, on the other hand, is the external agent or causer of the whole event, with the specific mode of causation (facilitation in the examples above) depending on the specific choice of light verb.

One can compare the 'permissive' complex predicate in (2a) above with the transitive version of the same verb, as in (3), where both sentences show the same type of valency addition.

(3)   naadyaa-ne   anjum-ko   nikaal-aa
       Nadya.F-ERG   Anjum.F-ACC   emerge-PERF.M.SG
       'Nadya pulled Anjum out.'

One of the ways in which these two constructions differ is in the existence of nominalizing morphology on the main verb in the permissive construction. The second is the fact that transitive verbs can themselves form a permissive, creating an extra argument, i.e. they do not 'lose' their original agent under the permissive construction.

More generally, the argument structure of a permissive is dependent on the valency and general properties of the main verb, with the obligatory addition of the one argument (external causer) contributed by the light verb itself. In other words, the permissive light verb construction seems like a genuine embedding of one verbal form within another. These constructions, therefore, seem to involve a recursion of the first phase, with the light verb taking a complement which embeds a whole potential *init*, *proc*, *res* sequence in its own right. This can be shown straightforwardly by the fact that roots already showing causative morphology (see next sections) can be embedded under a permissive light verb (4).

(4)   naadyaa-ne saddaf-ko   (Bill-se)   xat   likh-vaa-ne
       Nadya-ERG   Saddaf-ACC Bill-INSTR   letter.NOM   write-CAUSE-INF
       diiyaa
       give.PERF
       'Nadya let Saddaf have the letter written (by Bill).'

Intuitively, in the permissive, the notional agent or 'subject' of the infinitival verb 'raises to object position' and gets accusative case together with the thematic relation associated with undergoing the process of permission giving. The infinitival projection here must be porous enough to allow what has been called 'restructuring' in the literature (Rizzi 1978, Wurmbrand 2000), since Butt (1995) has shown very clearly that the permissive passes the tests for monoclausality with respect to agreement, anaphoric binding and control. Butt (1995) points out that the permissive construction differs minimally from control constructions where accusative case marking shows up on the infinitivally marked main verb. An example of the control construction is shown below in (5).

(5)   anjum-ne   saddaf-ko   [xat   likh-ne]-ko   kah-aa
       Anjum-ERG   Saddaf-ACC   letter.M.NOM   write-INF-ACC   say-PERF.M
       'Anjum told Saddaf to write the letter.'

As an example of the contrast, a feminine object of the embedded clause triggers feminine agreement on the permissive light verb as shown in (6), but does not give rise to feminine agreement on the matrix verb in the 'tell' construction in (7).

(6)   anjum-ne   saddaf-ko   ciṭhi   likh-ne   dii
       Anjum-ERG   Saddaf-ACC   letter.F.NOM   write-INF   give.PERF.F
       'Anjum let Saddaf write the letter.'

(7)   anjum-ne   saddaf-ko   [ciṭhi   likh-ne]-ko   kah-aa
       Anjum-ERG   Saddaf-ACC   letter.F.NOM   write-INF-ACC   say-PERF.M
       'Anjum told Saddaf to write the letter.'

Thus, it seems that the accusative-marked infinitival complement cannot 'restructure', and is fully biclausal, while the bare infinitival complement found with the permissive does restructure. I will assume that the permissive in Hindi/Urdu is to be analysed along the lines of Wurmbrand's (2000) VP complementation. The complement in question must be large enough to include initiational information but not so large that it includes an opaque phasal boundary. In fact, as pointed out in Butt and Ramchand (2005), the two verbs in the permissive construction can be independently negated; this is not true of the completive complex predicates discussed in chapter 5, and nor is it true of the morphological causative I will be treating next. I will not pursue the details of the restructuring analysis here, since it is beyond the scope of this book.

I have discussed the analytic 'causative' permissive in Hindi/Urdu first because it will be important to contrast its properties with the true 'first-phase' internal causatives that are the focus of this chapter. Also, I wish to emphasize that the main claims of this monograph do not involve ruling out recursion of elements within the first phase. In fact, one of the important current research questions involves establishing constraints on which pieces of structure can be recursed, and which morphological devices signal opacity within a recursive derivation (phase theory more generally). Such questions are important, but apply equally to all theories of syntax. They go beyond the narrow concerns of this book.

Since my aim here is to understand the basic building blocks of eventive predication, we must turn our attention to structures that are smaller and involve no recursion or restructuring. The morphological transitivizing suffixes of Hindi/Urdu contrast minimally with the analytic structures described above, and bear most directly on the event-building phase of the clause being explored here.

6.3   Overview of Hindi/Urdu transitivity alternations

Nearly every verb in Hindi/Urdu can undergo morphological causativization (Kachru 1980, Hook 1979, Masica 1991, Saksena 1982). Traditionally, these fall into three classes according to the nature of the morphology involved. The first, older stage of causativization in the language consists in a strengthening process applied to the internal vowel of the root. This gives rise to a closed class of intransitive–transitive pairs in the language. The second two morphological devices are more productive and will be the focus of this chapter. They are: (i) the addition of the *-aa* suffix to the root; and (ii) the addition of the *-vaa* suffix to the root, representing direct and indirect causation respectively.

6.3.1 Transitive–intransitive pairs via vowel alternation

In this section, I briefly outline the facts concerning this class of alternations, since it is the primary source in the language for nonsuffixed transitive verbs. An example of this alternation, taken from Bhatt (2003a), is given in (8) below.

(8)
    (a)   jaayzaad   bãṭ   rahii   hai
            property   divide   PROG.FEM   be.PRES
            'The property is dividing.'

    (b)   ram-ne   jaayzad   bããṭ   dii
            Ram-ERG   property   divide   give.PERF
            'Ram divided the property.'

According to Panini and the ancient grammarians, causatives were formed by root 'strengthening' (see Masica 1991 for a historical discussion). However, sound changes have obscured the predictability of the strengthening rule, because of a collapsing of vowel distinctions in the 'short' versions found in intransitives. Saksena (1982) and Bhatt (2003a) argue on the basis of predictability that the phonological alternation must go in the direction of 'transitive →
intransitive', instead suggesting, if anything, a synchronic anticausativization derivation. The vowel alternations in the root are tabulated below.

      aa → a
      ii → i
      uu → u
      o → u
      e → i

Saksena (1982) argues that there are cases of innovated intransitive forms in the history of Hindi/Urdu, back-formed from certain transitives, where the historical record does not support an original vowel-strengthening process. On the other hand, the alternation in the modern language does not appear to be particularly productive, and the pairs remain part of a closed class. I will remain agnostic as to whether there is a productive derivational process at work here, and concentrate in what follows on the suffixal forms. I will use the term 'base transitive' for the transitive members of the pairs discussed in this section (there are no other plausible candidates for 'base transitives' in Hindi/Urdu other than the 'ingestives' which will be described in a later subsection).

Thus, the vowel-alternating roots will not be considered 'causativization' for the purposes of this chapter. They will be important here only in so far as both transitive and intransitive alternants will be input to the suffixing causatives -*aa* and -*vaa*.

6.3.2   *Causativization using the -aa suffix*

Most roots in Hindi/Urdu are intransitive, and only become transitive
(causativized) by means of a suffix. We can see an example of this alternation in the following pair of examples from Butt (2003). Note that the gloss
in (9a) is forced into the passive due to the lack of an intransitive version of
'build' in English. However, this form is clearly not a passive in Hindi/Urdu –
it is a simple verb root with no additional morphology, and does not include the
'passive'-creating light verb 'go'.

(9)   (a)   makaan   ban-aa
              house   make-PERF.M.SG
              'The house was built.'
       (b)   anjum-ne   makaan   ban-aa-yaa
              Anjum-ERG   house   make-*aa*-PERF.M.SG
              'Anjum built a house.'

A list of some alternating forms is shown in the table in (10) below, taken
from Bhatt (2003a), to give the reader some sense of the productivity and
pervasiveness of the alternation.

(10)

Intransitive	Transitive	Gloss
bach-naa	bach-aa-naa	'be saved/save'
bah-naa	bah-aa-naa	'flow/cause to flow'
bahal-naa	bahl-aa-naa	'be entertained/entertain'
baiṭh-naa	biṭh-aa-naa	'sit/seat'
ban-naa	ban-aa-naa	'be made/make'
baṛh-naa	baṛh-aa-naa	'increase'
bhaag-naa	bhag-aa-naa	'run away/chase away'
bhiig-naa	bhig-aa-naa	'become wet/wet'
bichh-naa	bichh-aa-naa	'unroll'
biit-naa	bit-aa-naa	'elapse/cause to elapse'
bikhar-naa	bikhr-aa-naa	'scatter'
bujh-naa	bujh-aa-naa	'go/put out'
chamak-naa	chamk-aa-naa	'shine'
chaṛh-naa	chaṛh-aa-naa	'climb/cause to climb'
chipak-naa	chipk-aa-naa	'stick'
chÕk-naa	chÕk-aa-naa	'be startled/startle'
chhip-naa	chhip-aa-naa	'hide'
ḍar-naa	ḍar-aa-naa	'fear/scare'

ḍuub-naa	ḍub-aa-naa	'drown'
gal-naa	gal-aa-naa	'melt'
gir-naa	gir-aa-naa	'fall/cause to fall'
hil-naa	hil-aa-naa	'rock'
jaag-naa	jag-aa-naa	'wake up'
jam-naa	jam-aa-naa	'freeze'
jii-naa	jil-aa-naa	'be alive/cause to be alive'
lag-naa	lag-aa-naa	'be planted/attach'
leṭ-naa	liṭ-aa-naa	'lie/lay'
mil-naa	mil-aa-naa	'meet/introduce'
miṭ-naa	miṭ-aa-naa	'be wiped/wipe'
pahŭch-naa	pahŭch-aa-naa	'arrive/escort'
pak-naa	pak-aa-naa	'ripen'
phail-naa	phail-aa-naa	'spread'
pighal-naa	pighl-aa-naa	'melt'
ro-naa	rul-aa-naa	'cry/cause to cry'
saj-naa	saj-aa-naa	'be decorated/decorate'
saṛ-naa	saṛ-aa-naa	'rot'
so-naa	sul-aa-naa	'sleep/put to bed'
sulag-naa	sulg-aa-naa	'be lit/light'
sulajh-naa	suljh-aa-naa	'get simplified/simplify'
suukh-naa	sukh-aa-naa	'dry'
uṭh-naa	uṭh-aa-naa	'rise/raise'

One important thing to notice about the addition of the *-aa* suffix is that it triggers vowel shortening in the root that it attaches to, according to the same pattern of root vowel alternations seen in the transitive–intransitive pairs in section 6.3.1. However, in this case, because it is triggered by the addition of the suffix, it is the *transitive* version that ends up with the shortened root vowel.

It has been claimed in the literature that 'direct' or 'lexical' causatives tend to apply only to unaccusatives, and not to unergatives or to base transitives. However, this is not the case for *-aa* suffixation in Hindi/Urdu, since all intransitives undergo the process and some of them do indeed pass the tests of unergativity in the language. According to Bhatt (2003a), intransitives fall into two classes with regard to the following tests.

Diagnostics for unaccusativity

(i) The past participle of unaccusatives can be used in a reduced relative, unergatives cannot.

(ii) Unaccusatives can never form impersonal passives, while unergatives can.

(iii) Only unaccusatives form an inabilitative construction, unergatives (and transitives) require passive morphology to do so.

(11)   *Unergative in reduced relative*
    *hãs-aa   (huaa)   larkaa
    laugh-PERF   be.PERF   boy
    *'the laughed boy'

(12)   *Unaccusative in reduced relative*
    kat-e   (hue)   phal
    cut-PERF   be.PERF.M.PL   fruit
    'the cut fruit'

(13)   *Impersonal passive of unergative*
    calo   daur-aa   jaaye
    come.on   run-PERF   PASS
    'Come on, let it be run (let us run).'

(14)   *Passive of unaccusative*
    *calo   kat-aa   jaaye
    come.on   cut-PERF   PASS

In the inabilitative construction, there is an instrumental marked argument which is interpreted as the participant that a particular (in)ability is predicated of. For transitives and unergatives, the construction uses the same verbal complex form as the analytic passive (15) and (16) respectively; for unaccusatives no passive morphology is required to get the reading (17). This is thus another clear test that distinguishes unaccusative intransitives from unergative intransitives. (The test and the data here are taken from Bhatt 2003a).[3]

(15)   *Inabilitative based on passive of transitive*
    nina-se   dhabbe   mitaa-ye   nahĩ   gaye
    Nina-INSTR   stains.M   wipe-PERF.PL   not   PASS.PERF.MPL
    'Nina couldn't (bring herself to) wipe away the stains.'

---

[3] The inabilitative reading is facilitated by the presence of negation, and by the imperfective aspect. The instrumental-marked argument is preferentially initial, and has subject properties (see Bhatt 2003b and Butt 2003 for details). An actual analysis of this construction is beyond the scope of this book, however.

(16)   *Inabilitative based on passive of unergative*
        nina-se   daur-aa   nahĩı   gayaa
        Nina-INSTR   run-PERF   not   PASS.PERF
        'Nina couldn't run.'

(17)   *Inabilitative based on active of unaccusative*
        nina-se   dhabbe   nahĩı   miṭ-e
        Nina-INSTR   stains.M   not   wipe$_{intr}$-PERF.MPL
        'Nina wasn't able to wipe away the stains.'

Examples of intransitives in Hindi/Urdu that, according to Bhatt (2003a), satisfy the unergativity diagnostics are shown below, together with their 'causativized' alternants.

(18) | *Intransitive* | *Transitive* | *Gloss* |
        |---|---|---|
        | chal-naa | chal-aa-naa | 'move, walk/cause to move, drive' |
        | daur-naa | daur-aa-naa | 'run/cause to run, chase' |
        | hãs-naa | hãs-aa-naa | 'laugh/cause to laugh' |
        | naach-naa | nach-aa-naa | 'dance/cause to dance' |
        | ur-naa | ur-aa-naa | 'fly' |

While these verbs pattern as unergatives with respect to the tests, it is not clear whether the initiational interpretation on the original subject is actually retained when the verb is transitivized using the -*aa* suffix. In fact, the selectional restrictions on the object of these transitives seem to require a participant that is inanimate, or explicitly controllable (20) (data from Bhatt 2003a).

(19)   patang/chiriyaa   ur   rahii   hai
        kite/bird   fly   PROG.F   be-PRES.SG
        'The kite/the bird is flying.'

(20)   anjali   patang/*?chiriyaa   uraa   rahii   hai
        Anjali   kite/bird   fly   PROG.F   be.PRES.SG
        'Anjali is flying a kite/* a bird.'

Causativization of 'basic' transitives
In addition to being able to attach to basic unergatives, the -*aa* suffix also appears to attach to the transitives found in the vowel-alternating class discussed at the outset. In practice, it is quite difficult to tell whether the -*aa* suffix is attaching to the transitive or the intransitive alternant because vowel shortening obscures the length of the root vowel. In addition, the -*aa*-suffixed form has an extra

required argument when compared to the base intransitive *kaṭ*, but does not add another argument when compared to the transitive *kaaṭ*. Thus, it is not clear whether the alternation is as shown in (21), or as shown in (22) (data from Butt 1998).

(21)   (a)   paoda   kaṭ-aa
              plant   cut-PERF.M.SG
              'The plant got cut.'

       (b)   anjum-ne   paoda   kaṭ-aa-yaa
              Anjum-ERG   plant   cut-*aa*-yaa
              'Anjum cut a/the plant.'

(22)   (a)   anjum-ne   paoda   kaaṭ-a
              Anjum-ERG   plant   cut-PERF.M.SG
              'Anjum cut a/the plant.'

       (b)   anjum-ne   (saddaf-se)   paoda   kaṭ-aa-yaa
              Anjum-ERG   Saddaf-INSTR   plant   cut-*aa*-yaa
              'Anjum had Saddaf cut a/the plant.'

However, in (22), we can see that the *-aa*-suffixed version allows an instrumental adjunct interpreted as an intermediate agent, something not allowed in the base transitive version.[4]

Causativization of transitive 'ingestives'
With one small class of transitive verbs, causativization with *-aa* is possible with the *addition* of a required argument, to create a derived 'ditransitive'. The following table is taken from Bhatt (2003a).

(23)
Verb	*Verb-aa*	*Gloss*
chakh-naa	chakh-aa-naa	'taste/cause to taste'
dekh-naa	dikh(l)-aa-naa	'see/show'
khaa-naa	khil-aa-naa	'eat/feed'
pakaṛ-naa	pakṛ-aa-naa	'hold, catch/hand, cause to hold'
paṛh-naa	paṛh-aa-naa	'read/teach'
pii-naa	pil-aa-naa	'drink/cause to drink'
samajh-naa	samjh-aa-naa	'understand/explain'
siikh-naa	sikh-aa-naa	'learn/teach'
sun-aa	sun-aa-naa	'hear/tell'

---

[4] An instrumental-marked adjunct is in fact also allowed in the base transitive, but is interpreted as an instrumental, and cannot be used on an intermediate 'agent'.

As can be seen in the pair of examples below (from Butt 1998), an extra
-ko (dative)-marked argument becomes obligatory with the suffixed form of the
root. This argument could be seen as the 'demoted' subject of the base transitive
version (24), but it also gets the semantics of an 'affected' argument (cf. Alsina
1992). Note that this argument is obligatory, and cannot be expressed with the
instrumental *-se* morphology classically associated with unexpressed agents of
causatives.

(24)   saddaf-ne   khaanaa   kha-yaa
       Saddaf-ERG   food   eat-PERF.M.SG
       'Saddaf ate food.'

(25)   anjum-ne   Saddaf-ko/*se   khaanaa   khil-aa-yaa
       Anjum-ERG   Saddaf-ACC/*INSTR   food   eat-*aa*-PERF.M.SG
       'Anjum fed Saddaf food.'

Bhatt and Anagnostopoulou (1996) show that examples such as (25) above
behave in many subtle respects like base ditransitives such as 'give' in the
language, showing the same internal syntax.[5] Interestingly, the paraphrases of
these forms in English reflect their special semantics – a form such as (25) does
not mean 'Anjum caused Saddaf to eat food', it must mean that 'Anjum *fed*
Saddaf, directly affecting her in doing so.'

6.3.3   Causativization using the -vaa suffix
One of the striking things about causativization in *-vaa* is that it does not show
any obvious differences in distribution as compared to the *-aa* class. On the
other hand, the *-vaa* causative is traditionally considered to be the 'indirect'
causation marker, analysed by Kachru (1980) as a 'second' causative, and by
Shibatani (1973a, 1973b) as a 'syntactic' causative alongside a more 'lexical',
'first causative' *-aa*. If we consider the triple of examples in (26)–(28), it is easy
to find this representation of the facts tempting.

(26)   (a)   makaan   ban-aa
             house   be made-PERF.M.SG
             'The house was built.'

---

[5] For example, the *-ko* here is a real dative and cannot be dropped under conditions of
animacy (unlike the homophonous accusative); there is obligatory object shift when the
object is marked with overt accusative case.

(b) anjum-ne   makaan   ban-aa-yaa
    Anjum-ERG   house   be made-*aa*-PERF.M.SG
    'Anjum built a house.'

(c) anjum-ne   (mazdurõ-se)   makaan   ban-vaa-yaa
    Anjum-ERG   labourers-INSTR   house   be made-*vaa*-PERF.M.SG
    'Anjum had a house built by the labourers.'   (from Butt 2003)

However, once one looks at the data more closely, there are compelling reasons to reject this kind of account. The first embarassment for the idea that *-vaa* causatives are second causatives of *-aa* forms is the fact that the morphemes themselves do not stack, although they are both extremely regular and productive. One could of course postulate a productive deletion rule, but that would have no *independent* justification. Moreover, it would fail to make sense of the fact that the *-vaa* suffix already seems to contain the *-aa* suffix as a subcomponent, but on the wrong side of the root. In other words, if these morphological elements are to combine by any straightforward process respecting the mirror principle, one would expect the *-aa* to be embedded within *-v* suffixation.

Secondly, there are many cases where *-aa* suffixation and *-vaa* suffixation can both be applied, producing forms that seem virtually synonymous, and where both forms allow the addition of an instrumental *-se*-marked intermediate agent. This happens when suffixation applies to roots with transitive meanings, like *kaaṭ-* 'cut' (seen above in the discussion of *-aa* causativization). Parallel causatives in *-aa* and *-vaa* are shown here in (27) below.

(27)   (a)   mãi-ne   naukar-se   peṛ   kaṭ-aa-yaa
              I-ERG   servant-INSTR   tree   cut-*aa*-PERF
              'I had the servant cut the tree.'

        (b)   mãi-ne   naukar-se   peṛ   kaṭ-vaa-yaa
              I-ERG   servant-INSTR   tree   cut-*vaa*-PERF
              'I had the servant cut the tree.'   (from Saksena 1982)

Once again, it is difficult to tell whether the *-vaa* suffix is attaching to the transitive or to the intransitive stem, because of vowel shortening. However, Bhatt (2003) points out some consonant-changing idiosyncrasies which seem to indicate that, at least in some cases, it must be the transitive stem that is being used.

(28) *Intransitive* *Transitive* -vaa *causative* *Gloss*
       chhuuṭ-naa   chhoṛ-naa   chhuṛ-vaa-naa   'be free/free'
       phaṭ   phaaṛ-naa   phaṛ-vaa-naa   'be torn/tear'
       phuuṭ-naa   phoṛ-naa   phuṛ-vaa-naa   'be burst/burst'
       ṭuuṭ-naa   toṛ-naa   tuṛ-vaa-naa   'break'

The special class of 'ingestives' should also be considered here. Once again, the *-vaa* morpheme never creates more obligatory arguments than the *-aa* morpheme. The difference here is that (as in the base unaccusatives), the *-vaa* morpheme makes an instrumental intermediate agent possible, where the *-aa* form does not.

(29) (a) rita-ne   angur   khaa-e
           Rita-ERG   grape   eat-PERF.M.PL
           'Rita ate some grapes.'

      (b) rita-ne   sima-ko   angur   khil-aa-e
           Rita-ERG   Sima-DAT   grape   eat-*aa*-PERF.M.PL
           'Rita fed Sima some grapes.'

      (c) kala-ne   (rita-se)   sima-ko   angur   khil-vaa-e
           Kala-ERG   (Rita-INSTR) Sita-DAT   grape   eat-*vaa*-PERF.M.PL
           'Kala made Sima eat some grapes (through the agency of Rita).'
                                                        (from Butt 2003)

In general, then, *-vaa* and *-aa* attach to what appears to be the very same root/stem, with both transitives and intransitives of both kinds combining with both suffixes.

(30) *Base unaccusative* ban   ban-aa   ban-vaa
                           'get made' 'make'   'have s.t. made'
      Base unergative   hās   hās-aa   hās-vaa
                           'laugh'   'make laugh'   'have (s.o.) laugh'
      Base 'ingestive'   paṛh   paṛh-aa   paṛh-vaa
                           'read'   'teach'   'have s.o. study'
      Base transitive   kaaṭ   kaaṭ-aa   kaaṭ-vaa
                           'cut s.t.' 'have (s.o.) cut s.t.' 'have (s.o.) cut s.t.'

Thus, even though there are meaning differences between *-aa* causativization and *-vaa* causativization which might lead one to believe that the latter was the 'second causative' of the former, a closer look at the distribution shows that both suffixes attach to exactly the same root forms, and have exactly the same number of obligatory arguments when they do so. Semantically, there is a pervasive difference with respect to whether the causation is interpreted as 'direct' or 'indirect' (using these terms intuitively for the moment), which is related to the fact that an optional instrumental case-marked participant is interpreted as an instrument in the case of -*aa* causativization of intransitives, but as an intermediate agent in the case of -*vaa* causativization with the same roots.

Perhaps most devastating for the inner vs. outer causative analysis of -*aa* and -*vaa* is the fact that the -*vaa* form does not necessarily entail the truth of the -*aa* form. This can be seen most clearly in the examples involving ingestive verbs. As pointed out by Saksena (1982), the -*vaa* causative form in the (a) examples below does not entail the truth of the -*aa* causative in the (b) examples.

(31)   (a)   mãī-ne   laṛke-ko   do baje   khil-*vaa*-yaa
             I-ERG   boy-ACC/DAT   two o'clock   eat-*vaa*-PAST
             'I had the boy eat at two o'clock.'
       (b)   kisii-ne   laṛke-ko   do baje   khil-*aa*-yaa
             someone   boy-ACC/DAT   two o'clock   eat-*aa*-PAST
             'Someone fed the boy at two o'clock.'

(32)   (a)   mãī-ne   laṛke-ko   paṛh-vaa-yaa
             I-ERG   boy-DAT   study-*vaa*-PERF.M
             'I had the boy study.'
       (b)   mãī-ne   laṛke-ko   paṛh-aa-yaa
             I-ERG   boy-DAT   study-*aa*-PERF.M
             'I taught the boy.'   (from Saksena 1982)

From the point of view of productivity and idiosyncrasy too, the -*aa* and -*vaa* morphemes cannot be distinguished. They are both equally morphologically regular: they show no allomorphy and determine no stem allomorphy; both suffixes shorten the vowel in the stem when they attach; they both attach to any type of root.[6] As far as lexical idiosyncrasy is concerned, both forms seem to give regular and predictable meanings in the general case. However, there do exist a number of lexically idiosyncratic forms and selectional restrictions, for *both* types (data from Saksena 1982).

---

[6] There are some transitives that do not have -*aa* causatives, and some that do not seem to have -*vaa* causatives, but no real pattern for this has been discerned in the literature. Many transitives in fact have both versions, although speakers claim that they are virtually synonymous.

(33)   *Root (intr)*   *Idiomatic transitive*

        bul-naa   'speak'   bul-aa-naa   'call someone'

        pak-naa   'ripen'   pak-aa-naa   'cook'

        paṭ-naa   'get along'   paṭ-vaa-naa   'lay a floor/roof'

        le-naa   'take'   li-vaa-naa   'buy something for someone'

6.3.4   *Status of the causee*

As we have seen, under certain conditions, a *-se*-marked (instrumental) adjunct is licensed in Hindi/Urdu causatives, interpreted as an intermediate agent or 'causee'. This never seems to be possible with base intransitives and base (unsuffixed) transitives. However, the possibility of a causee does not cleanly distinguish the *-aa* forms from the *-vaa* forms in all cases. When it attaches to an intransitive root, *-aa* suffixation does not seem to license the presence of an instrumental-marked causee, while the *-vaa* form does.

(34)   (a)   makaan   ban-aa

            house   make-PERF.M.SG

            'The house was built.'

      (b)   anjum-ne   (*mazdurõ-se)   makaan   ban-aa-yaa

            Anjum-ERG   (*labourers-INSTR)   house   make-*aa*-PERF.M.SG

            'Anjum built a house.'

      (c)   anjum-ne   (mazdurõ-se)   makaan   ban-vaa-yaa

            Anjum-ERG   (labourers-INSTR)   house   make-*vaa*-PERF.M.SG

            'Anjum had a house built (by the labourers).'

Similarly, with the ingestives, an instrumental-marked causee is possible with the *-vaa* causative version, but not with the *-aa* causative version. The 'direct object' is not really a causee in (35) in the same sense, but a dative affected argument, and this argument is also obligatory with *-vaa*.

(35)   (a)   saddaf-ne   khaanaa   kha-yaa

            Saddaf-ERG   food   eat-PERF.M.SG

            'Saddaf ate food.'

      (b)   anjum-ne   (*ram-se)   saddaf-ko   khaanaa   khil-aa-yaa

            Anjum-ERG   Ram-INSTR   Saddaf-ACC   food   eat-*aa*-PERF.M.SG

            'Anjum fed Saddaf food (*through the intermediary of Ram).'

      (c)   anjum-ne   (ram-se)   saddaf-ko   khaanaa   khil-vaa-yaa

            Anjum-ERG   Ram-INSTR   Saddaf-ACC   food   eat-*vaa*-PERF.M.SG

            'Anjum had Saddaf eat food through the intermediary of Ram.'

                                      (from Butt 1998)

However, with many transitive roots, both *-aa* and *-vaa* allow a *-se*-marked causee, when they both exist.

(36)   anjum-ne   paoda   kaaṭ-a
        Anjum-ERG   plant   cut-PERF.M.SG
        'Anjum cut a/the plant.'

(37)   anjum-ne   saddaf-se   paoda   kaṭ-aa-yaa
        Anjum-ERG   Saddaf-INSTR   plant   cut-*aa*-yaa
        'Anjum had Saddaf cut a/the plant.'

(38)   anjum-ne   saddaf-se   paoda   kaṭ-vaa-yaa
        Anjum-ERG   Saddaf-INSTR   plant   cut-*aa*-yaa
        'Anjum had Saddaf cut a/the plant.'

To summarize, causees, in the sense of instrumental (*-se*) case-marked nominals interpreted as an 'intermediate agent' have the following properties: they are always optional; with *-vaa* causatives they are always possible; with *-aa* causatives they are possible only when the base is a (noningestive) transitive; they are never possible with the base transitives formed via vowel alternation. It is important to note that instrumental-marked adjuncts are actually nearly always possible with all verbal forms (interpreted as instruments), it is just their interpretation as intermediate agents that is at stake here.

6.3.5   Status of causer

There is also a difference between the two types of causative with respect to the nature of the surface subject, or causer, although this has not been pointed out in the literature before, as far as I am aware. It is true that English allows a much wider range of subjects/causers than most other languages, and Hindi/Urdu is no exception. However, the informants I consulted all accepted a certain limited number of stative and abstract causes in subject position. Strikingly, these were only possible with the causatives in *-aa*. Causatives in *-vaa* seemed only to be possible when the subject was an active instigator. Some causative pairs are shown below. In each case, both the *-aa* and *-vaa* causative were used in common natural speech by my informants, and in each case only the *-aa* causative was possible with that particular choice of subject.

(39)   *Pairs of near-synonymous transitives in* -aa *and* -vaa
        (a) ban-aa-naa/ban-vaa-naa 'build'
        (b) pak-aa-naa/pak-vaa-naa 'ripen'

    (c) suljh-aa-naa/suljh-vaa-naa 'simplify'
    (d) ubalaa-naa/ubal-vaa-naa 'boil'
    (e) dhul-aa-naa/dhul-vaa-naa 'wash'

(40)

Test sentence	-aa *causative*	-vaa *causative*
'John's money built that house.'	Yes	No
'The sun ripened the fruit.'	Yes	No
'The new arrangements simplified the problem.'	Yes	No
'The kettle boiled the water very fast.'	Yes	No
'The rain washed the clothes.'	Yes	No

6.3.6   Summary

So far, I have been at pains to describe the morphological system of a language that productively derives causative/transitive verbs. The point, however, is not merely to establish that there is a piece of morphology that is a plausible candidate for the initiation head in the first-phase decomposition argued for in this book. Nor even that it is also on the 'correct' side of the root, if it is to represent a morpheme in a structurally higher position than the root (consistent with the expectations of a Kaynian head-initial structure and the mirror principle). A typological examination of the world's languages (Julien 2000) shows that productive causative morphology, when it exists, indeed occurs closer to the root than tense or modality inflection. This supports a structural position for causation that is at least lower than tense, and higher than the root. Furthermore, the fact that this morphology also affects the argument-taking properties of the predication argues for the causational head being somehow inside the 'first phase', or the domain often referred to as the *v*P. But, so far, the facts are entirely consistent with many different implementations of the causative *v* head structures proposed by many recent researchers (Pylkkänen 1999, Kratzer 1996, Harley 2000).

    A more specific understanding of the processes involved is not possible from the evidence of morphological typology – a more detailed case study is required as offered here. Hindi/Urdu is an important test case because it is a language that shows highly regular and productive morphological exponence of causation, and has been reported to show the classic distinction between 'direct' and 'indirect' causation. This latter feature relates to the issue of 'recursion' of causational semantics, and to traditional claims about the lexical/syntactic dichotomy.

There are a number of questions any successful analysis of the Hindi/Urdu patterns should resolve. First and most basically, we need to understand the placement and productivity of these suffixes in attaching to roots that can be unergative and transitive in addition to unaccusative. Related to this, there is the question of why the 'ingestive' class of transitive roots is distinguished in actually giving rise to ditransitive causative structures. Secondly, if we are to take the order and productivity of morphemes seriously, is it possible to make sense of the fact that the *v* of the indirect causative is actually closer to the root than the *aa* piece of the morphology that the direct and indirect causatives share? Lastly, given that both suffixes seem to attach to the same roots, and have the same possibilities with regard to productivity on the one hand and lexical idiosyncrasy on the other, how can one make sense of the semantic differences between direct and indirect causation that have been noticed in the literature? In constructing an analysis that answers these questions, we can be more concrete about the details of lexical 'insertion' than our analysis of English alone could allow. The goal is to arrive at a theory of causativization that can then be generalized both to languages with 'synthetic' lexical items, like many English verbs, and those with more analytic systems.

6.4   Analysis

6.4.1   *Representing the verb classes in Hindi/Urdu*
The first step is to establish the first-phase representations of the individual root types in the language. We have seen that there are at least four broad classes of roots, based on certain robust language-internal diagnostics and distribution. We must first distinguish between the two different types of intransitive, designated informally by the labels 'unaccusative' vs. 'unergative'. The former type of intransitive can be used in reduced relatives, as we saw, while the latter cannot. In addition, the unergative roots can undergo impersonal passivization, unlike the unaccusatives. Although most transitive verbs are formed using the *-aa* and *-vaa* suffixes, there is, as I have been assuming, a class of base 'transitive' roots. These are the transitives that form pairs with intransitives by means of (unproductive) vowel alternation. These transitives are like the 'unergative' intransitives in that they passivize, and they require passivization in the inabilitative construction. I will therefore assume that what transitives and unergatives have in common is that they both have *init* features in their representation, thus licensing INITIATOR arguments.

On the other hand, the patterns of causativization in the language seem to be sensitive to a slightly different distinction, carving the verb types up a little differently. Basically, with respect to causativization, all intransitives pattern together, and together with the small class of transitive 'ingestives' in opposition to the core transitives. With the former class, the subject of the original verb becomes a direct structurally case-marked argument under (both types of) causativization, while with the latter class, the subject of the original verb does not appear at all, or appears as an optional instrumental adjunct. Another way of putting the generalization is to say that intransitives and ingestives increase their valency under causativization with *-aa* or *-vaa*, while transitives show no such valency increase (although allowing a 'causee' adjunct). I will interpret this pattern as meaning that the subject argument of the verbs that increase in valency is actually an UNDERGOER, and that this is what allows it to appear as the object argument of the causativized version. Notice that this means that both unergatives and ingestive transitives must have UNDERGOER–INITIATOR subjects, a possibility we saw already with motion verbs in English. Another way in which the 'ingestive' class appears to be similar to the intransitives is that they systematically allow unspecified object deletion (Saksena 1982) and are often thus used 'intransitively'. I will assume that this is because the 'object' argument of an ingestive is actually a PATH argument, whose content can be recovered from context.

To summarize, the basic verb root classes we find in Hindi/Urdu will be analysed as follows:

> *Verb classes in Hindi/Urdu*
> Unergatives (including intransitive motion verbs): single argument;
> INITIATOR–UNDERGOER
> Unaccusatives: single argument; UNDERGOER–RESULTEE
> Transitives: two arguments; INITIATOR and UNDERGOER
> Ingestives: two arguments; INITIATOR–UNDERGOER and PATH/RHEME.

6.4.2 *Direct vs. indirect causation*

The second step towards an analysis is to come up with an analysis of direct vs. indirect causation that does not involve actual recursion of the causative head. The reason that recursion seems wrong for Hindi/Urdu is that, as we have seen, there is no actual direct morphological recursion in evidence, and no productive semantic recursion (although, as we saw, there are some pairs that could be interpreted that way). In addition, there is no evidence that the 'indirect' causative *-vaa* is 'outside' or more syntactic than the *-aa* causative: they are both equally morphologically productive, attach to the same types of roots, and each have their own limited degree of lexical idiosyncrasy.

Fortunately, there is another potential way to capture the semantics of indirect causation without recursion of the *init* head in the first phase. To do so, we exploit the idea that causation more generally actually obtains between each pair of subevents in the first-phase decomposition – between the initiation and process, as well as between the process and result, if any.

As noted in the previous chapter on resultative formation, Levin and Rappaport-Hovav (1999) proposed a distinction between two types of resultative construction – a kind of direct vs. indirect result – that plays a role here. In their case, they correlate the idea of 'direct'-ness with a kind of temporal dependence between the two relevant subevents, calling only the 'indirect' or temporally independent subevents causational.

In the terms of this book, the relation between the *init* subevent and the *proc* subevent is one of causation, as is the relation between the *proc* subevent and the *res* one. In understanding the various types of resultative formation, I proposed a relationship between subevents that was geared to which morpholexical items identified which head in the first-phase decomposition. This temporal dependence hypothesis is repeated here in (41).

(41)   *Temporal dependence hypothesis*
        For a result subevent to be temporally dependent on a process, the
        same root must identify the two subevents.

This claim is relevant to any analysis of indirect causation, because the semantics of indirect causation is correlated with the potential lack of temporal dependence between subevents. It allows us to get the *effects* of embedding one cause within another cause without actually doing so: the idea will be that the subevents are asserted to be causally related while being temporally and lexically distinct, giving rise to the *inference* of an intermediary. Thus, I will claim in what follows that indirect causation does not involve recursion of the *init* head, but occurs whenever the morpheme identifying the *proc* head is lexically distinct from the morpheme lexically identifying *res*.

For ease of reference I also repeat the constraints on event composition I proposed in the previous chapter.

        Constraints on event composition
(42)   *Init-proc coherence*
        Given a decomposition $e_1 \rightarrow (e_2 \rightarrow e_3)$, some proper subpart of e_1
        precedes e_2.

(43)   *Proc-res coherence*
        Given a decomposition $e_1 \rightarrow (e_2 \rightarrow e_3)$, e_3 must *not* temporally
        overlap e_2, but may temporally abutt it.

The above constraints are assumed always to be in effect general coherence conditions; tighter temporal relations apply when a single lexical item co-identifies two heads in the structure. Thus, temporal independence in a causative structure will occur, as in resultatives, when the lexical item identifying the process part of the decomposition is distinct from that identifying the result portion.

6.4.3   Direct causativization in -aa

We now have the ingredients for an analysis of the Hindi/Urdu system. The natural assumption here must be that the *-aa* suffix is actually the *init* head, or, more precisely, it is a lexical item which possesses just an *init* feature, and has default/impoverished lexical-encyclopedic content. This lexical item will be able to combine unproblematically with an unaccusative root type (as in (44)) to build a maximal first-phase structure, as shown in (45) below.

(44)   (a)   makaan   ban-aa
              house   make-PERF.M.SG
              'The house was built.'

        (b)   anjum-ne   makaan   ban-aa-yaa
              Anjum-ERG   house   make-*aa*-PERF.M.SG
              'Anjum built a house.'

(45)   *Unaccusative plus -aa*

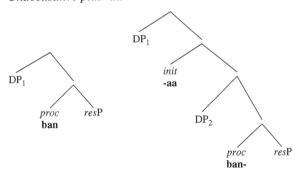

'ban': DP_1 *undergoes a making (DP1 gets made)*
'ban-aa': DP_1 *initiates, leading to DP_2 getting made (DP$_1$ makes DP$_2$)*

With the *-aa* initiation head, and the root that identifies *proc* and *res*, we have complementary ingredients for a transitive first-phase predication. In many languages, productive causative morphology only attaches to unaccusative roots, as might be expected from the assumption that each lexical item must satisfy all its category features.

However, we know already that this is not the situation in Hindi/Urdu and that *-aa* causativization attaches to roots of all types, even those that we have diagnosed as having *init* features themselves. So far, I have assumed that structure needs to be interpreted, but that underassociation is possible. Underassociation is constrained, however. It is not systematically possible to use intransitively any verb that appears in a transitive frame. We have already seen one such case in the discussion of particle constructions with punctual verbs. Recall that we analysed a verb like *break* as already possessing a *res* feature, while the particle head was also productively analysed as bearing a *res* feature. I argued then that allowing *break* to underassociate its own *res* was contingent on *res* actually still being present and identified, and on the two items being conceptually compatible. The same situation occurred with the light verb completive constructions.

Underassociation seems to occur in contexts where the unassociated feature carried by the root is actually morphologically preempted by another lexical item. Pursuing this line of thought, I suggested that features on a root may underassociate precisely when they are in an Agree relation with a syntactically present feature of the same type. I repeat the Underassociation rule once again as (46).

(46)   *Underassociation*
        If a lexical item contains an underassociated category feature,
        (i) that feature must be independently identified within the phase and linked to the underassociated feature by Agree;
        (ii) the two category features so linked must unify their lexical-encyclopedic content.

Specifically, then, if we turn to the situation where the *-aa* suffix attaches to a transitive root, we get a situation where the *-aa* will itself fill the *init* head and introduces its own argument, while the *init* feature of the root must remain unassociated. This means in turn that the lexical-semantic content of *init* can remain quite underspecified and any kind of causer is allowed. The root will identify the *proc* head directly and the two subevents will be interpreted via the general causational relation.

(47) (a) anjum-ne   paoda   kaaṭ-a
           Anjum-ERG   plant   cut-PERF.M.SG
           'Anjum cut a/the plant.'
      (b) anjum-ne   paoda   kaṭ-aa-yaa
           Anjum-ERG   plant   cut-*aa*-yaa
           'Anjum cut a/the plant.'

(48) *Base-transitives plus -aa*

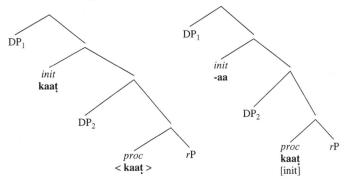

'*kaaṭ_{trans}*': DP₁ initiates cutting-wise and DP₂ undergoes a cutting
(also achieves result of cutting) (DP₁ cuts DP₂)
'*kaṭ_{trans}-aa*': DP₁ initiates, and DP₂ undergoes cutting and result of
cutting (DP₁ has DP₂ cut)

The analysis whereby the subject of the *-aa* causative is a general/vague causer, not necessarily encyclopedically associated with the root's lexical content, makes sense of the pattern we saw earlier, whereby *-aa* causatives can in principle have abstract or stative causers as their subjects. However, I have assumed that the lexical-encyclopedic content connected to the underassociated category feature is not lost, but somehow has to be conceptually unified with the category feature in the structure that it agrees with. Direct unification is an option here, and will be indistinguishable from the content of the underassociated feature on its own, since it is more specific than the general causational semantics given by the *-aa* morpheme. However, real-world knowledge in this case makes available a different kind of unification – one where the general causation expressed by the *-aa* head is distinct from that lexically identified by the underassociated feature. This does not mean that the latter information is not present, but that it is not considered to be the relevant initiational trigger. This analysis makes direct sense of the fact that 'causee' adjuncts are licensed with *-aa* causativization precisely when there is an unassociated root feature that would have that 'causee' as its subject. Thus, the actual initiation of cutting, the *doing* of the cutting by someone, as it were, is still part of the lexical-encyclopedic content of the root and accessed by the interpretational mechanisms, making the causee adjunct interpretation felicitous. Crucially, though, the surface subject of the causative verb is not necessarily the 'cutter' but merely someone who is responsible for a situation that does in fact lead to the 'plant undergoing the cutting'.

Consider now the case of unergatives. These verbal roots have a single argument that is an UNDERGOER–INITIATOR. Like the transitives, the addition of the -*aa* morpheme will lead to underassociation of the *init* feature of the root. Recall that these verbs are those in which the UNDERGOER of the process has some degree of control over their own motional or bodily function and will be coindexed with the root's INITIATOR – this indeed is still part of the semantics of the root. Under -*aa* causativization, however, some degree of volition is of necessity suspended, as the surface subject causer is interpreted as being able to control the physical functioning of the being undergoing the process. As reported in Bhatt (2003a) and Saksena (1982), objects of 'causativized' unergatives seem to have rather different felicity conditions regulating them than the subjects of the corresponding intransitive. In particular, it is often reported that these objects have to be children, invalids, nonhuman, or otherwise (contextually) controllable.

(49)   (a) patang/chiriyaa uṛ rahii   hai
            kite/bird   fly PROG.F be.PRES.SG.
            'The kite/the bird is flying.'

        (b) anjali   patang/*?chiriyaa uṛaa rahii   hai
            Anjali   kite/bird   fly   PROG.F   be.PRES.SG
            'Anjali is flying a kite/*a bird.'

(50)   *Unergatives*

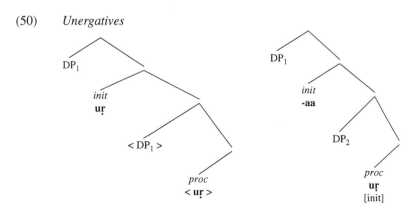

'*uṛ*': *DP*₁ *initiates/gives rise to flying motion and thus undergoes a flying motion (DP*₁ *flies)*
'*uṛ*'-*aa: DP*₁ *initiates, leading to DP*₂ *undergoing flying motion (DP*₁ *makes DP*₂ *fly)*

Ingestive transitives are just like the unergatives, by hypothesis, in having an initial subject that is an UNDERGOER–INITIATOR. Their internal argument is actually a PATH, not an UNDERGOER. Adding the -*aa* allows the initial subject to remain, but in UNDERGOER position. Crucially, the availability of the PATH position is unaffected, which is why these verbs retain their full set of arguments when causativized. This immediately predicts a ditransitive structure for these verbs under causativization. Recall that our analysis of ditransitives in English also involved generating one of the arguments in complement (i.e. rhematic or nonspecifier position). This is also what underlies the ditransitive structures created here. What is criterial of the ingestive class is that, even though they are transitive, their surface 'subjects' are also UNDERGOERS and affected in some way. The direct object in these events is not an UNDERGOER itself, but a PATH argument.

(51)   (a) saddaf-ne   khaanaa   kha-yaa
            Saddaf-ERG   food   eat-PERF.M.SG
            'Saddaf ate food.'

        (b) anjum-ne   (*ram-se)   saddaf-ko   khaanaa khil-aa-yaa
            Anjum-ERG Ram-INSTR Saddaf-ACC food   eat-*aa*-PERF.M.SG
            'Anjum fed Saddaf food (*through the intermediary of Ram).'

(52)   *Ingestive transitives plus* -aa

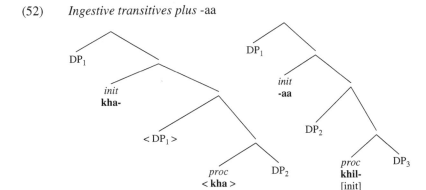

> '*kha*' : DP_1 initiates eating activity and thus undergoes an eating process/experience described by the PATH, DP_2 *(DP_1 eats DP_2)*
> '*khil*'-*aa*: DP_1 initiates, leading to DP_2 undergoing the eating process/experience as described by the DP_3 PATH *(DP_1 feeds DP_2 DP_3)*

All of the cases of -*aa* causativization involve the insertion of -*aa* under *init*. The causation asserted here will always be temporally dependent, since no disjunction between *proc* and *res* arises. On the other hand, the insertion of -*aa* will always add a causer to an otherwise noninitiation event, or, in the case of initiation events, optionally allow the expression of a 'pure' cause – one which is not necessarily experientially involved.

6.4.4   *'Indirect' causativization in* -vaa

The analysis I will be pursuing, in the absence of evidence for recursion in Hindi/Urdu morphological causativization, is that the semantics of 'indirect' causation arises from the way in which the subevents of the first phase are lexically identified. If Levin and Rappaport-Hovav (1999) are correct in distinguishing a class of indirect resultatives, where the most embedded result is temporally and lexically distinct from the description of the process that leads up to it, then it is plausible that -*vaa* causatives could be describing that very kind of event. Since -*vaa* is morphologically composed of -*aa* and -*v*, I will assume that it inserts to fill both the *init* and *proc* heads, leaving the root verb to just identify *res*. Also potentially relevant to this analysis is the observation in Bhatt (2003a) that the only base verbs that do *not* take -*vaa* in Hindi/Urdu are those that cannot occur in perfect participial form in combination with the 'light verb' *ja*- 'go', the so-called analytic passive.[7]

---

[7] Bhatt (2003) actually uses this fact to motivate an analysis of -*vaa* causativization which explicitly embeds passive substructure. I will pursue a different but related claim here, namely that the root identifies only the result subevent *res* in -*vaa* causativization, a fact that it has in *common* with the construction involving the 'passive' light verb 'go'. The reason I reject the idea of explicit passive substructure in -*vaa* causatives is that unaccusative intransitive roots do causativize in -*vaa* although they do not passivize. The fact that most verbs in Hindi/Urdu allow identification of *res*, even if they themselves are not normally telic, is initially surprising. However, it is perhaps relevant to note that the perfect participial form of the verb that appears in the completive complex predicate construction (as discussed in chapter 5) is actually indistinguishable from the bare root form. If these roots are actually perfect participles, the pattern is not so surprising, but it means that there may be more internal complexity involved. I abstract away from this problem here.

I will thus assume that *-v* merges as *proc* and that *-aa* merges as *init*, as before, where the two specifier positions are identified, giving rise to a single UNDERGOER–INITIATOR argument. The root fills the *res* head and encyclopedically identifies the final result attained by the single noncauser argument, the RESULTEE. Given that the *-vaa* suffix multiply inserts and takes up so much 'space' in the first-phase decomposition, any verb root that combines with it will have to leave some of its own category features unassociated. This will always be syntactically legitimate because of the presence of *init* and *proc* heads in the structure. No temporal overlap or common lexical content is asserted for the *proc* and *res* subevents in the case of *vaa* causativization; thus the whole event will be interpreted as involving an 'indirectly caused' result.

(53) anjum-ne   (mazdurõ-se)   makaan ban-vaa-yaa
      anjum-ERG labourers-INSTR house   be.made-*vaa*-PERF.M.SG
      'Anjum had a house built by the labourers.'

(54) *Unaccusatives plus* -vaa

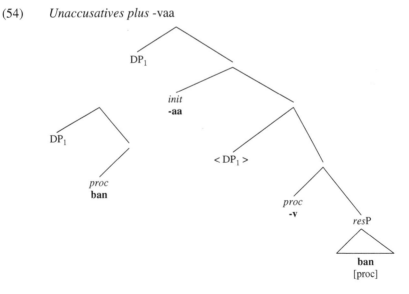

'*ban*': DP₁ *undergoes a making (DP₁ gets made)*
'*ban-vaa*' : DP₁ *initiates and undergoes some process so that DP₂ ends up getting made (DP₁ has DP₂ made)*

One possibly surprising feature of this analysis is the claim that the surface subject 'causer' is an UNDERGOER–INITIATOR, like the subjects of unergatives and motion verbs in English. However, distributional facts about the semantic selectional restrictions on the subjects of *-vaa* causatives suggest that this is not entirely implausible. Recall that causes can be abstract states in principle, but that abstract conditioning states cannot be conceived of as being, in addition, UNDERGOERS. Abstract conditioning states or inanimate causes turned out to be systematically impossible with *-vaa* causativization, as reported above. This would be a surprising fact from the point of view of an analysis that simply took *-vaa* as an 'outer' or more 'syntactic' causative. It is at least potentially explicable under the account proposed here: the 'subject' of a *-vaa* causative must be an UNDERGOER–INITIATOR regardless of the contextual causational process involved in the particular event. The subject must therefore be interpreted as an active 'experiencer' of the process, and therefore a deliberate and conscious participant. This in turn requires a volitional and sentient agent in subject position.

A simple, less decompositional alternative to this analysis is to claim that *vaa* is just a morpheme that multiply inserts as *init* and *proc*. Since it is a lexical item in its own right, we can assume it carries its own (fairly impoverished) lexical-encyclopedic content in identifying the process and initiation phases of the macro-event. A possible solution therefore is to claim that this lexical item carries the encyclopedic content associated with active volitional causation. The most important aspect of the proposal given here, however, is that the root in these cases identifies only the results of the action, and that therefore the relation between causational process and outcome is conceived of as indirect, as in Levin and Rappaport-Hovav's indirect resultatives.

Concretely, for the unergatives and transitive roots combining with *-vaa*, we find the root forced to identify just the *res* subevent while the *-vaa* takes up both *init* and *proc*, giving rise to the semantics of indirect causation.

(55)   Anjum-ne   Saddaf-ko   hãs-vaa-yaa
        Anjum-ERG   Saddaf-ACC   laugh-*vaa*-PERF.M.SG
        'Anjum made Saddaf laugh (by means of the clown).'

(56)   *Unergatives with* -vaa

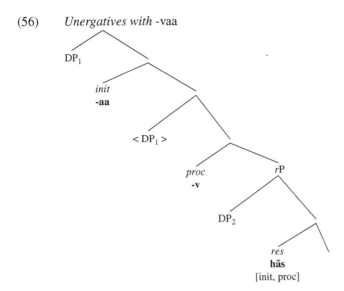

'*hãs*' -vaa: *DP*₁ *initiates and undergoes some process so as to bring*
*about the result of DP*₂ *laughing (DP*₁ *had DP*₂ *burst into laughter)*[8]

In the case of the unergative root 'laugh', we find the selectional restrictions
on the object are less than with the corresponding -*aa* causativization. This is
because in the latter case, the object is the UNDERGOER of the laughing process,
which is somehow being initiated by the subject. The 'laugher' must therefore
be conceived of as being directly controllable. However, with the -*vaa* causative,
no such direct relation exists since the process that the subject initiates is not
itself the laughing process– the causation is indirect, and therefore consistent
with actions like persuasion or a deliberate effort to be amusing.

(57)   anjum-ne   saddaf-se   paoda   kaṭ-vaa-yaa
          Anjum-ERG   Saddaf-INSTR   plant   cut-*vaa*-yaa
          'Anjum had Saddaf cut a/the plant.'

---

[8] Once again, the interpretation here seems to be related to the interpretation of the
corresponding perfect participle of 'laugh' rather than to the bare root. Since the two
are indistinguishable morphologically, it is not possible to show this conclusively, but I
will assume that it is this fact that makes such forms possible, given how much syntactic
space is taken up by the -*vaa* morpheme.

(58)   *Base transitives with* -vaa

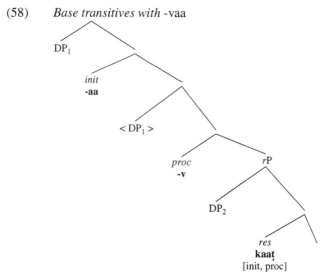

DP₁ *initiates and undergoes some process so that* DP₂ *can achieve the result of cuttedness (*DP₁ *had* DP₂ *cut)*

If we compare this latter situation with the analysis I gave for the *-aa* causative for 'cut', we can see that there is indeed a clear overlap in the situations that they describe. For the causative in *-vaa*, above, the result is indirect, but for *-aa* the result is a direct result of the process of 'cutting' and the relation between that process and the initiation is vague and contextually sensitive. The main difference between the two constructions would be that in the *-vaa* causative the deliberateness and volitionality of the causer are emphasized, and indeed obligatory, while the *-aa* causative is potentially compatible with abstract, stative or unintended causing.

When it comes to the ingestive transitives, once again the root only identifies the *res* portion of the macro-event. The two original arguments of the ingestive become the RESULTEE and RHEME OF RESULT respectively. The meaning of this form is that the causer intends, and brings about the final result of Saddaf's consumption of the food.

(59)   anjum-ne   (ram-se)   saddaf-ko   khaanaa   khil-vaa-yaa
        Anjum-ERG Ram-INSTR Saddaf-ACC food   eat-*vaa*-PERF.M.SG
        'Anjum brought it about that Saddaf ate food (through the intermediary
        of Ram).'

(60) *Ingestive transitives with* -vaa

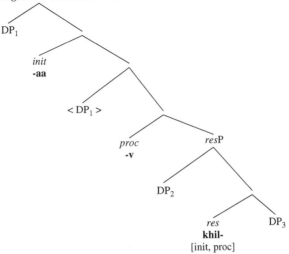

DP$_1$ initiated and experienced a process so that DP$_2$ could come to eat DP$_3$ (DP$_1$ had DP$_2$ eat DP$_3$)

6.4.5 *Event underassociation and the intermediate agent/causee*

To summarize the analysis given in the above subsections, the difference between direct and indirect causation for the two morphemes is captured by the difference in lexical specification for category features of the two different morphemes. The analysis is given again in encapsulated form in (61) below.

(61) *Direct causativization in* -aa
- The *-aa* suffix bears an *init* feature. It can form a structure together with roots of various different types.
- If the root in question also has an *init* feature, it will remain underassociated (implicit).
- Since *proc* and *res* are identified by the same lexical root, the complex causative structure will be interpreted as 'direct', or 'temporally dependent'.

'Indirect' causativization in -vaa
- The *-vaa* suffix bears both *init* and *proc* features. It can form a structure together with roots of various different types.
- *-vaa* always forces underattachment of the root's own category features. The root itself always identifies only *res*.

> • Since *proc* and *res* are always identified by different lexical items, the complex causative structure will be interpreted as 'indirect', or 'temporally independent'.

In this section, I will argue that the analysis in terms of underassociated category features representing subevents gives a better account of the distribution of the *-se*-marked adjunct than one that involves a correlation with suppressed or implicit agent arguments. One thing that is often only noted in passing in the literature on *-se* in this context is that it is always felicitous as an adjunct referring to an instrument, when attached to an inanimate DP. This is important to bear in mind and will be relevant to the proposal which emerges later. For now, the data I present on the interpretation of the *-se*-marked optional adjunct concerns whether it has an 'intermediate agent' reading.[9]

As one can see from (62), the intermediate agent reading is absent from a sentence containing a base transitive.

(62)   *Base transitive*
      anjum-ne   (*saddaf-se)   peṛ   kaaṭ-aa
      Anjum-ERG   Saddaf-INSTR   tree   cut-PERF.M.SG
      'Anjum cut the tree.'

The relevant reading is also completely impossible for *-aa* causativization of unaccusative roots (63). This is perhaps not surprising, since the structures and features I have offered for (62) and (63) respectively are identical.

(63)   *AA-causative based on unaccusative root*
      anjum-ne   (*mazdurõ-se)   makaan   ban-aa-yaa
      Anjum-ERG   labourers-INSTR   house   make-*aa*-PERF.M.SG
      'Anjum built a house.'

For *-aa* causatives based on unergatives, transitives and ingestives, we find an interesting dialect split. The forms cited in the literature (specifically Saksena 1982), and two of my informants accept the intermediate agent reading here (although they report a preference for the *-vaa* form in all cases).[10] One other speaker considers these ungrammatical.

---

[9] I thank Miriam Butt, Tafseer Khan Ahmed and Rajesh Bhatt for being the patient informants for this section of the chapter. All surviving misrepresentations and misunderstandings are self-created.

[10] The version with the base transitive is the worst of these three. The morphological form given here is actually ambiguous between being an *-aa* causative of a transitive as intended here, or the *-aa* causative of an unaccusative. On the latter interpretation, the *-se*-marked causee should be completely ungrammatical. I assume this is what is interfering with speaker judgements in this case.

(64) *AA-causative based on unergative root*
anjum-ne (% masxaraa-se) saddaf-ko hãs-aa-yaa
Anjum-ERG clown-INSTR Saddaf-ACC laugh-*aa*-PERF.M.SG
'Anjum made Saddaf laugh (% by means of the clown).'

(65) *AA-causative based on base transitive root*
anjum-ne (% ? saddaf-se) peṛ kaṭ-aa-yaa
Anjum-ERG Saddaf-INSTR tree cut-*aa*-PERF.M.SG
'Anjum cut the tree/ % ? had Saddaf cut the tree.'

(66) *AA-causative based on ingestive transitive root*
anjum-ne (% saddaf-se) ram-ko khaanaa khil-aa-yaa
Anjum-ERG Saddaf-INSTR Ram-ACC food eat-*aa*-PERF.M.SG
'Anjum had Saddaf feed Ram food.'

When we turn to the causatives in *-vaa*, we find that the *-se*-marked intermediate agent reading is available for *all* possible forms.

(67) *VAA-causative based on unaccusative root*
anjum-ne (mazduro-se) makaan ban-vaa-yaa
Anjum-ERG labourers-INSTR house make-*vaa*-PERF.M.SG
'Anjum had a house built (by the labourers).'

(68) *VAA-causative based on unergative root*
anjum-ne (masxaraa-se) saddaf-ko hãs-vaa-yaa
Anjum-ERG clown-INSTR Saddaf-ACC laugh-*vaa*-PERF.M.SG
'Anjum made Saddaf laugh (by means of the clown).'

(69) *VAA-causative based on base transitive root*
anjum-ne (saddaf-se) peṛ kaṭ-vaa-yaa
Anjum-ERG Saddaf-INSTR tree cut-*vaa*-PERF.M.SG
'Anjum had the tree cut by Saddaf.'

(70) *VAA-causative based on ingestive transitive root*
anjum-ne (saddaf-se) ram-ko khaanaa khil-vaa-yaa
Anjum-ERG Saddaf-INSTR Ram-ACC food eat-*vaa*-PERF.M.SG
'Anjum had Saddaf feed Ram food.'

The first point which emerges from this more careful look at the data is that a simple generalization in terms of suppressed or implicit agent is not possible.

If the existence of an implicit agent is diagnosed primarily by the loss of a participant argument in going from the base verb to its causativized version, we can see that the possibility of the causee reading for -*se* does not correlate with it.

(71)

Verb type	Se-causee	'Demoted' agent
Base trans.	*no*	*no*
aa-causative		
of unacc.	*no*	*no*
of unerg.	*%*	*no*
of trans.	*%*	*yes*
of ingestive	*%*	*no*
vaa-causative		
of unacc.	*yes*	*no*
of unerg.	*yes*	*no*
of trans.	*yes*	*yes*
of ingestive	*yes*	*no*

There is in fact independent evidence that a -*se* intermediate agent reading is not licensed by a demoted agent argument. In the passive of a simple transitive verb, a -*se* adjunct with the intended reading is not possible.[11]

(72)   *Passive of a transitive verb*
peṛ   (*anjum-se)   kaaṭ-aa   gay-aa
tree   Anjum-INSTR   cut(trans)-PASS   go-PERF.M.SG
'The tree was cut.'

Most colloquial speakers of Hindi/Urdu disprefer the expression of an agent at all in constructions such as (72) above. However, in more formal registers, if such a meaning is required, some (Hindi) speakers can use the postposition -*dwara*- 'by means of' for this use (never -*se*).[12]

---

[11] The -*se*-marked argument here can be interpreted as the holder of an ability. I will not explicitly address the abilitative reading of -*se* here. But see the conclusion of this section for some speculations.

[12] This basic fact is discussed in Bhatt (2003b), to whom I am also grateful for discussion.

(73)   *Passive of a transitive verb*
     per̥ (anjum-dwara) kaaṭ-aa   gay-aa
     tree Anjum-by   cut(trans)-PASS go-PERF.M.SG
     'The tree was cut by Anjum.'

On the other hand, if one tries to passivize a verb form that has already been causativized in *-vaa*, the intermediate agent *-se*-marked adjunct resurfaces as a possibility.

(74)   *Passive of* vaa-*causative of transitive verb*
     ram-se   per̥ kaṭ-vaa-yaa   ga-yaa
     Ram-INSTR   tree cut-*vaa*-PASS go-PERF.M.SG
     'The tree was cut through Ram's actions.'

However, the fact that this is not picking out the same argument as a true demoted agent is suggested by the fact that a *-dwara*-marked argument can actually be added to the sentence already containing the *-se*, as in (75).

(75)   *Passive of* vaa-*causative of transitive verb*
     anjum-dwara   ram-se   per̥   kaṭ-vaa-yaa   ga-yaa
     Anjum-BY   Ram-INSTR   tree cut-*vaa*-PASS go-PERF.M.SG
     'The tree was caused to be cut by Ram, by Anjum.'

The possibility of the *-se* as intermediate agent is directly connected to the *-vaa* morphology, and not to the passive, as the following minimal pair shows.

(76)   (a) *Passive of* aa-*causative of unaccusative verb*
       makaan   (*anjum-se)   ban-aa-yaa   ga-yaa
       house   Anjum-INSTR   build-*aa*-PASS go-PERF.M.SG
       'The house was built.'
     (b) *Passive of* vaa-*causative of unaccusative verb*
       makaan   (anjum-se)   ban-vaa-yaa   ga-yaa
       house   Anjum-INSTR   build-*vaa*-PASS go-PERF.M.SG
       'The house was built (through the actions of Anjum).'

This brief excursion into the passive construction confirms what we have seen already, namely that the possibility of the intermediate agent reading is (i) independent of the passive and (ii) not actually licensed by a demoted agent argument. What, then, is correlated with the appearance of this interpretation (other than the *-vaa* morphology itself)? If we chart the possibility of the causee reading against the implicit *subevents* in my analysis of each type, we get a much more regular picture.

(77) | Verb type | 'se'-causee | underassociated subevent |
|---|---|---|
| Base trans. | no | none |
| -*aa*-causative | | |
| of unacc. | no | none |
| of unerg. | % | *init* |
| of trans. | % | *init* |
| of ingestive | % | *init* |
| -*vaa*-causative | | |
| of unacc. | yes | *proc* |
| of unerg. | yes | *init, proc* |
| of trans. | yes | *init, proc* |
| of ingestive | yes | *init, proc* |

Thus, it seems to be that the possibility of the intermediate agent reading is correlated strongly with the existence of an underassociated/implicit *proc* feature in the structure. The dialect split also has a ready explanation: some speakers tolerate the reading if there is only an *init* subevent left implicit, although they all prefer the *proc* version.

An explicit semantics for the interpretation of adjuncts is beyond the scope of this book, but I will outline an intuitive proposal that would make sense of the correlation we have seen.

- The -*se* phrase is an adjunct which is a subevent modifier. In all cases, it is interpreted as information cotemporaneous with the subevent that it modifies.
- -*se* phrases can modify both present and underassociated subevental information: if it modifies the identified *proc* it is interpreted as 'instrument'; if it modifies *init* it can be a manner or means modifier; if it modifies an *implicit proc*, it is interpreted as an intermediate actor. For some speakers, modification of an implicit *init* can also give rise to this reading, but is more difficult.

The intermediate agent interpretation arises from a combination of factors. The -*vaa* suffix insertion ensures that the relation between the causational *proc* and the *res* identified in the first phase is indirect (no temporal abutment). The process that *would* be more temporally related to the lexically identified result remains implicit. Any modification of that more temporally related process is consistent with a reading in which the participant is intimately connected to that process. For some speakers, association with an implicit *init* is enough, but more difficult since the causation in this case is temporally direct, and it is hard to see how there would be 'room' for an intermediate agent.

One other feature about -*se* is important to mention: *se* phrases have obligatory anti-volitive or 'out of control' semantics. Even when they occur as animate 'causees', it is the true subject that is always the intentional controller. Because -*se* occurs in a structure where the causation chain is explicitly represented as belonging to the arguments introduced by -*vaa*, the -*se*-marked argument cannot be in control. I assume that this is part of the semantics of the -*se* lexical item, which makes it ideally suited to marked inanimate instruments, but semantically incompatible with genuine demoted agents in the passive. I note in passing that 'lack of control' is also a property of the -*se*-marked arguments of the abilitative construction, in both its 'accidental' and 'inabilitative' guises. I leave a unification of these uses of -*se* to further research.

6.4.6 Consequences

What I have shown in the previous sections is that a complicated distribution of direct vs. indirect causation interpretations can be accounted for with a small set of theoretical assumptions, many of which appear to be independently necessary in the analysis of other data. I argued that it is a mistake to analyse the two different causative morphemes in Hindi/Urdu in terms of a complete recursion of the first phase (or, equivalently, as a lexical vs. syntactic distinction). Instead, I claimed that the semantics of indirect causation can be achieved within the first phase itself by pursuing the logic of what it means for a particular root to identify a subevent/category head with its lexical-encyclopedic content. While the heads *init*, *proc* and *res* are uniformly linked by the general cause or leads-to relation, differences emerge depending on how the content of those subevents is lexically described. Specifically, if the process that leads to a result has different lexical-encyclopedic content from that result, then the two subevents are less organically related (more independent, less direct) and may even involve temporal disjunction even though cause and effect can be detected. The difference between -*aa* and -*vaa* causation is then that the former suffix fills the *init* head, while the -*vaa* suffix fills both the *init* and *proc* heads, causing a disruption/indirection between the process instigated by the causer and the actual final state caused.

The analysis I propose immediately accounts for the fact that there is no explicit morphological or semantic embedding found with the two morphemes in question, and that both suffixes attach in principle to the same types of roots, with the same effects on valency. In addition, the analysis makes sense of the fact that the -*vaa* morpheme actually includes the -*aa* suffix as a subpart, since it structurally includes it as well. Since both suffixes are internal to the first phase, we predict that both forms will be subject to idiomatic and lexicalized interpretations equally. This is indeed what we find – while both suffixes are reasonably regular and semantically compositional, coventionalized forms and meanings appear with either -*vaa* or -*aa* versions of a verb. I do not actually rule out recursion in principle. There may be languages and causational devices that do not occur within the first phase, or fully biclausal causative constructions. My purpose here has been to investigate the properties of the building blocks of subevental complexity, before such recursion is taken into account.

In constructing the analysis, I needed to make certain important assumptions about the way the system works, and in particular about the way in which different lexical or morphological pieces are allowed to combine. What we found in Hindi/Urdu is that root category features are allowed to remain unassociated provided they are licensed by the presence of those features in the syntactic structure anyway. I assumed that a mechanism similar to Agree is responsible for this descriptive generalization. As we saw, unassociated features remained semantically active and facilitated the presence of certain adjuncts.

6.5   Reinterpreting internal and external causation

One of the claims of the syntactic, or constructional, approach to verbal complexity is that the morphological/lexical independence of the subparts of the first phase is epiphenomenal, and that the very same syntactic structures can be expressed synthetically, morphologically, or analytically, depending on the language and the particular lexical items in its inventory.

Unlike Hindi, English is a language where transitive verbs are not systematically related to intransitive counterparts via a piece of morphology. In my terms, English expresses its complex event structures 'synthetically' in the core cases. So far, I have used the evidence of Hindi/Urdu morphological causatives to argue for the syntactic reality of the *init* head, and also to concretize my proposals about lexical attachment and subevent coherence. Now I wish to turn to the cases of labile alternating verbs in English and reinterpret the facts in the light of the kind of theory advanced here.

Given the general system in place for connecting the event-structure information within first-phase syntax with the encyclopedic knowledge of the lexical item, we are in a position to reconsider the variable behaviour verbs in English. We have seen that one class of verbs in English occurs in transitive–intransitive pairs. Levin and Rappaport Hovav (1995) argue that the transitive is the base form, and that the intransitive is derived by a lexical suppression of the CAUSE component in the item's lexical-conceptual structure. Since not all transitive verbs with a CAUSE component actually have intransitive counterparts, a lexicon-internal condition must be placed on the suppression mechanism. The conditions under which this suppression is supposed to be possible seem unconvincing to me. Basically, L&RH argue that CAUSE may be suppressed precisely when the verb can be conceived of as being able to take place without any external causation (a worryingly vague and unfalsifiable principle, but also one which would predict more contextual variability than there actually is). As for the principle itself, it seems unintuitive to say that these are the verbs that *must* have CAUSE in their lexical representation in the first place, since they are the very ones where we can conceive of the event without it! Reinhart (2002), who also takes the transitive-to-intransitive position, is forced to claim that intransitive unaccusative verbs with no transitive counterpart do nevertheless have a transitive counterpart in the lexicon which is 'frozen' and never surfaces. In the case of English, a far more satisfying system emerges if we take the derivation to occur in the other direction: while many causative transitives fail to have intransitive counterparts, only a small number of unaccusatives, if any, fail to causativize. Even a lexicon-internal rule of causativization would do a better job of predicting the pairs that exist than a suppression account.

Since I am working within a nonlexicalist set of assumptions, a 'lexicon-internal' rule of concept suppression (or addition) is not available. On the other hand, since structure can contribute interpretation in this system, causational semantics when it occurs does not have to inhere in the lexical semantics of the root in question.

Under the system so far, these were the verbs that did *not* already possess an *init* feature in their syntactic information, at least in their intransitive uses. The idea is that intransitive verbs that are more volitional, and already have specification of *init*, will resist further causativization.[13]

In the current system, there are at least two ways to approach the variable behaviour of a verb like *break* that participates in the alternation shown in (78).

(78)   (a) The stick broke.
         (b) John broke the stick.

---

[13] Here I will claim that so-called unaccusative verbs like 'arrive' and 'fall' that fail to causativize in English are actually *init, proc, res* verbs with a single composite argument and are not counter-examples to the principle that all non-*init* verbs will causativize in English.

One strategy is to say that verbs of this type have an 'optional' *init* feature in their specification.

(79)   Lexical entry of *break*: [(init) proc$_i$, res$_i$]

This is a possibility, but in addition to expanding the logic of the system greatly, it also misses a potentially important generalization – namely that a substantial majority of verbs of the unaccusative type have a causative version. If the few exceptions can be explained away, one is tempted to the conclusion that the addition of an initiational subevent, with its own independent argument, seems to be a systematic possibility for *all* noninitiational verbs in English. There are a couple of other suspicious facts that should be accounted for: the INITIATOR that is added is always independent of the other arguments of the intransitive verb and has very general and unconstrained semantics with respect to encyclopedic content, in other words, the verb *break* doesn't seem to impose much in the way of semantic selectional restrictions on the external argument. English is quite unusual crosslinguistically in the availability of a wide range of abstract causers in the subject position of most verbs.

(80)   (a) Alex broke the window.
(b) The storm broke the window.
(c) Mary's carelessness broke the window.

Given the stated aims of this framework to eliminate lexicon-internal processes and primitives, and given the need to express this peculiar property of English in a simple way that would account for the possibility of crosslinguistic variation, we have one clear option open to us. I have suggested that English possesses a lexical item (unpronounced) which possesses default causational semantics and which can be associated under *init* in the general case, and which triggers incorporation of the verbal root into it, much like the Hindi/Urdu *-aa* suffix.

The analysis for English therefore lists intransitive *break* as a lexical item with just the *proc* and *res* category features.

> *break*: [proc$_i$, res$_i$]
> *run*: [init$_i$, proc$_i$]
> Ø: [init]

The null *init* head can be built on top of a structure where *break* has already merged, but not on top of a structure where *run* has merged, so that only the former will have a transitive counterpart. Under this analysis, English is very like Hindi/Urdu, except for the fact that in English *-aa* is unpronounced, and that English has a larger class of base transitives.

In fact, it is not strictly true that *run* in English cannot transitivize. There are at least two kinds of contexts where it does: one, where an explicit resultative subevent is added to the verb phrase; the other, where more abstract, non-leg-motion running is involved (81).

(81)   (a) John ran the bathwater.
      (b) John ran the meeting.
      (c) John ran Mary's life.

In fact, we already have an explanation for these facts in place if we pursue the analogy to Hindi/Urdu *-aa* to its logical conclusion. Recall that *-aa* could attach to unergatives and to transitives as well as to unaccusatives, thereby forcing the category root features to be unassociated. If we assume that the same is possible in English (except that of course one wouldn't see any addition of morphology), then *run* should be able to take the null causative morpheme as well. However, when it does so, (i) the lexical-encyclopedic content of *run* would no longer be able to identify the initiational subevent, (ii) the UNDERGOER of the process would have to be distinct from the INITIATOR, and (iii) the UNDERGOER could not be a volitional or undergoing a process he/she has implicit control over. I claim that these constraints can only be met under a metaphoricization or bleaching of the meaning of *run* (reducing to something like 'continuous dynamic activity typical of undergoer'). Where this is conventionalized, transitivization will be possible with the null *init* head for those verbs. In addition, one could imagine a different unification of the conceptual content of *run* with the null causational suffix in English, if it were possible to demote the running initiational impulse to that of an irrelevant triggering state which is not deemed to be the underlying cause of the event. Consider a case where John gets small furry animals to run through a maze as part of his experiments on rodent intelligence. He could set up a piece of cheese at the end of the track and then lift a trapdoor, thus releasing the rat. My judgement is that, in such a case, it is perfectly felicitous to say (82), even though it is the rats doing the running, not John at all. This is the same effect that we get with some uses of *-aa* in Hindi/Urdu.

(82)   John ran the rats through the maze.

More generally, it is also plausible that the general causational *init* head is what is merged when transitive verbs in English do appear with abstract causes as subjects instead of subjects with the expected active involvement in the event (83).

(83)   (a) This sofa seats three.

(b) The wind threw the clothes from the washing line.

(c) The crime situation reduced the revenues from tourism.

It is well known that English is quite special in allowing this kind of range of abstract subjects for verbs. I speculate that this is a consequence of the null *init* head that it possesses, with such impoverished encyclopedic content. The system makes such constructions possible, but I assume that in each specific case, real-world information will conspire to make them felicitous or infelicitous. I leave the investigation of this line of thought to further research.

6.6   Conclusion

Against the recent dominant view in the theoretical literature, I have argued for a view of causativization that involves 'structure building', as opposed to 'lexical subtraction'. I have given an analysis of the patterns of Hindi/Urdu morphological causativization from a constructional viewpoint, where the suffixes found in this language actually morphologically spell out heads in the first-phase syntax that I have been proposing. Specifically, the *-aa* suffix in Hindi/Urdu was argued to be a pure *init* head, while *-vaa* spelled out *init* plus *proc* together. In accounting for the difference between direct and indirect causativization in Hindi/Urdu, I argued that recursion is not necessary to capture the difference in the relatedness of the subevents involved. In doing so, I made some specific proposals concerning the relationship between subevental integration and lexical identification. Once again, the notion of underassociation turned out to be important for this analysis, suitably constrained. The claim was that category features on a lexical item can fail to 'associate' or directly identify structure, provided the feature did actually appear in the syntax. Thus, both Merge and Agree seemed to be possible as mechanisms to satisfy the category requirements of a lexical item, in addition to some less well-understood constraints on the felicity of unifying the encyclopedic content of the features involved. In the final part of the chapter I returned to the case of English alternating verbs to argue that they could be given the same kind of analysis as the Hindi/Urdu suffixation strategy. The main difference between the two systems was that the 'pronunciation' of the Hindi/Urdu *-aa* suffix was null in English.

7 Conclusion

7.1 Summary of the system

In this book, I have tried to work through some of the details of a very specific proposal concerning the decomposition of verbal meaning. Following the intuitions of Hale and Keyser (1993), Borer (2005) and others, I have argued that event structure and event participants are directly represented in syntax. The first-phase syntax explored here is a binary branching structure for a particular functional sequence of heads, where structure and category label correspond systematically to meaning. In particular, specifiers are interpreted as the semantic subject of a head–complement complex, and embedded eventuality descriptors are interpreted as being unified by a generalized 'cause' or 'leads-to' relation. The other important semantic correlate of structure within the event domain is 'homomorphic unity': a phrase in the complement of an event-denoting head must co-describe that event, and I have proposed that natural language does this by imposing a matching requirement between the event-scale and a scale introduced by that complement. The first-phase syntax and the rules of combination that I have argued for are repeated here as a summary.

(1)

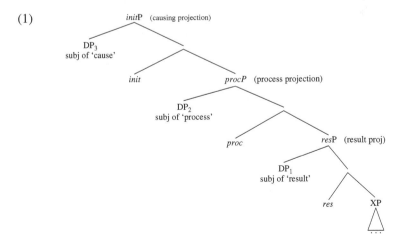

193

The specifiers of 'event' projections

- *init*P introduces the causation event and licenses the external argument ('subject' of cause = INITIATOR)
- *proc*P specifies the nature of the change or process and licenses the entity undergoing change or process ('subject' of process = UNDERGOER)
- *res*P gives the 'telos' or 'result state' of the event and licenses the entity that comes to hold the result state ('subject' of result = RESULTEE)

Initiation, process/transition and result derived from event composition

(2)   *Event Composition Rule*

$e = e1 \rightarrow e2$: e consists of two subevents, e1, e2 such that e1 causally implicates e2

(cf. Hale and Keyser 1993)

Assume that there are two primitive subsorts of eventuality:
a. State(e) : e is a state
b. Process(e): e is an eventuality that contains internal change

(3)   IF $\exists e_1, e_2[\text{State}(e_1) \& \text{Process}(e_2) \& e_1 \rightarrow e_2]$, then by definition Initiation(e_1)

(4)   IF $\exists e_1, e_2[\text{State}(e_1) \& \text{Process}(e_2) \& e_2 \rightarrow e_1$] then by definition Result(e_1)

Toy semantic denotations for event heads

(5) $[[res]] = \lambda P\lambda x\lambda e[P(e) \& res'(e) \& \text{State}(e) \& \text{Subject}(x,e)]$

(6) $[[proc]] = \lambda P\lambda x\lambda e\exists e_1,e_2[P(e_2) \& proc'(e_1) \& \text{Process}(e_1) \& e = (e_1 \rightarrow e_2) \& \text{Subject}(x,e_1)]$

(7) $[[init]] = \lambda P\lambda x\lambda e\exists e_1,e_2[P(e_2) \& init'(e_1) \& \text{State}(e_1) \& e = e_1 \rightarrow e_2 \& \text{Subject}(x,e_1)]$

In the case of *proc* combining with a nonevent head, the complement must bear the PATH role, where being a path requires the existence of a set of measures associated with the phrase. To fulfil the PATH role, the following two entailments must hold. This is a definition inspired by Krifka (1992) original Mapping-to-Objects and Mapping-to-Events.

(8) $\text{P}_{\text{ATH}}(x, e) =_{def} \exists R \exists D_x [\ \forall e,d,d'[R(e,d)\ \&\ d' \le d \to \exists e'[e' \subseteq e\ \&$
      $R(e',d')]$ (mapping to measures) $\&$
      $\forall e,e',d'[R(e,d)\ \&\ e' \subseteq e \to \exists d'[d' \le d\ \&\ R(e',d')]$ (mapping to events)

(9) $[[proc]] = \lambda y \lambda x \lambda e[\text{Path}(y,e)\ \&\ proc'(e)\ \&\ \text{Process}(e)\ \&\ \text{Subject}(x,e)]$

In fact, during the course of this book, a slightly weaker, more informal
definition of PATH was used, under the principle that I call *homomorphic unity*.

(10)   **Homomorphic unity**: when two event descriptors are syntactically
       merged, the scalar structure of the complement must unify with the
       scalar structure of the head by means of a homomorphism (i.e. the rel-
       evant scales must be synchronized and unified to describe the complex
       event).

Another important aspect of the system defended here is that participant
relations can be (and most often are) composite. This means that a small number
of event-structure primitives and corresponding syntactic positions can be used
to describe a larger number of different participant types, by simple rules of
combination. The entailments corresponding to each participant type simply
unify. In the early part of the book, I tried to show how the different verb types
in English could be distinguished using the primitives given by the system.
While this cursory examination of necessity had to sacrifice depth of analysis for
breadth of coverage, it at least gives some idea of the flexibilities and predictions
of the system. I repeat the table of verb types in English and their participant
relations below in (11). I leave more detailed analysis and refinements to further
research.

(11)   [*init, proc*]

I	Transitive	INITIATOR, UNDERGOER	*drive, push, paint*
	Transitive	INITIATOR, PATH	*eat, read, paint*
II	Intransitive	INITIATOR$_i$, UNDERGOER$_i$	*run*
	[*init, proc, res*]		
III	Transitive	INITIATOR, UNDERGOER$_i$, RESULTEE$_i$	*throw, defuse*
	Transitive	INITIATOR$_i$, UNDERGOER$_i$, RESULT–RHEME	*enter*

IV	Intransitive	INITIATOR$_i$,	*arrive, jump*
		UNDERGOER$_i$, RESULTEE$_i$	
V	Ditransitive	INITIATOR, UNDERGOER	*give, throw*
		RESULTEE	
	[proc]		
VI	intransitive	UNDERGOER	*melt, roll, freeze*
	[proc, res]		
VII	intransitive	UNDERGOER$_i$, RESULTEE$_i$	*break, tear*
	[init, proc, N]		
VIII	N-conflation	INITIATOR$_i$, UNDERGOER$_i$	*dance, sleep*
	[init, proc, A]		
IX	A-conflation	UNDERGOER	*dry, clear*

The Vendler classes

'Activities' correspond to either [init, proc] or [proc] verbs; 'Accomplishments' are [init, proc] verbs with incremental theme or PATH complements; 'Achievements' are [init, proc, res], or [proc, res]; Semelfactives are verbs ambiguous between [proc] and [proc, res]; Degree achievements are [proc] verbs with an implicit property-scale path.

The system proposed in this book is generative–constructivist in spirit, in that it allows the semantics of event structure and participanthood to be built up compositionally as opposed to being explicitly stated in the lexical entries of verbs. I have tried to construct a system which does not rely on the lexicon as a module in the sense of lexicon-internal primitives, rules or operations. On the other hand, the lexical entries themselves are not totally devoid of syntactic information. I thus do not subscribe to the 'naked roots' view espoused by Marantz (1997a, 1997b) and Borer (2005). Rather, the lexical item does come with syntactic information, but *only* that of category features – primitives that the syntax is independently known to manipulate. This syntactic 'tagging' information on the lexical entry is the syn–sem relevant information that allows the item to be deployed in the computational system. The lexical entry itself is a crossmodular bundle of associations, containing, among other things, lexical-encyclopedic information. Lexical-encyclopedic information must be sharply distinguished from compositional-semantic information under this system: only the semantic interpretation of structure is systematic and rule driven; the lexical-encyclopedic content is formless from the point of view of the linguistic system (although it may be structured in more general cognitive terms). Syntactic category features on the lexical items sanction their Merge in particular syntactic positions, and conversely, syntactic category needs to be identified by specific encyclopedic content in order to create well-formed propositions which actually say something about the world.

In the system I have been advocating, lexical items have multiple category features and lexicalize chunks of trees. This means, in effect, that in order to capture the effects of competition among lexical items, a 'superset principle' needs to be assumed (Caha 2007). This principle states that a lexical item may insert to spell out a sequence of heads if its category signature is a contiguous superset of the sequence to be spelled out. In place of the combination of the 'subset principle' and rules of fission and fusion (as in Distributed Morphology), I have used a superset principle together with constraints on when features are allowed to underassociate or not.

(12)   *Underassociation*
       If a lexical item contains an underassociated category feature,
       (i) that feature must be independently identified within the phase and linked to the underassociated feature, by Agree;
       (ii) the two category features so linked must unify their lexical-encyclopedic content.

The flexibilities built into this system are designed to account for the various argument-taking and aktionsartal flexibilities that we find in language, without invoking either multiple homophonous lexical entries, or lexical redundancy rules. The idea is that the syntactic information on the root (i.e. the category features) underspecifies the number of structures that can be built with it, but is still constrained enough to rule out certain impossible forms.

The last main point of the book concerns morphology and the crosslinguistic spell-outs of these verbal structures. I have tried to show that even when different languages use different lexical resources, the same syntactic and semantic structuring principles are involved. Specifically, it turns out that English consistently uses 'synthetic' lexical items, i.e. items which bear more than one category feature and thus Merge in more than one position (ReMerge). On the other hand, we also saw the very same structures spelled out by individual pieces of morphology (Slavic lexical prefixes or Hindi/Urdu causatives), or by separate analytic pieces (Scandinavian and English verb–particle construction, completive complex predicates in Bengali and Hindi/Urdu). While I do not necessarily claim that there is no important difference between words, morphemes and phrases within the grammar, I do claim that these differences do not bear on the syn–sem structures that are being spelled out.

7.2   The connection to tense

The verbal decomposition I have been arguing for is logically independent of tense, and hence of telicity or boundedness per se. However, the nature of the event built up is a central ingredient to subsequent tense interpretation. Given the internal causal and topological complexity of events, an important question to ask is how that complex event is anchored to the speech time which is conceived of as a single moment. The speech time is the pivotal moment around which tense relations are defined, but whether that speech time is directly related to the internal dynamic portion of the event, or to its initial or final transitions, is a matter that has been traditionally seen as the domain of Aspect. I will follow this general intuition here as well and assume that an aspectual head (or heads) embeds the eventuality-building component of the clause by introducing a time variable which is anchored in a specific way to the event (as in Giorgi and Pianesi 1997, Demirdache and Uribe-Etxebarria 2000).

Giorgi and Pianesi (1997) hypothesize that various tenses are the result of a composition of a relation of the first type with a relation of the second type (table repeated from Giorgi and Pianesi 1997).

(13)   Relation 1:   S_R   future   Relation 2:   E_R   perfect
                        R_S   past   R_E   prospective
                        (S,R) present   (E,R) neutral

Demirdache and Uribe-Etxebarria (2000) propose a similar system in which an event time (EV-T) is ordered with respect to an assertion time (AST-T), and then the latter is ordered with respect to an utterance time (UT-T) (after Klein 1994). The former is the analogue of Giorgi and Pianesi's Relation 2 (relating E to R) and the latter of their Relation 1 (relating S to R).

(14)   (Adapted from Demirdache and Uribe-Etxebarria 2000)
        (a) [+ *central coincidence*]: (FIGURE within GROUND)
            Present Tense: UT-T within AST-T
            Progressive Aspect: AST-T within EV-T
        (b) [− *central, + centripetal coincidence*]: (FIGURE before/towards
            GROUND)
            Future Tense: UT-T before AST-T
            Prospective Aspect: AST-T before EV-T

(c) [− *central*, + *centrifugal coincidence*]: (FIGURE after/from
   GROUND)
   Past Tense: UT-T after AST-T
   Perfective Aspect: AST-T after EV-T

Demirdache and Uribe-Etxebarria (D&U) (2000) work with intervals as opposed to time instants in this model, and they claim that there is an analogy between tense and aspect relations in terms of the topological configurations they determine. Like Giorgi and Pianesi (1997), D&U assume that the event gives a particular time directly. This is not consistent with the semantics of the first phase argued for in this book, where the *init*P denotes a pure predicate over events. While I agree with the current literature that both an Asp head and a T head are necessary in expressing tense and outer aspect of the clause, giving this idea a slightly different implementation would allow us to maintain the first phase as a domain of pure event structuring, independent of tense. Basically, I assume that the existence of a time variable is provided by the Asp head (Assertion time head) itself. Consequently, the assertion time in D&U's terms cannot be specified as preceding or following the run time of the event, but must somehow be linked integrally to that run time, the complication being that the events in our first-phase composition are actually internally complex.

The crucial phase boundary between *init*P and the T/Asp phrase-structural domain requires the establishment of a relation between the extended event topology which makes no direct reference to times, and the actual time variable which is only introduced at Asp. In general, we can assume that t and e are related formally by a temporal trace function $\tau(e)$ (as found in Krifka 1992) which maps an event to the 'time line' that it occupies. In any actual predication, the time variable introduced by Asp will be related in a particular way to the event that it embeds via a temporal trace function. In formal terms, we can represent this restriction as:

(15)   t *in* $\tau(e)$ (the reference time of the predication is one of the time moments in the temporal trace function of e)[1]

Assuming that *init*P denotes some predicate over events, the aspectual head combines with it to bind the event variable, introduce t, and to specify the relationship between the two. The actual relationship specified will depend on

---

[1] In this implementation, I am treating the reference time introduced in Asp as a linguistic instant, as is the speech time, although the temporal trace function of the event clearly represents an interval.

the particular Asp head. The general property of the Asp head, therefore, is to bind the event variable, and create a predicate over times related to that event. The particular content of the Asp head will vary, ranging from very specific conditions on the relation between the time variable and the event, to a very simple minimal condition, as shown in (15) above. Further up the clause, in a completely parallel way, the tense head combines with the predicate over times to bind that time variable and relate it (anchor it) to the speech time in a particular way. The general compositional schema is shown in the annotated tree below (16). For concreteness in the illustration I have chosen a default inclusive Asp head and the T_{past} form.

(16)

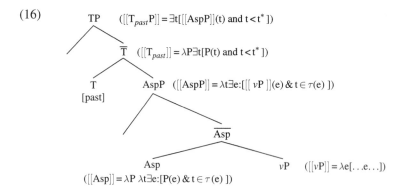

This system can be used to model many instances of external aspectual operators which were beyond the scope of this book.[2] I have given the phrase structure here for concreteness since temporal and aspectual issues interact with many of the phenomena taken up in this book.

During the course of this book, I argued that there are some general semantic felicity conditions on event–event relationships which bear on how they are eventually anchored to tense.

(17)   *Init-proc coherence*:
        Given a decomposition $e_1 \rightarrow (e_2 \rightarrow e_3)$, e_1 may temporally overlap e_2.

---

[2] But see Ramchand (2004) for an analysis of the 'perfective'/'imperfective' contrast in Russian and its relation to prefixation. In fact, the analysis claims that perfectivity (more particularly, the perfectivity diagnostics) is sensitive to the existence of a *definite* event time given by AspP, as opposed to an *indefinite* event time given by AspP.

(18)   *Proc-res coherence*:
        Given a decomposition $e_1 \rightarrow (e_2 \rightarrow e_3)$, e_3 must *not* temporally
        overlap e_2.
        (although they may share a transition point).

While these conditions are fairly loose, I have argued that they become rigid
requirements when the same lexical 'word' identifies multiple subevents.[3]

(19)   *Temporal dependence and lexical identification*
        Temporal dependence is required for subevents identified by the *same*
        lexical content.

We saw the notion of temporal dependence and lexical identification at work
both in the examination of resultatives in chapter 5 and in the morphological causatives in chapter 6. Here at least is one area in which the nature of
the spell-out options have implications for the semantics of the clause and
further operations. In general, we found that subevents that were identified
by separate analytic pieces had more temporal independence than those that
were identified by a single lexical item. The hope is that these generalizations
will fall out without stipulation once a precise theory of the relation between
tense features on roots and the higher functional structure of the clause is
articulated.

It is important to stress that there is no single projection in this system which
carries a [+telic] feature. Rather, telicity emerges from a number of different
interacting factors. In the absence of secondary aspectual modification, the
existence of *res*P does give rise to telicity. Class III, IV, V and VII are default
telic and are also punctual. Class I is telic when the PATH argument is bounded,
class VI, when there is an endpoint on the scale of change implied (as in Hay,
Kennedy and Levin 1999). Class III, IV, V and VII in the list of English verbs
above are default telic and are also punctual because *proc* and *res* subevents are
identified by the same root. Class I is telic when the PATH argument is bounded,
class VI, when there is an endpoint on the scale of change implied (as in Hay,
Kennedy and Levin 1999).

Telicity is no longer a homogenous concept in this system but arises from the
interaction of many ingredients: the existence of a *res* head gives a final bound

---

[3] I speculate that this intuition can be implemented using a theory of tense-feature specification of a lexical item – since one t value needs to be chosen by the Asp head to be
linked to the speech time, that t value must be contained in every single subevent that
the lexical item identifies.

for a dynamic event; the existence of an *init* head gives an initial bound for a dynamic event and both of these are available for anchoring to tense in principle. In addition, in the absence of a *res* head, a bounded path in the complement position of a process head (whether it be a bounded directional PP or a quantized DP) can also provide a bound to the event that can be located temporally. If we now reconsider the traditional tests used in English for 'telicity', we can see that they are sensitive to different aspects of this system. The 'in an hour' test measures a time scale leading up to a definite bound or transition. Thus it is grammatical with bounded paths (20c, d) as well as *res*P decompositions (20e, f), but not with unbounded processes (20a, b).

(20)   (a)*Michael drove the car in an hour.
        (b)* Karena danced in an hour.
        (c) Michael walked the trail in an hour.
        (d) Alex ate the mango in ten minutes.
        (e) Ariel ran her shoes ragged in one hour.
        (f) Katherine painted the wall red in an hour.

To the extent that (21a, b) are possible in English, the 'in an hour' measures the time span up to the initiation transition of the event, this being the only transition determined by the event decomposition.

The 'for an hour' test is not the converse of the 'in an hour' test, it seems rather to be a test for the explicit existence of a *res*P. It is sharply ungrammatical only with decompositions that have a *res* either synthetically or analytically (21e, f). Contrary to many claims in the literature (see also Smollett 2005), 'for an hour' is pretty acceptable for most speakers with bounded paths (21c, d). It also seems independently to require some sort of nontrivial duration, so that even a *proc* decomposition is ungrammatical if its PATH complement represents a short spatial transition, as in (21g).

(21)   (a) Michael drove the car for an hour.
        (b) Karena danced for an hour.
        (c) Michael walked the trail for an hour.
        (d) Alex ate the mango for an hour.
        (e)*Ariel broke the box for an hour.
        (f) ??Katherine ate the mango up for an hour.
        (g) *Michael drove the car into the garage for two minutes. (under the intended reading)

I will therefore assume the following as general diagnostics in English:

(22)   (i) 'for X time' incompatible with decompositions that include *res*P, and decompositions without duration;
         (ii) 'in X time' incompatible with decompositions that do not include a final temporal bound.

I have included a discussion of the traditional tests here because of their ubiquity in the literature, and because the way they are traditionally deployed goes against the way in which I have divided up the verb classes in this book. I hope to have shown, however, that notions of telicity based on these common diagnostics are seriously flawed, and conflate event-structure boundedness with aspectual boundedness, and even pragmatic boundedness, if not carefully applied.

More careful investigation of the relationship between event structure and temporal/aspectual structure must await further research.

7.3   Open questions

There are a number of intriguing issues relevant to this work that I simply have not been able to address in the context of this book. First and foremost, the relation between argument structure and case has not been discussed in any deep way. In the recent literature, tantalizing connections have been made between tense and nominative case on the one hand (Pesetsky and Torrego 2001) and aspect and accusative case on the other (Kratzer 2004, Pesetsky and Torrego 2004, Svenonius 2002, Kiparsky 1998, de Hoop 1992). An important further issue for investigation will be to what extent the decompositions proposed here in this book can provide the foundation for a semantically grounded understanding of the structural cases found in natural language. It would have been impossible to do justice to such issues here.

Another issue concerns the unaccusative–unergative distinction, which I have generally assumed is real and corresponds to the absence or presence respectively of the *init* head in the first-phase decompositions of the two classes. What I have not been able to address systematically is the relation between these structures and the specific diagnostics that have been proposed in the literature for different languages. My intuition is that the diagnostics currently used are as heterogeneous as the standard telicity tests, and will decompose into being sensitive to slightly different things, once looked at carefully. The hope is that the system of primitive distinctions found in this book will be able to make sense of when tests converge and when they interestingly diverge.

Perhaps the most glaring omission in this book has been stative verbs. I have nothing interesting to say about statives, far less the relevant and fascinating relationship between stative verbs, adjectives and participles. Clearly, no theory of verbal decomposition would be complete without addressing these central questions of category and eventuality type.

Many questions remain to be investigated, but I must leave them to further research. As one concrete working out of a constructivist agenda for argument and event structure, I hope that this book can provide a useful starting point for deeper investigation.

References

Ackema, Peter, Neeleman, Ad and Weerman, Fred. 1993. Deriving functional projections. *Proceedings of NELS 23*, 17–31.

Adger, David. 2003. *Core Syntax*. Oxford: Oxford University Press.

Åfarli, Tor A. 1985. Norwegian verb particle constructions as causative constructions. *Nordic Journal of Linguistics* 8:75–98.

Alsina, Alex. 1992. On the argument structure of causatives. *Linguistic Inquiry* 23:517–55.

Babko-Malaya, Olga. 1999. Zero Morphology: a study of aspect, argument structure and case. PhD thesis, Rutgers, the State University of New Jersey.

Baker, Mark C. 1988. *Incorporation: A Theory of Grammatical Function Changing*. Chicago: University of Chicago Press.

Baker, Mark C. 1996. *The Polysynthesis Parameter*. Oxford Studies in Comparative Syntax. New York: Oxford University Press.

Baker, Mark C. 1997. Thematic roles and syntactic structure. In L. Haegeman, ed., *The Elements of Grammar*, 73–137. Dordrecht: Kluwer.

Baker, Mark C. 2003. *Verbs, Nouns, and Adjectives: Their Universal Grammar*. Cambridge Studies in Linguistics 102. Cambridge: Cambridge University Press.

Batsiukova, Volha. 2003. Aspectual expression of attenuation in Russian and Spanish: a lexical semantic approach. Ms., Universidad Autónoma de Madrid.

Belletti, Adriana and Rizzi, Luigi. 1988. Psych-verbs and θ-theory. *Natural Language and Linguistic Theory* 6:291–352.

Bhatt, Rajesh. 2003a. Causativization in Hindi. Class handout, March 2003.

Bhatt, Rajesh. 2003b. Passive in Hindi. Class handout, March 2003.

Bhatt, Rajesh and Anagnostopoulou, Elena. 1996. Object shift and specificity: evidence from -*ko* phrases in Hindi. In L. M. Dobrin, K. Singer and L. McNair, eds., *Papers from the 32nd Regional Meeting of the Chicago Linguistic Society*. Chicago: Chicago Linguistic Society.

Borer, Hagit. 1998. Deriving passive without theta roles. In Steven G. Lapointe, Diane K. Brentari and Patrick M. Farrell, eds., *Morphology and its Relation to Phonology and Syntax*, 60–99. Stanford, CA: CSLI Publications.

Borer, Hagit. 2005. *Structuring Sense: An Exo-Skeletal Trilogy*. New York: Oxford University Press.

Bowers, John. 1993. The syntax of predication. *Linguistic Inquiry* 24:591–656.

Bresnan, Joan. 1982. Control and complementation. In Joan Bresnan, ed., *The Mental Representation of Grammatical Relations*, 282–390. Cambridge, MA: MIT Press.

Bresnan, Joan. 2001. *Lexical-Functional Syntax*. Malden, MA, and Oxford: Blackwell.

Bresnan, Joan and Moshi, Lioba. 1990. Object asymmetries in comparative Bantu syntax. *Linguistic Inquiry* 147–85.

Bury, Dirk. 2003. Phrase structure and derived heads. PhD thesis, University College London.

Burzio, Luigi. 1986. *Italian Syntax: A Government-Binding Approach*. Dordrecht: Reidel.

Butt, Miriam. 1995. *The Structure of Complex Predicates in Urdu*. Dissertations in Linguistics, Stanford, CA: CSLI Publications.

Butt, Miriam. 1998. Constraining argument merger through aspect. In E. Hinrichs, Andreas Kathol and T. Nakazawa, eds., *Complex Predicates in Nonderivational Syntax*, 73–113. New York: Academic Press.

Butt, Miriam. 2003. The morpheme that wouldn't go away. Handout, University of Manchester seminar series.

Butt, Miriam and Lahiri, Aditi. 2005. Historical stability vs. historical change. Ms., University of Konstanz.

Butt, Miriam and Ramchand, Gillian. 2005. Complex aspectual structure in Hindi/Urdu. In Nomi Erteschik-Shir and Tova Rapoport, eds., *The Syntax of Aspect*, 117–53. Oxford: Oxford University Press.

Caha, Pavel. 2007. The superset principle. Ms. University of Tromsø, GLOW presentation 2007.

Carrier, Jill and Randall, Janet H. 1992. The argument structure and syntactic structure of resultatives. *Linguistic Inquiry* 23:173–234.

Chierchia, Gennaro. 2004. Scalar implicatures, polarity phenomena and the syntax/pragmatics interface. In Adriana Belletti, ed., *Structures and Beyond*, 39–103. Oxford: Oxford University Press.

Chierchia, Gennaro and Turner, Raymond. 1988. Semantics and property theory. *Linguistics and Philosophy: An International Journal* 11:261–302.

Chomsky, Noam. 1965. *Aspects of the Theory of Syntax*. Cambridge, MA: MIT Press.

Chomsky, Noam. 1970. Remarks on nominalization. In Roderick A. Jacobs and Peter S. Rosenbaum, eds., *Readings in English Transformational Grammar*, 184–221. Washington, DC: Georgetown University Press.

Chomsky, Noam. 1981. *Lectures on Government and Binding*. Studies in Generative Grammar 9. Dordrecht: Foris.

Chomsky, Noam. 1995. *The Minimalist Program*. Cambridge, MA: MIT Press.

Chomsky, Noam. 2000. Minimalist inquiries: the framework. In Roger Martin, David Michaels and Juan Uriagereka, eds., *Step by Step: Minimalist Essays in Honor of Howard Lasnik*, 89–155. Cambridge, MA: MIT Press.

Chomsky, Noam. 2001. Derivation by phase. In Michael Kenstowicz, ed., *Ken Hale: A Life in Language*, 1–52. Cambridge, MA: MIT Press.

Croft, William. 1998. Event structure in argument linking. In Miriam Butt and Wilhelm Geuder, eds., *The Projection of Arguments*, 1–43. Stanford, CA: CSLI Publications.

Davidson, Donald. 1967. The logical form of action sentences. In Nicholas Rescher, ed., *The Logic of Decision and Action*, 81–95. Pittsburgh, PA: University of Pittsburgh Press.

de Hoop, Helen. 1992. Case configuration and noun phrase interpretation. PhD thesis, Rijksuniversiteit Groningen.

Déchaine, Rose-Marie. 2003. Morphology as the intersection of phonology and syntax: evidence from roots. Talk presented at CASTL Workshop on Morphology, Tromsø, 30-31 May.

Demirdache, Hamida and Uribe-Etxebarria, Myriam. 2000. The primitives of temporal relations. In Roger Martin, David Michaels and Juan Uriagereka, eds., *Step by Step. Essays on Minimalist Syntax in Honour of Howard Lasnik*, 157–86. Cambridge, MA: MIT Press.

den Dikken, Marcel. 1995. *Particles: On the Syntax of Verb-Particle, Triadic, and Causative Constructions*. New York: Oxford University Press.

Di Sciullo, Anna-Maria and Williams, Edwin. 1987. *On the Definition of Word*. Linguistic Inquiry Monographs 14. Cambridge, MA: MIT Press.

Doron, Edit. 2003. Agency and voice: the semantics of the Semitic templates. *Natural Language Semantics* 11:1–67.

Dowty, David R. 1979. *Word Meaning and Montague Grammar: The Semantics of Verbs and Times in Generative Semantics and in Montague's PTQ*. Dordrecht: Reidel.

Dowty, David R. 1989. On the semantic content of the notion 'thematic role'. In B. Partee, G. Chierchia and R. Turner, eds., *Properties, Types and Meaning*, 69–129. Dordrecht: Reidel.

Dowty, David R. 1990. Thematic proto-roles and argument selection. *Language* 67:547–619.

Dubinsky, Stan and Simango, Sylvester Ron. 1996. Passive and stative in Chichewa: evidence for modular distinctions. *Language* 72:749–81.

Embick, David and Noyer, Ralf. 2001. Movement operations after syntax. *Linguistic Inquiry* 32:555–95.

Emonds, Joseph E. 1976. *A Transformational Approach to English Syntax: Root, Structure-Preserving, and Local Transformations*. New York: Academic.

Folli, Raffaella. 2003. Deriving telicity in English and Italian. PhD thesis, Oxford University.

Folli, Raffaella and Harley, Heidi. 2004. Flavors of *v*: consuming results in Italian & English. In Roumyana Slabakova and Paula Kempchinsky, eds., *Aspectual Inquiries*, 95–120. Dordrecht: Kluwer.

Folli, Raffaella and Harley, Heidi. 2006. On the licensing of causatives of directed motion: waltzing matilda all over. *Studia Linguistica* 60:1–35.

Forsyth, J. 1970. *A Grammar of Aspect: Usage and Meaning in the Russian Verb*. Cambridge: Cambridge University Press.

Giorgi, Alessandra and Pianesi, Fabio. 1997. *Tense and Aspect: From Semantics to Morphosyntax*. New York: Oxford University Press.

Goldberg, Adele. 1995. *Constructions: A Construction Grammar Approach to Argument Structure*. Chicago: University of Chicago Press.

Grimshaw, Jane. 1979. Complement selection and the lexicon. *Linguistic Inquiry* 10: 279–326.

Grimshaw, Jane. 1990. *Argument Structure*. Linguistic Inquiry Monographs 18. Cambridge, MA: MIT Press.

Gruber, Jeffrey Steven. 1965. Studies in lexical relations. PhD thesis, MIT, Department of Modern Languages.

Guéron, Jacqueline. 1987. Clause union and the verb-particle construction in English. *Proceedings of NELS 17*.

Hale, Ken and Keyser, Jay. 2000. On the time of Merge. Ms., MIT.

Hale, Ken and Keyser, Samuel J. 1987. A view from the middle. Lexicon Project Working Papers 10. Center for Cognitive Science, MIT.

Hale, Kenneth and Keyser, Samuel Jay. 1993. On argument structure and the lexical expression of syntactic relations. In Kenneth Hale and Samuel Jay Keyser, eds., *The View from Building 20: Essays in Linguistics in Honor of Sylvain Bromberger*, 53–109. Current Studies in Linguistics 24. Cambridge, MA: MIT Press.

Hale, Ken and Keyser, Samuel Jay. 2002. *Prolegomenon to a Theory of Argument Structure*. Linguistic Inquiry Monographs 39. Cambridge, MA: MIT Press.

Halle, Morris and Marantz, Alec. 1993. Distributed morphology and the pieces of inflection. In Kenneth Hale and Samuel Jay Keyser, eds., *The View from Building 20: Essays in Linguistics in Honor of Sylvain Bromberger*, 111–76. Cambridge, MA: MIT Press.

Harley, Heidi. 1995. Subjects, events, and licensing. PhD thesis, MIT.

Harley, Heidi. 2000. Possession and the double object construction. Ms., University of Arizona.

Harley, Heidi. 2002. Possession and the double object construction. *Yearbook of Linguistic Variation* 2:29–68.

Harley, Heidi and Noyer, Rolf. 2000. Licensing in the non-lexicalist lexicon. In Bert Peeters, ed., *The Lexicon/Encyclopaedia Interface*, 349–74. Amsterdam: Elsevier.

Haspelmath, Martin. 1993. *A Grammar of Lezgian*. Mouton Grammar Library 9. Berlin: Mouton de Gruyter.

Hay, Jennifer, Kennedy, Christopher and Levin, Beth. 1999. Scalar structure underlies telicity in 'Degree Achievements'. In Tanya Matthews and Devon Strolovitch, eds., *Proceedings of SALT IX*, 127–44. Ithaca, NY: CLC Publications.

Higginbotham, James. 1985. On semantics. *Linguistic Inquiry* 16:547–93.

Higginbotham, James. 2001. Accomplishments. Ms., Oxford University.

Hoekstra, Teun. 1984. *Transitivity: Grammatical Relations in Government-Binding Theory*. Dordrecht: Foris.

Hoekstra, Teun. 1988. Small clause results. *Lingua* 74:101–39.

Hoekstra, Teun. 1992. Aspect and theta theory. In I. M. Roca, ed., *Thematic Structure: Its Role in Grammar*, 145–74. Berlin: Foris.

Hoekstra, Teun and Mulder, René. 1990. Unergatives as copular verbs. *Linguistic Review* 7:1–79.

Hook, Peter. 1979. *Hindi Structures: Intermediate Level*. University of Michigan, Ann Arbor: Michigan Papers on South and South East Asia 16.

Isačenko, Alexander. 1960. *Grammatičeskij stroj russkogo jazyka. Morfologija. Častj vtoraja*. Bratislava: Vydavatelstvo Slovenskej Akadémie vied.

Jackendoff, Ray. 1983. *Semantics and Cognition*. Cambridge, MA: MIT Press.

Jackendoff, Ray. 1990. *Semantic Structures*. Current Studies in Linguistics 18. Cambridge, MA: MIT Press.

Johnson, Kyle. 1991. Object positions. *Natural Language and Linguistic Theory* 9:577–636.

Julien, Marit. 2000. Syntactic heads and word formation: a study of verbal inflection. PhD thesis, University of Tromsø.

Kachru, Yamuna. 1980. *Aspects of Hindi Syntax*. Delhi: Manohar Publications.

Kamp, Hans. 1980. Some remarks on the logic of change: Part I. In C. Rohrer, ed., *Time, Tense and Quantifiers*, 135–79. Tübingen: Niemeyer.

Kaufmann, Ingrid and Wunderlich, Dieter. 1998. Cross-linguistic patterns of resultatives. Theorie des Lexikons. Sonderforschungsbereich 282, Bericht 109, University of Düsseldorf.

Kayne, Richard S. 1985. Principles of particle constructions. In Jacqueline Guéron, Hans-Georg Obenauer and Jean-Yves Pollock, eds., *Grammatical Representation*, 101–40. Dordrecht: Foris.

Kearns, Kate. 2006. Telic senses of deadjectival verbs. Ms., to appear in *Lingua*.

Kennedy, Chris. 1999. Gradable adjectives denote measure functions, not partial functions. *Studies in the Linguistic Sciences* 29.1.

Kennedy, Christopher and McNally, Louise. 2005. Scale structure and the semantic typology of gradable predicates. *Language* 81.2: 345–81.

Kenny, Anthony. 1963. *Action, Emotion and Will*. London: Routledge and Kegan Paul.

Kiparsky, Paul. 1973. 'Elsewhere' in phonology. In Paul Kiparsky and Steven Anderson, eds., *A Festschrift for Morris Halle*, 93–106. New York: Holt, Rinehart and Winston.

Kiparsky, Paul. 1982. Lexical morphology and phonology. In The Linguistic Society of Korea, ed., *Linguistics in the Morning Calm*, 1–91. Seoul: Hanshin.

Kiparsky, Paul. 1998. Partitive case and aspect. In Wilhelm Geuder and Miriam Butt, eds., *The Projection of Arguments: Lexical and Compositional Factors*, 265–307. Stanford, CA: CSLI Publications.

Koeneman, Olaf. 2000. *The Flexible Nature of Verb Movement*. PhD thesis, Utrecht University. LOT dissertations in Linguistics. Utrecht: LOT.

Koopman, Hilda. 1995. On verbs that fail to undergo V-second. *Linguistic Inquiry* 26:137–63.

Koopman, Hilda. 2000. Prepositions, postpositions, circumpositions, and particles. In Hilda Koopman, ed., *The Syntax of Specifiers and Heads*, 204–60. London: Routledge.

Kracht, Marcus. 2002. On the semantics of locatives. *Linguistics and Philosophy* 25:157–232.

Kratzer, Angelika. 1996. Severing the external argument from the verb. In Johann Rooryck and Laurie Zaring, eds., *Phrase Structure and the Lexicon*, 109–37. Dordrecht: Kluwer.

Kratzer, Angelika. 2004. Telicity and the meaning of objective case. In Jacqueline Guéron and Jacqueline Lecarme, eds., *The Syntax of Time*, 398–425. Cambridge, MA: MIT Press.

Krifka, Manfred. 1987. Nominal reference and temporal constitution: towards a semantics of quantity. In Jeroen J. Groenendijk, Martin Stokhof and Frank Veltman, eds., *Proceedings of the 6th Amsterdam Colloquium*, 153–73. Amsterdam: Institute of Linguistics, Logic and Information, University of Amsterdam.

Krifka, Manfred. 1989. Nominal reference and temporal constitution and quantification in event semantics. In P. van Emde Boas, R. Bartsch and J. van Bentham, eds., *Semantics and Contextual Expression*, 75–115. Dordrecht: Foris.

Krifka, Manfred. 1992. Thematic relations and links between nominal reference and temporal constitution. In Ivan A. Sag and Anna Szabolcsi, eds., *Lexical Matters*, 29–53. Stanford, CA: CSLI Publications.

Larson, Richard K. 1988. On the double object construction. *Linguistic Inquiry* 19:335–91.

Levin, Beth. 1993. *Verb Classes in English*. Cambridge, MA: MIT Press.

Levin, Beth. 2006. Dative verbs: a crosslinguistic perspective. Ms., Stanford University.

Levin, Beth and Rappaport, Malka. 1998. Building verb meanings. In Miriam Butt and Wilhelm Geuder, eds., *The Projection of Arguments: Lexical and Compositional Factors*, 97–134. Stanford, CA: CSLI Publications.

Levin, Beth and Rappaport Hovav, Malka. 1995. *Unaccusativity: At the Syntax-Lexical Semantics Interface*. Cambridge, MA: MIT Press.

Levin, Beth and Rappaport-Hovav, Malka. 1999. Two structures for compositionally derived events. In *Proceedings of SALT 9*, 199–223, Ithaca, NY: CLC Publications.

Link, G. 1983. The logical analysis of plurals and mass terms: a lattice-theoretical approach. In R. Bäuerle, C. Schwarze and A. von Stechow, eds., *Meaning, Use and Interpretation of Language*, 302–23. Berlin: Walter de Gruyter.

Marantz, Alec. 1984. *On the Nature of Grammatical Relations*. Linguistic Inquiry Monographs 10. Cambridge, MA: MIT Press.

Marantz, Alec. 1997a. 'cat' as a phrasal idiom: consequences of late insertion in Distributed Morphology. Ms., MIT.

Marantz, Alec. 1997b. No escape from syntax: don't try morphological analysis in the privacy of your own lexicon. In Alexis Dimitriadis and Laura Siegel, eds., *Proceedings of the 21st Annual Penn Linguistics Colloquium*, University of Pennsylvania Working Papers in Linguistics, 201–25. Philadelphia: University of Pennsylvania.

Marantz, Alec. 2001. Words. Ms., MIT.

Masica, Colin. 1991. *The Indo-Aryan Languages*. Cambridge: Cambridge University Press.

McIntyre, Andrew. 2001. Argument blockages induced by verb particles in English and German: event modification and secondary predication. In Nicole Dehé and Anja Wanner, eds., *Structural Aspects of Semantically Complex Verbs*, 131–64. Frankfurt/Berlin/New York: Peter Lang.

Napoli, Donna Jo. 1992. Secondary resultative predicates in Italian. *Journal of Linguistics* 28:53–90.

Neeleman, Ad. 1994. Complex predicates. PhD thesis, Utrecht University.

Oehrle, Richard. 1976. The grammatical status of the English Dative alternation. PhD thesis, MIT.

Parsons, Terence. 1990. *Events in the Semantics of English: A Study in Subatomic Semantics*. Cambridge, MA: MIT Press.

Partee, Alice ter Meulen, Barbara H. and Wall, Robert, eds. 1990. *Mathematical Methods in Linguistics*. Dordrecht: Springer.

Perlmutter, David. 1978. Impersonal passives and the unaccusative hypothesis. *Proceedings of the Fourth Annual Meeting of the Berkeley Linguistics Society*, 157–89.

Pesetsky, David. 1982. Paths and categories. PhD thesis, MIT.

Pesetsky, David. 1995. *Zero Syntax: Experiencers and Cascades*. Cambridge, MA: MIT Press.

Pesetsky, David and Torrego, Esther. 2001. T to C movement: causes and consequences. In Michael Kenstowicz, ed., *Ken Hale: A Life in Language*, 355–426. Cambridge, MA: MIT Press.

Pesetsky, David and Torrego, Esther. 2004. Tense, case, and the nature of syntactic categories. In Jacqueline Guéron and Jacqueline Lecarme, eds., *The Syntax of Time*, 495–537. Cambridge, MA: MIT Press.

Pinker, Steven. 1989. *Learnability and Cognition: The Acquisition of Argument Structure*. Cambridge, MA: MIT Press.

Pollock, Jean Yves. 1989. Verb movement, universal grammar, and the structure of IP. *Linguistic Inquiry* 20:365–424.

Pustejovsky, James. 1991. The syntax of event structure. *Cognition* 41:47–81.

Pylkkänen, Liina. 1999. Causation and external arguments. In Liina Pylkkänen, Angeliek van Hout and Heidi Harley, eds., *Papers from the UPenn/MIT Roundtable on the Lexicon*, 161–83. WPL 35. Cambridge, MA: MIT Press.

Ramchand, Gillian. 1993. Aspect and argument structure in modern Scottish Gaelic. PhD thesis, Stanford University.

Ramchand, Gillian. 1997. Questions, polarity and alternative semantics. In *Proceedings of NELS 27*, 383–96. Amherst: GLSA.

Ramchand, Gillian. 2004. Time and the event: the semantics of Russian prefixes. In Peter Svenonius, ed., *Nordlyd*, University of Tromsø, www.ub.uit.no/munin/nordlyd/.

Ramchand, Gillian and Svenonius, Peter. 2002. The lexical syntax and lexical semantics of the verb-particle construction. In Line Mikkelsen and Chris Potts, eds., *Proceedings of WCCFL 21*, 387–400. Somerville, MA: Cascadilla Press.

Ramchand, Gillian and Svenonius, Peter. 2004. Prepositions and external argument demotion. Paper presented at workshop on 'Demoting the Agent', Oslo, Dec. 2004.

Rappaport-Hovav, Malka and Levin, Beth. 2000. Classifying single argument verbs. In M. Everaert, P. Coopmans and J. Grimshaw, eds., *Lexical Specification and Insertion*, 269–304. Amsterdam: John Benjamins.

Reinhart, T. 2002. The theta system– an overview. *Theoretical Linguistics* 28:229–90.

Ritter, Elizabeth and Rosen, Sara Thomas. 1998. Delimiting events in syntax. In Miriam Butt and Wilhelm Geuder, eds., *The Projection of Arguments: Lexical and Compositional Factors*, 135–64. Stanford, CA: CSLI Publications.

Rizzi, Luigi. 1978. A restructuring rule in Italian syntax. In Samuel Jay Keyser, ed., *Recent Transformational Studies in European Languages*, 113–58. Cambridge, MA: MIT Press.

Rizzi, Luigi. 1997. The fine structure of the left periphery. In Liliane Haegeman, ed., *Elements of Grammar: Handbook in Generative Syntax*, 281–337. Dordrecht: Kluwer.

Romanova, Eugenia. 2004. Superlexical vs. lexical prefixes. *Nordlyd*, University of Tromsø, www.ub.uit.no/munin/nordlyd/.

Romanova, Eugenia. 2006. Perfectivity in Russian. PhD thesis, University of Tromsø.

Rothstein, Susan. 2004. *Structuring Events: A Study in the Semantics of Aspect*. Oxford: Blackwell.

Saksena, Anuradha. 1982. *Topics in the Analysis of Causatives with an Account of Hindi Paradigms*. Los Angeles: University of California Press.

Schwarzschild, Roger. 2002. The grammar of measurement. In Brendan Jackson, ed., *Proceedings of SALT 12*. Ithaca, NY: CLC Publications.

Schwarzschild, Roger. 2005. Measure phrases as modifiers of adjective. *Recherches Linguistiques de Vincennes* 35:207–28.

Shibatani, Masayoshi. 1973a. Lexical versus periphrastic causatives in Korean. *Journal of Linguistics* 9:209–383.

Shibatani, Masayoshi. 1973b. A linguistic study of causative constructions. PhD thesis, University of California, Berkeley.

Singh, Mona. 1994. Perfectivity, definiteness and specificity: a classification of verbal predicates in Hindi. PhD thesis, University of Texas, Austin.

Smith, Carlota S. 1991. *The Parameter of Aspect*. Studies in Linguistics and Philosophy 43. Dordrecht: Kluwer.

Smith, Carlota S. 1995. *The Parameter of Aspect*, revised edition. Studies in Linguistics and Philosophy 43. Dordrecht: Kluwer.

Smollett, R. 2005. Quantized direct objects don't delimit after all. In Henk Verkuyl and Henriette de Swart, eds., *Perspectives on Aspect*. Dordrecht: Kluwer.

Son, Minjeong. 2006. Directed motion and non-predicative pathp. *Nordlyd: Tromsø Working Papers on Language and Linguistics*, 176–99, special issue on adpositions, ed. Peter Svenonius.

Starke, Michal. 2001. Move dissolves into merge: a theory of locality. PhD thesis, University of Geneva.

Stiebels, Barbara and Wunderlich, Dieter. 1994. Morphology feeds syntax: the case of particle verbs. *Linguistics* 32:913–68.

Svenonius, Peter. 1994a. C-selection as feature-checking. *Studia Linguistica* 48:133–55.

Svenonius, Peter. 1994b. Dependent nexus: subordinate predication structures in English and the Scandinavian languages. PhD thesis, University of California at Santa Cruz.

Svenonius, Peter. 1996. The verb-particle alternation in the Scandinavian languages. Ms., University of Tromsø.

Svenonius, Peter. 2002. Icelandic case and the structure of events. *Journal of Comparative Germanic Linguistics* 5:197–225.

Svenonius, Peter. 2004a. Slavic prefixes inside and outside VP. Ms., University of Tromsø; to appear in *Nordlyd*: www.ub.uit.no/munin/nordlyd/.

Svenonius, Peter. 2004b. Spatial prepositions in English. Ms., University of Tromsø; http://ling.auf.net/lingBuzz/000001.

Talmy, Leonard. 1978. Figure and ground in complex sentences. In Joseph H. Greenberg, ed., *Universals of Human Language*, volume 4, 625–49. Stanford, CA: Stanford University Press.

Talmy, Leonard. 1985. Lexicalization patterns: semantic structure in lexical forms. In Timothy Shopen, ed., *Language Typology and Syntactic Description, I: Clause Structure*, 57–149. Cambridge: Cambridge University Press.

Taylor, B. 1977. Tense and continuity. *Linguistics and Philosophy* 1.2:199–220.

Tenny, Carol. 1987. Grammaticalizing aspect and affectedness. PhD thesis, MIT.

Travis, Lisa. 2000. Event structure in syntax. In Carol Tenny and James Pustejovsky, eds., *Events as Grammatical Objects: The Converging Perspectives of Lexical Semantics and Syntax*, 145–85. Stanford, CA: CSLI Publications.

van Hout, Angeliek. 1996. Event semantics of verb frame alternations: a case study of Dutch and its acquisition. PhD thesis, Tilburg University, published in 1998 by Garland Publishing, New York.

van Hout, Angeliek. 2000a. Event semantics in the lexicon-syntax interface. In Carol Tenny and James Pustejovsky, eds., *Events as Grammatical Objects*, 239–82. Stanford, CA: CSLI Publications.

van Hout, Angeliek. 2000b. Projection based on event structure. In M. Everaert, P. Coopmans and J. Grimshaw, eds., *Lexical Specification and Insertion*, 397–422. Amsterdam: John Benjamins.

van Riemsdijk, Henk. 1990. Functional prepositions. In H. Pinkster and I. Gene, eds., *Unity in Diversity*, 229–41. Dordrecht: Foris.

van Riemsdijk, Henk and Huybregts, Riny. 2002. Location and locality. In Marc van Oostendorp and Elena Anagnostopoulou, eds., *Progress in Grammar: Articles at the 20th Anniversary of the Comparison of Grammatical Models Group in Tilburg*, 1–23. Amsterdam: Meertens Instituut.

Van Valin, Robert D. 1990. Semantic parameters of split intransitivity. *Language* 66:221–60.

Vendler, Zeno. 1967. *Linguistics in Philosophy*. Ithaca, NY: Cornell University Press.

Verkuyl, Henk J. 1972. *On the Compositional Nature of the Aspects*. Dordrecht: Reidel.

Verkuyl, Henk J. 1989. Aspectual classes and aspectual composition. *Linguistics and Philosophy* 12:39–94.

Verkuyl, Henk J. 1993. *A Theory of Aspectuality: The Interaction between Temporal and Atemporal Structure*. Cambridge: Cambridge University Press.

Wasow, Thomas. 1977. Transformations and the lexicon. In Peter Culicover, Thomas Wasow and Joan Bresnan, eds., *Formal Syntax*, 327–60. New York: Academic Press.

Wechsler, Stephen. 2001. An analysis of English resultatives under the event-argument homomorphism model of telicity. *Proceedings of the 3rd Workshop on Text Structure*, 1–17.

Wechsler, Stephen. 2005. Resultatives under the 'event-argument homomorphism' model of telicity. In N. Erteschik-Shir and T. Rappoport, eds., *The Syntax of Aspect*, 255–73. Oxford: Oxford University Press.

Williams, Edwin. 1980. Predication. *Linguistic Inquiry*. 11: 203–38.

Wurmbrand, Susi. 2000. The structure(s) of particle verbs. Ms., McGill University.

Zaenen, A. 1993. Unaccusativity in Dutch: an integrated approach. In J. Pustejovsky, ed., *Semantics and the Lexicon*, 129–61. Dordrecht: Kluwer.

Zeller, Jochen. 1999. Particle verbs, local domains, and a theory of lexical licensing. PhD thesis, University of Frankfurt.

Zubizarretta, Maria-Luisa and Oh, Eunjeong. 2006. On the syntactic composition of manner and motion. To appear, MIT Press.

Zwarts, Joost. 2003. Vectors across spatial domains: from place to size, orientation, shape and parts. In Emile van der Zee and John Slack, eds., *Representing Direction in Language and Space*, 39–68. Oxford: Oxford University Press.

Zwarts, Joost. 2005. Prepositional aspect and the algebra of paths. *Linguistics and Philosophy* 28.6:739–79.

Zwarts, Joost and Winter, Yoad. 2000. Vector space semantics: a model-theoretic analysis of locative prepositions. *Journal of Logic, Language, and Information* 9:169–211.

Index

Note. In this index entries in italics indicate the author's own terminology; page numbers in bold type indicate places where a definition is given.

Printed in Great Britain by Amazon.co.uk, Ltd., Marston Gate.